The undergraduate terrain can be landscaped _____ _____ _____ than classroom species, genres native to the terra_____ research culture, ones which take root and flourish in its particular combination of soil nutrients and climate conditions, these being the values, experience, attitudes of the research faculty who are also teachers. Native species can draw on these resources.

In this terrain, the reading and representation of others' research—what others have said, the story of a research conversation—is native. The very act of saying "others have said this, in these ways, with these agreements and these differences, in these contexts, with these prospects for further inquiry" is a rhetorical action radically indigenous to research culture. And students can do it, if nurtured. It's a first and authentic step for students making the transition from schoolroom culture, a first step in taking a position, joining a conversation. This action, so deep-rooted in research culture, is a main focus of *Academic Writing: An Introduction*.

Landscaping Materials

The undergraduate terrain *is* landscaped, not naturally occurring. It arranges the four-year undergraduate education with courses, year-levels, exams and quizzes, prerequisites, and degree requirements. Even though we are planting with indigenous species, we *are* planting. Those genres do not arise naturally—or "naturally/socially," to reconcile the botanical metaphor—out of activities already under way. Even indigenous species, transplanted, need tending, some added nutrients, protection, and extra watering to help them take root, to tide them over during inclement conditions, and to resist invasive species.

Academic Writing: An Introduction provides materials to prepare the terrain for indigenous species. It presents many samples of academic expression from a range of disciplines in the humanities, social sciences, and natural sciences, offering opportunities for comparison and providing perspectives from which to observe these ways of writing to discover their function in spheres of activity. These perspectives are landscaping materials. They are not naturally occurring. Researchers do not carefully compare the writing in their discipline to writing in other disciplines, although they will have an unexpressed sense of differences. (When a student writes like an historian in philosophy class, the professor will notice.) Genre theory tells us that most of what people know about their

own ways of writing and speaking is tacit, that is, unspoken and unde-
clared. (Would coaches be able to express usefully the principles of their
coach-talk? Probably not.) Moreover, this tacit knowledge can be very
awkward in its expression, even misleading, and also tending to unhelp-
ful generalities: *make sure your essay has a coherent argument.*

Explicit awareness of genres' features doesn't occur naturally. *Academic Writing: An Introduction,* however, cultivates this awareness, helping students to nurture the new plantings in the landscaped terrain, and
to resist invasive species. Confronted with the array of styles and intentions in a typical first- or second-year course of studies, and untrained
to observe the differences or informed that good writing has universal
features, student writers can soon resort to the classroom essay, with for
example its dictates for a thesis statement for which evidence is sought.
Awareness of characteristic features of academic writing and their function can ward off invasive species like the classroom essay.

Instructors can take further measures to resist invasive species by
replacing classroom genres with genres from the research habitat. For
example, instead of distributing a list of topics from which students
choose in order to fulfill an assignment, instructors can issue a Call for
Papers—a genre from research culture—for a class colloquium. The
theme of the colloquium is the line of inquiry that has developed in the
course. Instructors can read the proposals as if they were a conference
organizer—that is, responsible for its success, mindful that people will
want to hear good-quality presentations. Rather than read with a rule-
book in hand, instructors can read the proposals with research-culture
questions in mind: does the proposal address the lines of inquiry that
have developed in the course, that is, will people be interested? Will the
presentation speak to them? Does the proposal demonstrate enough
familiarity with relevant research that people won't say, haven't you read
such-and-such, it deals with exactly what you're talking about? In other
words, will the paper take up the course readings this audience will have
in mind. (There's no need to make up a rule—*refer to at least THREE
course readings*—because the rhetorical situation, derived from research
culture, will coach the uptake.) Does the proposal suggest something
fresh—a new question or perspective, something others can use in their
own thinking? By the methods proposed, is it reasonable to expect that
a useful product will be delivered on time? What is the plan for getting
this done? There will be a mark, reflecting how some proposals will be

better than others, just as they are in the research habitat. But mainly the response is a constructive estimate of real-world feasibility, before a real audience, not only a teacher. The genre of Call for Papers mobilizes the teacher's experience as a participant in research culture. No rules are needed.

Another genre resource that can be introduced into the landscaped terrain is a version of the review article, the account of the state of knowledge in a field—to replace a final exam and to extend the arena of reception for students' writing and speaking. After students have presented their work-in-progress—their five-minute presentations with handouts and questions from the audience—they submit an account of work in this community of scholarship: say, "Trends in research on international security: the view from [course number and name]." Instructors can read these reports as they would a review article in their field: not just for information, for they know the field being reported, but for synthesis, perspective, analysis. Student authors of these submissions detect patterns of inquiry (did everyone consult UN reports? why might that be?), or contrasts in methodologies, in uptake of published research (did everyone in the class seize one theory and overlook others?), in research sites amongst their fellow students, or in findings—how do they add up? do they conflict? To report and analyze this way, students have to listen attentively and collegially to their fellow scholars, just as professional scholars listen to one another. And, with the review pieces posted on the course website, students also get to hear how they themselves have been heard. Introducing this genre extends and enhances audience, offering response beyond the teacher's marking, and enriching writers' sense of their work being used by others, not just rated by a teacher.

The Call for Papers, the brief presentation of work-in-progress, and the review of research trends are indigenous species, but adapted. The adaptations respect this terrain as being landscaped, not wild. Some genres of research culture will not transplant to the terrain of undergraduate education, even if adapted: the keynote address or the job talk, for example, although students may attend these as spectators. Instructors might want to think about the viability of the research article as a transplant. In research culture, it's typically the result of months if not years of work, and typically a passage in a research program. Even with adaptations, planting that genre in the undergraduate landscape might be like moving a three-metre conifer with wide and deep roots to a narrow hole dug in a new space: chances are slim for its flourishing. When we assign 15-page "term papers," are we just expanding the notion of the "essay," or are we attempting this kind of unwieldy transplant? The six-page script for a panel presentation, or two-slide PowerPoint with handouts and talk might be better candidates for transplanting, more likely to address an audience beyond the teacher and draw response from extended inter-action. Or students might prepare annotated bibliographies for use by future students, a student committee selecting the most useful for future dissemination.

There are many more possibilities of adapted transplants to be drawn from the grounds of research culture: the op-ed piece, for example, where a member of an academic community addresses the broader public from a position of expertise on a topic of public concern; ethics approval forms, including consent for research described and justified to both evaluators and participants; explanations of inquiry carried on in a field or sub-field to a multi-disciplinary audience—students explaining what they are doing in one course to students in another course.

Each of these suggestions, as well as the samples—the tasting menu of academic expression—in *Academic Writing: An Introduction*, offers stu-dents a glimpse of what's going on in the domain they step into when they enroll in courses. It's possible that, even today, with innovations in curriculum, this scene is still curtained off by the student genres: the exam, the quiz, even innovations like reading journals (how does the journal work? what does it do, or prepare its writer to do? how does it contribute to a sphere of activity?). A question the first author of this book asks herself when she thinks about introducing a new writing activ-ity: is there a parallel in research culture, a native species? What are the interactional conditions of its flourishing? For if there is not a parallel native species, rules will have to be devised to keep the writing alive.

Academic Writing: An Introduction provides some landscaping mate-rials to prepare the terrain for indigenous species—those suggested here, and others occurring in the habitats adjacent to students' coursework. Like others, we find that reporting research conversations is a core activ-ity to all disciplines, and also that it is a site of meaningful differences amongst them. Along the same lines, and again like others, we find that means of qualifying and limiting statements is crucial to participation in research culture, not as a formality but as a practical recognition of the means of making knowledge in the disciplines. These rhetorical actions are at the heart of work in any discipline, and they afford a view of disciplinarity itself.

Even so, *Academic Writing: An Introduction* is not on its own a course of study. It is meant to contribute to the cultivation of a community of new scholars. It is meant to support students—beginning or beyond—in their collegial inquiries. *Academic Writing: An Introduction* can accompany multi-disciplinary studies; or it can accompany materials from courses students have in common. Where the course is stand-alone, materials for inquiry—that is, research conversations—could engage topics active not only in multiple research domains but in public consciousness as well: for example, international security; migration and transnational youth, settlement and identity; labour markets and international trade; the ethics and politics of sustainability; media and dissent, media history; homelessness and income inequality; the science of climate change and its public dissemination. In some settings, an institution may afford a unique archive, local and compelling, for students' disciplined exploration and preparation for report to other scholars or to an interested public. If instructors feel these areas are beyond their expertise, *Academic Writing: An Introduction* offers to them a field guide to exploring new territory, just as it offers students such a guide as they enter the undergraduate terrain.

Janet Giltrow

1

Introducing Genre

1A Hearing Voices

The seven passages below are in English. The observation that they are all written in English may be less important than the grounds on which they differ. As you read them, think about what they have in common and how they differ from one another. Issuing from decidedly different moments in North American life, each passage voices a different **cultural situation**. No one could say which of these passages is "best," or which is proper English and which is not. But we can think about how each voice—each style of expression—serves the **situation** from which it arises.

PASSAGE 1

Research on stigma management strategies has examined the many ways that discredited persons, or those of low status, attempt to maintain self-worth and dignity (see Anderson and Snow 2001 for a review). In *Stigma*, Goffman outlined "passing," in which the discreditable person conceals the stigma through "information control," and "covering," which involves making "a great effort to keep the stigma from looming large" (1963a:102). Numerous studies have enhanced the understanding of the processes of passing and covering (e.g., Charmaz 1991, 1995; Herman 1993; Anderson, Snow, and Cress 1994; Nack 2008). When neither strategy is possible, especially when one has reached one's limits, defiant behavior

1

becomes an option, and the stigmatized engage in "reactive, entailing actions and verbalizations meant to reject humiliating moral assaults or ridicule" (Anderson et al. 1994:134).

Irvine, Kahl, and Smith 2012: 25.

PASSAGE 2
CanuckDriver
2:33 PM on 15 July 2013

Trust the G&M to keep flogging this dead horse. There has been no—repeat—NO—global warming since 1998. There has been a slight cooling trend.

A major recent study shows a direct correlation to CFC's in the Earth's atmosphere interacting with solar radiation as the cause. CFC concentrations are declining and with their decline so are temperatures.

Besides, only ice on land need be considered when talking about melting ice caps. If it's in the water already, it does not affect the levels. Don't believe me, take a glass of water and put an ice cube in it. Mark the water level. Wait for the ice to melt, then check the level.

More of the IPCC's utter balderdash.

8 replies

PASSAGE 3
My name is Jersey and I am only 15 weeks old. My mom is Amy and she is just 1 year old. My mom and I are best buds and are always found together! Why won't people adopt us together? Please don't make us be adopted separately, we want to stay together!! Come meet us and you'll see! We are both awesome and you'll have endless entertainment ... mom sometimes likes to talk so maybe she'll tell you a story? We are currently hangin with VOKRA so please go to the site and fill out an adoption application if you are interested in us....

PASSAGE 4
In baseball, the home run is a sure way to score and the problem of hitting the ball as far as possible is as old as the game. An analysis of the problem consists of two phases: impact and flight. Many previous

investigations have considered one or both of the phases of this problem. Briggs[1] investigated the effects of velocity and spin on the lateral deflection of a curve ball. Baseballs spinning about a vertical axis were dropped through a horizontal wind tunnel. The lateral deflection of the ball was found to be proportional to the spin and the square of the translational velocity for speeds up to 150 ft/s and spins up to 1800 rpm. Achenbach[2] characterized the drag on spheres as a function of the Reynolds number Re and the surface roughness. He showed that there is a critical Reynolds number at which the drag coefficient C_D decreases dramatically and that this critical Reynolds number decreases as the roughness increases. Although a baseball is not uniformly rough, the spinning seams cause boundary layer behavior similar to that of a rough surface.

Sawicki and Hubbard 2003: 1152.

PASSAGE 5

Executive living in this LIKE NEW, upgraded, spacious 1 bdrm & den (could be 2nd bdrm), 2 full baths home in a boutique complex. Absolutely fantastic water & mountain views. Just steps to the seawall, marina, parks, restaurants and shopping. Featuring stunning Brazilian tiger wood H/W flrs, upgraded doors, mouldings & baseboards. Upgraded appliances incl 5-Star gas range, Fisher & Pakel fridge, Asko top of the line dishwasher & Panasonic Genius microwave, Caesar Stone counters & breakfast bar with California glass tile backsplash. Bathrms with travertine floors & walls, granite accents & counters, Kohler sinks & Grohe trims. Plush carpet, custom lighting built-in custom storage & closet. $879,000.

PASSAGE 6

1.2 Unless otherwise agreed in writing with Google, your agreement with Google will always include, at a minimum, the terms and conditions set out in this document. These are referred to below as the "Universal Terms." Open source software licenses for Google Chrome source code constitute separate written agreements. To the limited extent that the open source software licenses expressly supersede these Universal Terms, the open source licenses govern your agreement with Google for the use of Google Chrome or specific included components of Google Chrome.

PASSAGE 7

"Memories give me the strength I need to proceed, the strength I need to believe." Puff Daddy. This babygirl faced many challenges & brings with her wisdom, strength & sweet memories. Much luv to God & her loving parents. FM's: B&E's, YB '95–97 crew, Vox/R#17, fireworks, 290 guy (Minty? Sarah?), car races (boom!) eject'n seat/ Chungism w/Mike, killing 007/starfish w/Ho, who's Paul?, Summer Jam, jon z's w/evil one & STM grad/ 101 w/Brian. Shouts: my girl 2107 (&pops), Jenn, Geoff, Ang, Bear (you're mine! 112 hugs), all my buddies & bad boyz [sic]! FP: skydive, be happy & live the good life!

Exercise 1

Name the types of writing exemplified in Passages 1–7. Can you identify the distinct occasion or cultural situation which each serves? A cultural situation connects writers and intended readers, so begin by trying to identify the writer and reader for each passage. How does this situation shape the writer's choices?

1B Hearing Genres

The passages above not only serve the cultural situations in which they arise; they also embody them. They represent distinct occasions in our culture; at the same time, people recognize and respond to them in ways that can be recognized as typical. So, when we hear these different voices, we also "hear" the setting in which they operate. The sounds of these passages indicate typical moments which culture has produced: occasions of professional publication, online debate, or legal agreement. In each case, the situation has left its mark on, or *imprinted*, English. It has pressed into the general shape of the language features—for example, patterns of word choice and sentence construction—which mark it for use in particular contexts. The **imprint** makes language characteristic: something we recognize as typical of how people communicate with one another in particular circumstances.

To name the types and situations for each of these passages, you have to call upon your knowledge of North American culture. Perhaps Passage 3 escaped you: your life experience may not have included contact with the situation which has produced this particular kind of pet-adoption advertisement. Or, you may never have encountered highly condensed yearbook profiles of the kind that appears in Passage 7. Hearing and speaking, reading and writing, we enact our experience of the world as that experience has been shaped by culture.

As the diversity of the seven passages shows, language is sensitive to situation. Moreover, the way we use language changes as new situations arise. For example, new technologies have given rise to new situations and new ways of using language, such as texting. In this situation, instead of using conventional spelling and full sentences, we often use single letters, numbers, and emoticons; and our friends recognize this way of writing as a typical and appropriate, not incorrect, use of English. In recent years, this sensitivity to situation has been captured and studied in new ways of thinking about **genre**. This book takes advantage of these recent developments.

Before sketching new ideas about genre, let us glance at old ones. Chances are that when you hear the word "genre," you think of music or movies. For example, you may think of the difference between hip hop and technopop, or between slasher movies and psychological thrillers. Or you heard the word in the high-school classroom in connection with literary studies. Genre was, for instance, a way of saying that poems, novels, and plays are different. So the notion of genre helped school boards make their curriculum orderly. Now at university, some of your English courses may be organized according to genre: one course is about poems, another is about novels. For these purposes, genre has been a useful concept, tending toward traditional descriptions of literary form.

But then, at the end of the twentieth century, more and more scholars began to think about the social and political contexts of knowledge. Scholars considered the ways in which the characteristics of statements about the world depended on who was making the statement and who was being addressed. Alert to new opportunities, genre offered itself as a way of thinking about the context-dependency of language—the ways in which language depends upon and responds to the social and political contexts that produce it.

While old ideas of genre had slipped into regarding only **form**, the new ideas insisted that it was not form alone that constituted genre, but situation and form:

situation + form = genre

Or, to put it another way, the situations that writers find themselves in *give rise* to genres.

This new understanding of genre gave researchers a way of talking about similarities of form not as rules but as signs of common ground among communities of readers and writers: shared attitudes, practices and habits, positions in the world. Forms of speaking are connected to social contexts where people *do* things—like renting an apartment or finding a pet. Different routines of social behaviour—habits of acting in the world—create different genres of speech and writing.

In this light, consider the thank-you note as a genre. People who know this genre not only know how to compose the note—what to mention, how much to say, how to begin, how to conclude, what kind of writing materials to use—but also *when* to do all this: soon after receipt of a certain type of gift from a person in a certain relation to the recipient. (So, in all probability, you would not send a thank-you note to your parents for the gift of a laptop computer or to the Students' Union for the daily planner you were handed as you walked across campus on the first day of classes. And if you delay sending a thank-you note where one is called for, you will feel—consciously or unconsciously—that you are failing to comply with the genre's norms, no matter how perfectly you compose the note itself.) The thank-you note genre is made up not only of a characteristic type of written expression but also of the situation in which it occurs. It is a way of acting in the world. People with know-how in this genre understand not only its form but also its situation. We could even say that, at some deep, perhaps unconscious level, these people also share an understanding of the role of the genre in larger social or cultural situations—systems of relationship amongst family and friends, symbolized by the exchange of gifts and expressions of recognition and gratitude.

Once scholars began to consider genre outside traditional literary studies, it became clear that English classes weren't its only, or even its best, place of work. Increasingly, other kinds of writing began to be thought of in terms of genre: auditors' reports, news accounts of violent crime, case reports in publications in veterinary medicine, architects' proposals, primary school show-and-tell sessions, and—most impor-tant to our interests—**academic writing**. At all these sites, genre was a means of investigating similarities in documents occurring in similar situations.

Genre theory gave researchers a way of talking about these similarities not as rules but as signs of common ground among communities of readers and writers: shared attitudes, practices and habits, positions in the world. So the style of Passage 5, the real estate ad, comes about not because somebody followed rules, but because it embodies a widely recognized situation—property transaction in a market economy—through its typical, list-like naming of qualities that the users of this genre recognize as valued and translatable into dollars. Views are good, and so is proximity to the city's seawall and marina. The document assumes that readers recognize the value of custom-built storage and the prestige associated with various brand names. It trusts that readers will interpret the wide array of materials—tiger wood, granite, travertine, and glass—as indicators of luxury and taste rather than as revealing a haphazard approach to construction. It also assumes that readers are familiar with the customary practice of buying and selling a dwelling—contacting a broker specializing in this kind of transaction. Note that such knowledge is not universal but cultural. In another culture, where people inherit their homes from their parents, or share them with co-workers, such a genre would not exist at all. Or some culture, somewhere, might value a home not for its brand name appliances but for its human history: while in urban North America people exchange homes with strangers, dwellings in some other place might be identified with their residents. Then the genre accompanying property transactions might develop techniques for describing the dwelling's current or past occupants in appealing or prestigious terms. In each case, the genre suits the cultural situation.

Perhaps, a hundred years from now, historians will examine personal ads or rental agreements to piece together vanished systems of association amongst people. Or they will look at the genres which report research in physics or social history to understand the systems of professional interaction and knowledge production which held academic communities together at the turn of the millennium.

Exercise 2

Consider one of the following pairs of popular genres, or come up with your own pair:

- the romantic comedy and the spy film;
- the half-hour infomercial and the brief television ad;
- manga and the American-style comic book;
- email and texting;
- hip hop and electronic dance music.

What are some differences in form between the two genres you've chosen? How do those differences embody the different social situations that those genres serve?

1C High-School vs. University Writing

Genre theory predicts that diversity of expression will reflect the complexities of social life, whether that life takes place in a chat room or on a hockey rink or in a university classroom. Because people interact for a lot of different purposes, they write and speak in a lot of different ways. And, as the world changes, so too will ways of writing and speaking. If we apply genre theory to the kinds of writing produced by university researchers, we can better understand what communities of scholars do and how they typically communicate with one another. For the student just beginning a university career, there are huge benefits to understanding how communities of scholars interact.

Writing *instruction*, however, has tended to focus on one type of writing: the schoolroom essay. Different kinds of assignments may produce different versions of the essay—the "argument" essay, for example, or the "expository" essay—but, generally, when students arrive at college or university, they are experienced in producing forms of writing which serve the high-school classroom. Along with this experience, they absorb—from teachers, from handbooks, from public sentiments—ideas about writing. It should be "clear" and "concise," for example; it should not be "vague" or "wordy." Writing should also be "logical" and "well organized."

But then, at university, students encounter writing that would not be "clear" to most people (consider Passage 4), and writing that most people would not call "concise" (Passage 1). And what seems to be "logical" in one discipline might not seem "logical" from the perspective of another.

For example, a physics student, recording findings from an experiment, may be expected to privilege unbiased observation and objective recording of data, while an anthropology student, writing a report on the behaviour of a community, may be asked to recognize that the community needs to accept and even edit results. "Organization" in a book review written for a history class is not "organization" in a psychology lab report, and neither resembles "organization" in an argument essay in high school. After their long experience with the schoolroom essay, and long contact with rules and pronouncements about good writing, university students suddenly face many examples of expression that contradict the schoolroom tradition.

Genre theory tells us that the schoolroom essay—in its style—serves its situation. Inspecting the situation, we might look for connections between the kinds of features prized in student essays and the broader function of the schoolroom itself. We might consider the schoolroom's role in socializing youth, in controlling the time of young people, in scheduling some students for further education—in well-paid occupations that structure and regulate social life—and scheduling others for vocational or service occupations. Since the essay is a persistent genre, it must be doing an adequate job of defining, and serving, and maintaining schoolroom situations.

But the schoolroom and the university classroom are different situations. Accordingly, the kind of writing that suits the schoolroom tends not to suit the university classroom. That is, these two kinds of writing represent two different genres—that is, two different blends of *situation* and *form*.

Exercise 3

Develop a list of features that, in your experience, define essays you wrote in high school. Consider in particular anything that may have been presented as a rule. (For example, "never refer to yourself in the first person.") In each case, try to identify the social function the feature served in the high-school classroom. (Did it encourage—or discourage—certain kinds of stances, attitudes, or tones?) Present your list to the class and have your instructor comment on how many of these features pertain to writing that experienced university students—or, for that matter, university researchers—produce.

1D **The University as Research Institution**

The most important distinction between high-school and university situations is that the latter are located in research institutions—that is, institutions that produce new knowledge through observation, experimentation, and interpretation of the natural world and humanity, or that apply, integrate, or mobilize existing knowledge for other sectors of society. While students may see themselves as learners rather than researchers, they nevertheless do their learning under the direction of people who are trained as researchers and who read and write research publications. The knowledge that university students acquire is the kind of knowledge that comes from the techniques of inquiry developed by the various **academic disciplines**. We could go so far as to say that in the university the very wording of the facts and concepts students must absorb derives from research practice: the routines, habits, and values which motivate scholars to do the work they do. This wording represents research communities' beliefs and their members' shared techniques for interpreting the world. At the same time, such wording is also the medium in which students must work.

If university students are not writing schoolroom essays, what are they writing? What uses of language or wordings will represent the student's position in the university situation? While it would be too much to say that students should write research articles, it is not too much to say that their writing shares features of the **research genres**. After all, while the undergraduate curriculum readies most students for careers outside the university, it prepares some to assume positions as researchers in universities and other institutions. It's not surprising, then, that the information students encounter in their university courses is shaped by the research situations or academic disciplines that produced it. So, as students work with a particular type of research information—experimental data, archaeological artefacts, philosophical concepts—the style of that research genre becomes the most appropriate for them to adopt. And while the wording of research writing shares some features with the schoolroom essay—both are, after all, English—for our purposes the differences are more meaningful than the similarities. (Equally, the styles of the different disciplines share many features, but the differences are meaningful and have consequences.) This book puts student writers in touch with the language of the research genres, and in doing so it invites students to enter the **discourse communities** where researchers conduct their work. It shows student writers what the salient, or distinguishing, features of scholarly expression are—features which distinguish the scholarly genres and which we recognize as typical of academic situations. At the same time, it encourages students to develop informed perspectives on scholarly styles and situations. As sites for shared understandings, and shared means of interpreting the world, genres can seem like worlds unto themselves—self-justifying and removed from the concerns of everyday life. But the research genres (like other genres) are not worlds unto themselves. They are involved in all the social and political complexities of their times.

Exercise 4

The styles of expression in Passages 1 to 7 differ in many respects. In the chapters which follow, you will acquire means of identifying and using salient features of 1 and 4—the two passages from research genres. But you might begin to develop your awareness of style here by inspecting and comparing all seven samples. First, and most broadly, what distinguishes 1 and 4 from the others? Second, and more narrowly, can you distinguish between the styles of 1 and 4? In approaching these tasks, you might take into account these features:

- ways the writers are represented in the text (most obviously, do they mention themselves?);
- words—their commonness (would they show up in, for example, conversation between neighbours?), their recurrence (to what degree do these writers repeat the same words?); and sentences—their length, completeness;
- capital letters, parentheses, names, dates.

How would you describe the relation between writer and reader in each of these passages?

From what you know (or can guess) about the ways of life surrounding each of these samples, estimate how each of the writers learned to write this way (on the job? in class? on a weekend seminar?).

2

Citation and Summary

In Chapter 1 we considered genre in terms of social and cultural situations with which writers and readers—users of the genre—are familiar. We have seen that genres involve patterns of form and style which represent common ground (shared purposes) between writers and readers. Sharing that common ground, writers and readers recognise its features. We could say that successful writing depends upon readers' recognition of features of the genre.

In the next two chapters we head for **summary**—an important and highly recognizable feature of the research genres. Summary may not seem, at first, an attractive destination, or a serious one. With its schoolroom role as a check to see if you've done assigned reading, or its role in exams in seeing if you understand what you read ("List the three main points the author makes. Write in complete sentences."), summary can appear to be a mechanical exercise. But for scholarly writers, summary fulfils quite different functions. In summarizing, academics identify with a community of researchers, establish what **positions** have been taken by others, and take a position themselves. All of these activities allow them to construct new knowledge. In this sense, summary is a central activity of scholarly life.

So, to put summary in the context of research itself and to show how summary is part of the scholarly community of practice, we are going to begin by examining how **citation** occurs in different disciplines, noting similarities and differences in citation practices. We will also look at how citation in scholarly discourse differs from citation in everyday conversation and other situations.

2A Introducing Scholarly Citation

Here is a way of writing which somebody unaccustomed to scholarly writing in archaeology might find peculiar:

PASSAGE 1

It is widely believed that the archaeological traces of the last Neanderthal and earliest anatomically modern human populations in western Europe are represented by the Chatelperronian and Aurignacian cultures, respectively.[1-10] The Chatelperronian culture is confined essentially to western France and northern Spain, and shows strong technological links with the immediately preceding Mousterian technologies. The Aurignacian culture is distributed over the whole of western, central and eastern Europe, and apparently reflects a major population dispersal across these regions (deriving ultimately from the Near Eastern region) over the period approximately 43,000–36,000 before present (BP) (uncalibrated radiocarbon years).[9] Skeletal remains associated with the Chatelperronian and Aurignacian industries, although not abundant, bear out these correlations.[1,2,9,11,12]

Notes

1 Bar-Yosef, O. The Upper Paleolithic revolution. *Annu. Rev. Anthropol.* 31, 363–393 (2002).

2 Hublin, J.-J. in *The Geography of Neandertals and Modern Humans in Europe and the Greater Mediterranean* (eds Bar-Yosef, O. & Pilbeam, P.) 157–182 (Peabody Museum, Harvard Univ., Cambridge, 2000).

3 Klein, R.G. Archaeology and the evolution of human behaviour. *Evol. Anthropol.* 9, 7–36 (2000).

4 Conard, N. & Bolus, M. Radiocarbon dating the appearance of modern humans and the timing of cultural innovations in Europe: new results and new challenges. *J. Hum. Evol.* 44, 331–371 (2003).

5 Zilhaõ, J. & d'Errico, F. The chronology and taphonomy of the earliest Aurignacian and its implications for the understanding of

Neanderthal extinction. *J. World Prehist.* 13, 1–68 (1999).

6 Zilhaõ, J. & d'Errico, F. (eds) *The Chronology of the Aurignacian and of the Transitional Technocomplexes: Dating, Stratigraphies, Cultural Implications* (Instituto Português de Arqueologia, Lisbon, 2003).

7 Mellars, P.A. The Neanderthal problem continued. *Curr. Anthropol.* 40, 341–364 (1999).

8 Mellars, P.A. in *The Geography of Neanderthals and Modern Humans in Europe and the Greater Mediterranean* (eds Bar-Yosef, O. & Pilbeam, P.) 35–48 (Peabody Museum, Harvard Univ., Cambridge, 2000).

9 Mellars, P.A. Neanderthals and the modern human colonization of Europe. *Nature* 432, 461–465 (2004).

10 Mellars, P.A. The impossible coincidence: a single species model for the origins of modern human behaviour in Europe. *Evol. Anthropol.* 14, 12–27 (2005).

11 Gambier, D. in *The Human Revolution: Behavioural and Biological Perspectives on the Origins of Modern Humans* (eds Mellars, P.A. & Stringer, C.) 194–211 (Edinburgh Univ. Press, Edinburgh, 1989).

12 Churchill, S. & Smith, F. Makers of the early Aurignacian of Europe. *Yb. Phys. Anthropol.* 43, 61–115 (2000).

Brad Gravina, Paul Mellars, and Christopher Bronk Ramsey 2005 "Radiocarbon dating of interstratified Neanderthal and early modern human occupations at the Chatelperronian type-site." *Nature* 438 (3): 51–56, 51.

But this kind of citation—using superscripts at the ends of sentences—isn't peculiar to archaeologists. Other researchers—physicists and historians, for instance—write this way, too. Sociologists, by contrast, include the names of cited authors within sentences:

PASSAGE 2

In spite of the well-worn nature of critiques of utopian and dystopian arguments surrounding information and communication technologies (ICTs) and new media in academic circles (see Bingham 1996; Bingham, Valentine and Holloway 1999; Hinchliffe 1996; Holloway and Valentine 2003; May and Hearn 2005; Pain et al. 2005; Woolgar 2002) and tendencies to understand machines more as "troublesome companions" rather than as salvations or threats (Bijker, Hughes and Pinch 1987, cited in Thrift 1996), dualistic interpretations persist, particularly in the popular media. In the case of technologies that are used by children and young people, these interpretations tend toward the dystopian, for example some New Zealand schools have banned the use of cell phones because of fears of "text bullying" and disruptions to school work. The purpose of this paper is an analysis of the widespread use by young people of cell phones and text messaging or SMS (short message service).

Lee Thompson and Julie Cupples 2008 "Seen and not heard? Text messaging and digital sociality." *Social & Cultural Geography* 9 (1): 95–108, 95.

Neanderthals may be unfamiliar as a topic of discussion for most of us, while cell phones and text messaging are probably exceedingly familiar. But both of these passages share ways of talking about their topic which may strike us as surprising, even baffling. For example, both topics are referred to using somewhat rare wording: "earliest anatomically modern human populations in Western Europe" and "critiques of utopian and dystopian arguments surrounding information and communication technologies." There are also some conspicuous formal features—clusters of superscripts in Passage 1 and long parenthetical interruptions to the sentences in Passage 2, with only names and years in them. Why do Gravina, Mellars, and Ramsey write, "Skeletal remains ... bear out these correlations[1,2,9,11,12]"? Why do Thompson and Cupples write, "(see Bingham 1996; Bingham, Valentine and Holloway 1999; Hinchliffe 1996; Holloway and Valentine 2003; May and Hearn 2005; Pain et al. 2005; Woolgar 2002)"? What kind of writing finds such references so important?

These patches of parenthetical references and superscripts are a condensed, concentrated way of telling us that somebody other than the present writer has said something: they signal citation. Other writers in different research disciplines use different citing strategies. They **unpack** the clumps of names and dates, show us that these statements have been uttered by other speakers, and even permit us to hear their actual words. In the next passage, Ann Taylor Allen, an historian, is beginning a discussion of what others have said about moods of uncertainty in the early part of the twentieth century (people feeling insecure and alienated). We've used bold type to emphasize the **reporting expressions** which attribute statements about those moods to writers other than Allen.

PASSAGE 3

Most of the literature on European and North American intellectual history at the turn of the century emphasizes the problematic
and disorienting effects of (**as Everdell puts it**), "the impossibility
of knowing even the simplest things that the nineteenth century
took for granted."[1] In fact, **the characterization of** the period from
1890 to 1914 as an era of pessimism, alienation, and anxiety has
become a cliché of intellectual history. In German political thought,
Fritz Stern describes a mood of "cultural despair";[2] for the social
sciences, **writes Lawrence Scaff**, "the central problem appears to be
the same in every case: a sense that unified experience lies beyond
the grasp of the modern self and that malaise and self-conscious guilt
have become inextricably entwined with culture."[3] **Eugen Weber
remarks** that, in France at the turn of the century, "the discrepancy
between material progress and spiritual dejection reminded me of
my own era."[4] In Britain, **the literary critic Terry Eagleton refers**
to a "cataclysmic crisis of Victorian rationality."[5]

Notes

1   William R. Everdell, *The First Moderns: Profiles in the Origins of Twen-
    tieth-Century Thought* (Chicago, 1997), 10–11.
2   Fritz Stern, *The Politics of Cultural Despair: A Study in the Rise of the
    Germanic Ideology* (1961; rpt. edn., New York, 1965).
3   Lawrence A. Scaff, *Fleeing the Iron Cage: Culture, Politics, and Moder-
    nity in the Thought of Max Weber* (Berkeley, Calif., 1989), 80.
4   Eugen Weber, *France: Fin de Siècle* (Cambridge, Mass., 1986), 3. For
    other examples, see [...].
5   Terry Eagleton, "The Flight to the Real," in *Cultural Politics at the Fin
    de Siècle*, Sally Ledger and Scott McCracken, eds. (Cambridge, 1995),
    13.

Ann Taylor Allen 1999 "Feminism, social science, and the meanings of modernity: The debate
on the origin of the family in Europe and the United States, 1860–1914." *The American
Historical Review* 104 (4): 1085–1113, 1085–86.

We might compare the way names of cited authors, numbers in super-
script, and notes are used by an historian with the forms of citation used
by a literary critic. In the following passage, Joyce Irene Middleton discusses what others have said about the work of Toni Morrison, a Nobel

prize–winning American novelist. We've used bold type to emphasize the reporting expressions by which Middleton attributes statements about Morrison's novels to writers (including Morrison herself):

PASSAGE 4

Literary critics praise Toni Morrison's novels as "modernist" and "experimental," but **such criticism overlooks** the extent to which her fiction draws on the oldest literary tradition of all, that of oral storytelling. Morrison's achievement has been to illuminate the values of an ancient form within the modern novel. By using this highly literate and literary genre, she privileges oral memory and the oral culture of the African-American community and dramatizes the cultural conflicts between oral and literate traditions. **Morrison herself emphasizes** the traditional elements of her work **and distinguishes** herself from the lineage of the modern novel, **asserting in an interview with the African-American literary scholar Nellie McKay,**

> I am not *like* James Joyce; I am not *like* Thomas Hardy; I am not *like* Faulkner. I am not *like* in that sense ... I am not experimental, I am simply trying to recreate something out of an old art form in my books. (426–27)

Toni Morrison's novels are especially rich in participatory oral forms such as songs, poetic language, formulaic features, the language of ritual and oral epic, which appeal for audience involvement and do not support an aesthetic view of art for art's sake. Furthermore, a central concept in her work is that of oral memory, highly valued in an oral culture but ignored and devalued in a highly literate one.

Joyce Irene Middleton 1993 "Orality, literacy, and memory in Toni Morrison's *Song of Solomon*." *College English* 55 (1): 64–75, 64 (italic emphasis in the original).

Unlike research in history, where names of cited authors and details of publication are made available at the bottom of the page, Passage 4 uses a list of references at the end of the paper. These references, however, are recorded in a format quite different from the references in the archaeologists' article on Neanderthals or the sociologists' study of text messaging.

But whether researchers refer to cited authors by number, by name and date, or simply by name, the practice of citation—the attributing of a statement to another speaker—produces one of the distinctive sounds (and looks) of scholarly writing. The distinctiveness of this way of writing could lead to one or two views of scholarly writing that may be overly simple and misleading. The first is that the only people who repeat the words and ideas of others are scholars. The second is that scholarly citations are a shortcut to "authority," simply a way to support an argument, and that scholarly writing is a platform for those who have a knack for repeating the words of others. We discuss each of these views below.

Exercise 1

Compare your experience reading passages 1–4 above. How do the different ways of citing affect your reading and comprehension of the passages? Does one style of citation seem more familiar to you than another? What do the different approaches to citation—the information the citation styles emphasize, the different ways the writer refers to previous researchers and their work—suggest about what the different academic disciplines see as especially noteworthy?

2B Is Citation Unique to Scholarly Writing?

So commonly do people in everyday conversation repeat the sayings of others that specialists in language studies investigate this speech habit. For example, Wallace Chafe (1994) focuses on how speakers' representations of others' words involve awareness of contexts distant from the setting of the conversation; Patricia Mayes's study of citation in spoken English finds that "at least half of the direct quotations are not authentic renditions, and many are the invention of the speaker" (1990: 358); and Greg Myers (1999) proposes methods to classify the many functions of citation, showing that the speech technique of representing the words of others involves complex purposes and, on the listener's part, subtle interpretive schemes. These are all studies of citation in commonplace settings: people telling about their experiences and feelings, explaining themselves, or passing on information about others.

And, if we consult our own experience, we too can readily tune in to citation in our daily encounters, as in the two following passages:

> So this guy comes over and says is that your car and I'm like yeah
> and he goes you gonna leave it there and I'm like—*what???*

> The weather channel says showers in the morning but then clearing.

Sometimes we encounter second-hand and even third-hand reports.
In the following passage, a speaker ("I") recounts what her friend Pat
reported Sally said, and Pat's account of what she said in reply:

> Pat's friend Sally is breaking up with her boyfriend. Apparently Sally
> is very upset and phones Pat all the time, and Pat is getting really
> tired of this. I guess Sally is always saying, Why me? So Pat finally
> said, Why not you? I think Pat's getting a bit frustrated.

Why is citation so common in everyday conversation? Possibly
because much of what we know about the world we learn only from
what others have said, and because conveying this knowledge as coming
from a particular source gives us a chance to take a position in relation
to other people's positions in the world. For example, the speaker in the
first passage above takes an oppositional stance vis-à-vis the other speaker
("this guy") he cites, while the speaker in the second passage uses citation
to show the source of his prediction about the weather.

How people cite others has an important effect on the listener's
understanding. Sometimes writers in non-academic genres—in the next
example, a writer of a letter to the editor of a small-town newspaper—
use citation to typify what they take to be a general message from other
sources (in this case, sources with which the writer strongly disagrees) by
putting words in others' mouths:

> Disincentives are everywhere for drivers.... "take transit so we can
> clog our arteries with fuel-hogging buses." I don't like it, and there
> is nothing I can do about it.
>
> Letter to the editor. *Tri-City News* 26 April 2000.

In the following passage, the speaker is one of a group of British working-class men who are on probation after having been convicted of
money-related crimes:

> They can rip off millions and pay nothing, then someone gets caught,
> twenty, thirty pounds DSS an' "they're a criminal scum-bag."
>
> Sara Willott and Chris Griffin 1999 "Building your own lifeboat: Working-class male offenders
> talk about economic class." *British Journal of Social Psychology* 38: 445–60, 451.

Notice that the speaker is *not* stating that small-time thieves are criminal scum-bags. He is stating that *others* (what we might call Big Interests) *say* that small-time thieves are criminal scum-bags, and he aligns himself in opposition to these others: his citation distinguishes his interests from the interests of those he perceives as embezzling and pillaging on a large scale. On the other hand, the next speakers (from the same group) self-cite not to oppose others but to establish solidarity amongst themselves:

> Mark: always said, right, you don't take from somebody who's just as bad off as you. I'd rather take from somebody who could *afford* to lose.
> Andy: What you say, "you don't take off your own kind."
> Mark: Exactly.
> Steve: Your own doorstep.
> Andy: Yup, your own doorstep ...
>
> Willott and Griffin 1999: 456.

Sometimes in everyday conversation, we simply repeat what we have heard, sewing it with invisible stitches into our utterances. Someone who has himself conducted no studies of climate change and has not visited South Asia could say—

> There are droughts in South Asia ... global warming

—and his listeners could infer that he read this somewhere, or heard it on television.

Other times, a view of our own gets a boost from citing a source people consider authoritative:

> He was black and blue from head to toe, the doctor says it was a miracle he survived.

Much of our performance as speakers is citation—repeating what others have said, attributing statements to those with authority, or those with whom we disagree: naming some of our sources (e.g., Pat), typifying others ("the doctor," "the weather channel"), leaving some anonymous ("they say," "this guy"), or leaving some cited claims unattributed. Some citation is more or less verbatim; some is paraphrase; some is invented.

Seeking recognition and sympathy for our position, or spreading the news or playing our part in rumour and hearsay, we repeat what others have said.

Exercise 2

Consider again the first example of non-scholarly citation we discussed:

> So this guy comes over and says is that your car and I'm like yeah and he goes you gonna leave it there and I'm like—*what???*

Here is an account of how this passage manages **reported speech**: "So this guy (speaker) comes over and says (reporting expression) is that your car (reported speech) and I (speaker)'m like (reporting expression) yeah (reported speech) and he (speaker) goes (reporting expression) you gonna leave it there (reported speech) and I (speaker)'m like (reporting expression)—*what???* (reported speech)."

In the two following passages apply the same notation to locate the speaker (or source of information) and the reported speech:

PASSAGE 5

Judy—you know, from Student Loans—she called me the other day, and she says they haven't received my cheque. And I say, I sent it last week. And she says, Oh.

PASSAGE 6

[My mother] took—she's got these two Dobermans who are really unruly but very sweet. She took them for a walk on the beach one day, and this was at the height of the Rottweiler scare, and this jogger's running along the beach at Liverpool, and Sophie, her dog that she can't control, decided to run along after the jogger and bit him on the bottom. And this man was going absolutely mad, and my mother started off by being nice to him and saying, "I'm terribly sorry; she's only a pup and she was just being playful," and so on, and he got worse, so the more she tried to placate him, the more he decided he was gonna go to the police station and create a scene about it. So she said, "Let me have a look," and she strode over to him and pulled his <LAUGHS> pulled his tracksuit bottoms down, and said, "Don't be so bloody stupid, man, there's nothing wrong with you, you're perfectly all right." At which point he was so embarrassed he just jogged away.

Cited in Jennifer Coates 1996 *Women talk: Conversation between women friends.* Cambridge: Blackwell, 100–01.

Exercise 3

Citation in everyday conversation: Without intruding on anyone's privacy, listen to discussions you overhear or in which you participate: listen for, and record, two or three instances of citation in everyday conversation. How does this speaker (who might be you) attribute his or her cited statement to a source? Is the source named ("Barb," "Prince Charles"), typified ("the Registrar's Office," "the vet"), anonymous ("I heard ...," "they")? What role does the citation play in the conversation?

Exercise 4

Citation in news genres: Citation not only plays a part in many conversational situations, it also has a major role in newspaper reports, in Western cultures especially. To get a sense of its importance in constructing public information, read the passage below and identify the statements that are citations. Which are paraphrase? Which are presented word for word? Which cited speakers are fully identified? Which are typified or anonymous? How would the reader's understanding of the trial change if we removed the expressions attributing statements to others?

THE PICKTON TRIAL—TESTIMONY

A close friend of Robert Pickton saw lots of blood everywhere in Mr. Pickton's trailer on one occasion in the mid-1990s, the jury at the first-degree murder trial heard yesterday.

However, the jury was not told anything else about the bloody scene. Mr. Pickton's friend, Ingrid Fehlauer, was not asked to elaborate on her testimony.

Instead, her credibility became an issue for the jury to consider.

Ms. Fehlauer had testified earlier yesterday that she did not see anything unusual when she was cleaning Mr. Pickton's trailer in late 1996 or early 1997. "Just the amount of dirt on the carpet," Ms. Fehlauer said with a chuckle.

But in cross-examination by Crown prosecutor Mike Petrie, Ms. Fehlauer agreed that she saw "lots of blood everywhere." She told the court she did not say anything about the blood earlier because defence lawyers had told her the matter would not be mentioned in court.

Ms. Fehlauer agreed with Mr. Petrie that, despite taking an oath to tell the truth, she chose to say something that she knew was untrue.

Mr. Justice James Williams told jurors to consider Ms. Fehlauer's credibility. "She answered in a way that was not truthful," Judge Williams said. The defence lawyers did not do anything improper in telling her that the matter would not be mentioned in court, he added, without explaining the basis for the lawyers' advice.

Ms. Fehlauer was the seventh witness for the defence to testify at Mr. Pickton's trial. A middle-aged mother of two children, she had known Mr. Pickton since she was a youngster of five or six. She lived across the street from the Pickton farm in the mid-1990s and did housecleaning for Mr. Pickton on six or seven occasions. Her sister was the common-law wife of Mr. Pickton's brother.

Robert Matas "Witness admits seeing 'lots of blood' in trailer." *The Globe and Mail* 6 September 2007: A7.

2c Why Do Scholars Use Citation?

In the last section we saw that citation is a feature of everyday conversation; it is therefore not peculiar to scholarly writing. It is nevertheless *conspicuous* in this kind of writing. It is a salient feature: it sticks up or stands out; it makes academic research recognizable from a distance. Citation is a feature these genres don't seem to be able to do without.

But what about the claim—or, as it's sometimes expressed, the accusation—that scholarly writers repeat others simply to support their claims or sound impressive? Do citations merely serve the purpose of making the writer sound authoritative—learned and important?

Let's look at an analysis by two sociologists of the effect of neighbourhoods on the behaviour of young people:

Initial skepticism over the impact of neighborhood conditions and neighborhood contexts on the behavior of adolescents and young adults (Jencks and Mayer 1990) has spurred considerable research purportedly documenting such effects (Aneshensel and Sucoff 1996; Billy, Brewster, and Grady 1994; Corcoran et al. 1992; Duncan 1994; Duncan, Connel, and Klebanov 1997; Elliott et al. 1996; Entwisle, Alexander, and Olson 1994; cf. Evans, Oates, and Schwab 1992).

Scott J. South and Kyle D. Crowder 1999 "Neighborhood effects on family formation: Concentrated poverty and beyond." *American Sociological Review* 64: 113–32, 113.

Notice that South and Crowder *don't* claim that neighbourhoods have good *or* bad effects, or no effects, on the young people who live in them. Instead, they report that others (Jencks and Mayer) have said that neighbourhoods may not have much effect on the young, and that some skeptical researchers (the remaining citations) reacted and set out to test this possibility. Are South and Crowder skeptical themselves? No, they attribute the skepticism to these other researchers. But the adverb "purportedly" suggests that they do not necessarily occupy the same position as those whose work has challenged that skepticism.

In the next sentence, South and Crowder interpret the eight clusters of speakers (appearing at the end of the sentence) as having been influenced by yet another speaker—the author of what they call a "prominent treatise":

> Grounded primarily in Wilson's (1987) prominent treatise on *The Truly Disadvantaged*, several recent studies have examined the impact of neighborhood disadvantage on family-related events, including the timing of first sexual activity (Billy et al. 1994; Brewster 1994; Brewster, Billy, and Grady 1993), first marriage (Hoffman, Duncan, and Mincy 1991; Massey and Shibuya 1995), and nonmarital and/ or teenage childbearing (Billy and Moore 1992; Brooks-Bunn et al. 1993; Crane 1991).

South and Crowder 1999: 113.

So why do scholars use citation? Have South and Crowder gained authority by citing others? So far, they have told a story of others speaking, and they have taken a reserved position, neither disputing nor accepting others' statements. In fact, rather than imparting an authoritative status, in this case the citations seem to cultivate a stance of **uncertainty**, which is elaborated as South and Crowder's discussion continues:

> While a general consensus appears to be emerging that, net of individual and family attributes, at least some neighborhood characteristics significantly influence these and other life-course events, thus far these studies have generated inconsistent findings regarding the existence, strength, and functional form of neighborhood effects on marriage and nonmarital childbearing.
>
> South and Crowder 1999: 113.

South and Crowder don't say that neighbourhoods *do in fact* influence young people's "family-related" behaviour, but that, from a certain position (theirs), you can see that researchers might be beginning to agree that some aspects of neighbourhoods *can* have some effect. Note how the use of "while," "appears," and "at least some" casts doubt on the "general consensus" and prepares the reader for an alternative position. Then, in the second part of the sentence, the writers make a claim of their own—and it turns out to be not about neighbourhoods, but about the **state of knowledge** (i.e., what researchers working in the field have said) about neighbourhoods. What they claim is that findings are "inconsistent": taken together, these studies do not provide a clear answer to questions about the influence of neighbourhoods on young people growing up in them. They continue with more **assertions** of their own:

> More important, several key elements in Wilson's theory relating neighborhood socioeconomic disadvantage to family formation patterns have been treated only cursorily, if at all. And virtually all prior studies of neighborhood effects on marriage and childbearing suffer from one or more methodological deficiencies that limit their contribution to our knowledge in this area.
>
> South and Crowder 1999: 113–14.

What is South and Crowder's position on this topic? Neither embracing nor disputing any of the studies they refer to, South and Crowder assemble the findings of a group of speakers and, taking these findings together, estimate the state of knowledge on a topic: in this case they find that the current understanding of the subject is incomplete—there is a **knowledge deficit**. Moreover, at the same time they position their own voice amongst these other voices—they see *themselves* as being among the researchers whose understanding is incomplete: "*our* knowledge in this area" is limited by "methodological deficiencies" (emphasis added). Collectively, all these speakers, including South and Crowder, own the knowledge (such as it is).

See Chapter 6 (p. 109) and Chapter 8, Sections 8D and 8E (pp. 179–86) for further discussion of state of knowledge and knowledge deficit.

Someone looking for answers to questions about "good" neighbourhoods and "bad" ones, desirable behaviour and undesirable, might be disappointed. **Experts** seem to be less sure of these things than **non-experts**.

Returning to Passage 3 above, we find, in the first sentence, that Allen does not say that it is impossible to know "even the simplest things," but that people *now say* that (other) people *thought* this way at the end of the nineteenth century and the beginning of the twentieth:

> Most of the literature on European and North American intellectual history at the turn of the century emphasizes the problematic and disorienting effects of (as Everdell puts it), "the impossibility of knowing even the simplest things that the nineteenth century took for granted."
>
> Allen 1999: 1085.

She goes on to bring other speakers to the page who seem to agree that, at that time, people felt that way. While she arranges for these voices to converse with one another, and come to an agreement, she positions herself at some distance from these views, referring to them as "a cliché of intellectual history." Although in this passage Allen does not explicitly identify a gap in our understanding of this period of Western thought, we can anticipate that she will show that, despite this apparent agreement amongst experts, something has been missed. (Later, she will show us what it is.)

Do scholarly writers acquire authority by citing? Few (if any) of the citations we've looked at here back up the writer who refers to others, or who repeats the words of others. Moreover, the citations can add up to uncertainty rather than authority.

We will find cases, though, where scholarly writers do position themselves beside an important figure and share his or her authority or prestige. It would be wrong to say that scholarly writers don't acquire some status—and a right to speak—by citing others. By convening fellow scholars, and arranging for conversation amongst them, the writer gets to

- report the current state of knowledge about the subject at hand;
- take a position in relation to the other researchers;
- identify himself or herself as a member of a group collectively;
- point out deficiencies in the current understanding;
- take a turn in the conversation;
- construct knowledge.

In other words, citation in the research genres represents and enables a range of actions: listening to the statements of others; identifying the position from which the statement comes; evaluating established knowledge and paying attention to the possibility that it may be incomplete, contradictory, or even wrong; and watching for opportunities to improve the state of knowledge.

Exercise 5

In this passage, the expressions which attribute a statement to another speaker have been emphasized with bold type.

> Within the context of the tecato subculture, **previous researchers have linked** machismo almost exclusively to hypermasculine aspects of drug use and aggression. Thus **Bullington (1977: 108, 115) regards** machismo as both an adaptive, efficacious attitude in navigating through prison experience and an underlying variable related to the expression of criminal behavior. Likewise **Casavantes (1976), in his study of "el tecato" [the male Mexican heroin addict], emphasizes** the hypermasculine aspects of this model. **He notes** that "... machismo in its exaggerated form [includes] fighting, drinking, performing daring deeds, seducing women, asserting independence from women, and ... bragging about escapades" (**Casavantes, 1976: 149**).

> Gilbert A. Quintero and Antonio L. Estrada 1998 "Cultural models of masculinity and drug use: 'Machismo,' heroin, and street survival on the U.S.–Mexican border." *Contemporary Drug Problems* 25: 147–65, 151.

In the following passage these expressions have been removed.

Within the context of the tecato subculture, machismo is connected with hypermasculine aspects of drug use and aggression. Machismo is both an adaptive, efficacious attitude in navigating through prison experience and an underlying variable related to the expression of criminal behavior. Machismo in its exaggerated form includes fighting, drinking, performing daring deeds, seducing women, asserting independence from women, and bragging about escapades.

In general, how does removing citation alter the reader's understanding of the state of knowledge? In particular, how does the absence of reporting expressions alter the degree of certainty the writer expresses?

Exercise 6
Identify the reporting expressions in this passage, and rewrite the passage removing these reporting expressions.

The problem of teenage parenthood, acknowledged to be a significant social problem in the United States since the late 1960s, has been the subject of much study (Alan Guttmacher Institute, 1985; Chilman, 1980; Furstenberg, Lincoln, and Menken, 1981; Lancaster and Hamburg, 1986; Hayes, 1987). Efforts to understand its causes have generally focused on the issue of individual choice regarding the decision to engage in sexual behavior (Chilman, 1978; Pete and DeSantis, 1990) and to use contraceptive devices (Finkel and Finkel, 1975; Goldsmith, Gabrielson, and Gabrielson, 1972). The association of teenage motherhood with dropping out of school prematurely (Gray and Ramsey, 1986; Roosa, 1986), not being employed (Trussell, 1976), and becoming dependent on government subsidies (Klerman, 1986; Moore, 1978) is well-documented. In general, consideration of how schools and educational policies contribute to the high rate of teenage motherhood has been limited to how dropping out affects the likelihood of a girl becoming pregnant, how pregnancy affects the probability of dropping out, and the relationship between education aspirations and pregnancy rates (Moore, Simms, and Betsey, 1986).

Helen Rauch-Elnekave 1994 "Teenage motherhood: Its relationship to undetected learning problems." *Adolescence* 29 (113): 91–103, 91–92.

3

Summary

At the beginning of the last chapter we mentioned that we needed to examine citation in order to understand summary. This is because we can look at each cited statement as a tiny summary. Consider these two sentences from the beginning of an article on rumour, gossip, and urban legends:

> The study of rumors has a long history in all the major social sciences, including psychology, social anthropology, geography, sociology, sociolinguistics, and folklore (Allport & Lepkin, 1945; Allport & Postman, 1945, 1947; Arno, 1980; Besnier, 1994; Brunvand, 1979, 1984; Cantril, 1940; Comwell & Hobbs, 1992; Cox, 1970; Lienhardt, 1975; Neubauer, 1999; Rosnow, 1991). Research has also been applied to practical problems of rumor-mongering (Bordia & Rosnow, 1998; Declerque, Tsui Abul-Ata, & Barcelona, 1986; Deodhar, Yemul, & Banerjee, 1998; Difonzo, Bordia, & Rosnow, 1994; Fine, 1986; Harrington & Beilby, 1995; Herr, Kardes, & Kim, 1991; Iyer & Debevec, 1991; Prasad, 1935, 1950; Rutenberg & Watkins, 1997; Scanlon, 1977; Singh, 1990; Sinha, 1952; Tishkov, 1995).
>
> Bernard Guerin and Yoshihiko Miyazaki 2006 "Analyzing rumors, gossip, and urban legends through their conversational properties." *Psychological Record* 56(1): 23–33, 23.

In the first sentence, Guerin and Miyazaki summarize thirteen books and articles published over almost fifty years by characterizing the focus of their research. The second sentence then zooms in on applications of the research—specifically "practical problems of rumor-mongering"—and cites fifteen books and articles that adopt such an approach. Each of these citations works as a miniature summary. These are very brief summaries indeed, and they work in concert to situate Guerin and Miyazaki's focus in relation to past research.

As they begin to discuss how rumour has been studied, Guerin and Miyazaki expand one of these citations (Allport and Postman, 1947) into a more extensive summary:

> One of the most influential theories of its day was Allport and Postman's (1947). They were concerned with rumors during World War II, and the effect these had on the morale of both troops and civilians. Their theory was based on two assumptions: (a) that people exert effort to find meaning in things and events and (b) that, when faced with ambiguity in an important matter, people try to find some meaning by the retelling of related rumors. This meant that *rumor importance* and *rumor ambiguity* were the key variables that predicted whether a rumor would be transmitted or not.

Without summary, Guerin and Miyazaki would not be able to introduce Allport and Postman into their article. With summary, they identify Allport and Postman as early researchers trying to understand rumour, and they introduce their readers to the basic findings of Allport and Postman. Immediately following this summary, they turn to another citation from the initial list (Rosnow, 1991) and summarize his research. In this way, Guerin and Miyazaki arrange for these different writers to take their turn. In effect, they recreate key aspects of a scholarly conversation that has been going on for more than fifty years.

Just as conversations in daily life differ, so do scholarly conversations. And we might predict that summaries will change accordingly. Guerin and Miyazaki are not the only sociologists to summarize Allport and Postman. Looking at another summary of Allport and Postman, this time by Kieffer, will prepare you to appreciate (a) how important summary of even well-known works is to scholarly discussion, and (b) how each summary is a *new* version for *new* purposes and emphases.

> Gordon Allport (Allport & Postman, 1947), a social psychologist who pioneered the study of rumor, stressed that in ambiguous and threatening situations, individuals tend to refer back to the group

for help in understanding the situation and for directions about how to act—a form of *group think* that fosters the discussion of rumors, particularly in the absence of formal information. That is, groups tend to seek clarity and safety through a process of informal interpretation. Thus, a rumor is the product of the group's process of interpretation, although the content, structure, and transmission of the rumor are inevitably influenced by group norms and goals—which are often unconscious. Malicious, derogatory rumors are particularly likely to develop when a group feels that its identity and/or prestige are under attack (Allport & Postman, 1947).

Christine C. Kieffer 2013 "Rumors and gossip as forms of bullying: Sticks and stones?" *Psychoanalytic Inquiry* 33(2), 90–104, 91.

Although many researchers since 1947 have told the Allport-&-Postman story, Kieffer tells it again in 2013, reactivating its terms and ideas for a new application, and new conversation.

Summary isn't just for researchers and professors; it provides students too with a means to join scholarly conversations. While you may not be ready to cite 28 sources in two sentences, as Guerin and Miyazaki do at the beginning of their article, you can compose the kinds of summaries we see above, bringing to the page the voices you read. This chapter is devoted to helping you develop your skills as a summarizer of scholarly material, so that you can become involved in the kinds of activities that are enabled by and represented in the research genres. In the next two sections, you will study related methods for approaching summary: the first method notes for **gist** as you read; the second explores the original as an arrangement of levels—**levels of generality** and detail, of abstract and concrete reference.

3A Noting for Gist

Academic sources are often difficult to read, and not just for students. This level of difficulty means that readers need to develop strategies to confront the difficulty. Noting for gist is an active reading strategy that is designed to help readers engage with and comprehend sources.

In this method, we write as we read, noting what we predict should be remembered in preparation for writing. The notes answer this question: if I were reading this with the intention of going on to write, what would I estimate as important from each paragraph? Avoiding full sentences and straight copying, the notes capture the gist—the point or basis—of each section in a form that is temporary, pliable, ready for other uses.

Reading for gist, we produce a set of wordings that partly depend on the original wordings but are also partly free of the original, too. These wordings prepare for a new version of what has been said by someone else, incorporating ties to the first speaker but also putting a new accent on those words.

Social practices, norms, and institutions are designed to meet heterosexual systems' need to produce sex/gender dimorphism—masculine males and feminine females—so that desire can then be heterosexualized. Gendered behavioral norms, gendered rites of passage, a sexual division of labor, and the like, produce differently gendered persons out of differently sexed persons. Prohibitions against gender crossing (e.g., against cross-dressing, effeminacy in men, mannishness in women) also help sustain the dimorphism necessary to heterosexualize desire.

heterosexual systems: social norms → the masc. & fem. genders

Children and especially adolescents are carefully prepared for heterosexual interaction. They are given heterosexual sex education, advice for attracting the opposite sex, norms of heterosexual behavior, and appropriate social occasions (such as dances or dating rituals) for enacting desire. Adult heterosexuality is further sustained through erotica and pornography, heterosexualized humor, heterosexualized dress, romance novels, and so on.

children: social customs → preparation for heterosexuality

adults: gendered attitudes, clothes → sustain heterosexual desire

Heterosexual societies take it for granted that men and women will bond in an intimate relationship ultimately founding a family. As a result, social conventions, economic arrangements, and the legal structure treat the heterosexual couple as a single, singularly important, social unit. The couple is represented linguistically (boyfriend-girlfriend, husband-wife) and is treated socially as a single unit (e.g., in joint invitations or in receiving joint gifts). It is legally licensed and legally

expected, socially, legally, econ.: men & women in intimate couple, for family

social, linguistic convention: M/F couple

supported through such entitlements as communal property, joint custody or adoption of children, and the power to give proxy consent within the couple. The couple is also recognized in the occupational structure via such provisions as spousal health care benefits and restrictions on nepotism. Multiple practices and institutions help heterosexual individuals to couple and create families and support the continuation of those couples and couple-based families. These include dating services, match-makers, introductions to eligible partners, premarital counseling, marriage counseling, marriage and divorce law, adoption services, reproductive technologies, family rates, family health care benefits, tax deductions for married couples and so on.

law: M/F couple

economic & institutional structures: M/F couple

The sum total of all the social, economic, and legal arrangements that support the sexual and relational coupling of men with women constitutes heterosexual privilege. And it is privilege of a peculiar sort. Heterosexuals do not simply claim greater socio-political-legal standing than non-heterosexuals. They claim as natural and normal an arrangement where only heterosexuals have socio-political-legal standing. Lesbians and gay men are not recognized as social beings because they cannot enter into the most basic social unit, the male-female couple. Within heterosexual systems the only social arrangements that apply to nonheterosexuals are eliminative by nature. The coercive force of the criminal law, institutionalized discrimination, "therapeutic" treatment, and individual prejudice and violence is marshalled against the existence of lesbians and gay men. At best, lesbians and gay men have negative social reality. Lesbians are not-women engaged in nonsex with nonrelationships that may constitute a nonfamily.

all this ("multiple") → privilege for heterosexual couple seems normal, natural

the privilege makes non-heterosexuals unrecognizable ...

... except as something to be "fixed"

only negative social standing for nonheterosexuals

Cheshire Calhoun 1994 "Separating lesbian theory from feminist theory." *Ethics* 104: 558–82, 579–80.

Exercise 1

Practise taking gists on the following passages. You can write directly in the right margin or perhaps on a separate sheet of paper with the paragraphs numbered. The gists should not add information or record your thoughts about the passage. Instead, distil what you think is most important by isolating or rephrasing key points.

PASSAGE 1

Science fiction has frequently been identified as a literature of estrangement. "One of the supreme functions of SF as a genre," Fredric Jameson has argued, is "the 'estrangement,' in the Brechtian sense, of our culture and institutions—a shocked renewal of our vision such that once again, and as though for the first time, we are able to perceive their historicity and their arbitrariness, their profound dependency on the accidents of man's historical adventure" (29). In this article, I want to propose that the estrangement effect generated by science fiction can be especially unsettling if it suggests more than simply that the apparently solid culture and institutions characteristic of capitalist society will be different at some scarcely conceivable time in the future but also insinuates the suspicion that, incipiently at least, they are already different. Effective SF can demonstrate that an inchoate future is already germinating in the present, changing it, and making it other than itself.

Matthew Beaumont 2006 "Red Sphinx: Mechanics of the uncanny in 'The Time Machine.'" *Science Fiction Studies* 33(2): 230–50, 230.

PASSAGE 2

Semiotics is generally described as the "study of signs." For a sign to exist, there must be meaning or content (the *signified*) manifested through some form of expression or representation (the *sign*).

[…]

Signs exist within semiotic systems. For example, the green light in a traffic signal is a sign meaning "go" within the semiotic system of traffic control; words are signs in the semiotic system of language; gestures are signs within the semiotic system of nonverbal communication; and so on. Because semiotic systems encompass the entire range of human practices,

> Semiotics provides us with a potentially unifying conceptual framework and a set of methods and terms for use across the full range of signifying practices, which include gesture, posture, dress, writing, speech, photography, film, television, and radio.... As David Sless notes, "we consult linguists to find out about language, art historians or critics to find out about paintings, and anthropologists to find out how people in different societies signal to each other through gesture, dress or decoration. But if we want to know what all these different things have in common then we need to find someone with a semiotic point of view, a vantage point from which to survey our world." (Chandler 2001)
>
> It is this cross-cutting vantage point that allows professional communicators to compare and contrast objects from two different semiotic systems—language and imagery—and make a valid, useful analysis.
>
> Claire Harrison 2003 "Visual social semiotics: Understanding how still images make meaning." *Technical Communication* 50(1): 46–60, 47–48.

3B Recording Levels

Using nothing but the gists we recorded, we could write a summary of Calhoun's discussion of how social practices reinforce gendered, heterosexual norms. But, doing so, we might be missing an opportunity to get a better picture of the original, or leaving to chance some of our recollection of that original. You might notice that the passage is full of details that our gist notes eliminate—"cross-dressing," for example, "dances," "romance novels," "family rates." Eliminating all of these details might render our summary confusing, particularly for readers who haven't already read Calhoun on their own.

In our everyday conversational "summarizing," we also eliminate details. For example, we'd probably say—

A. How was your cruise?
B. Excellent, very well organized, good food and tours at each port.

—instead of—

> A. How was your cruise?
> B. On the third night I had a delicious salmon terrine with juni-
>   per berries, followed by a peach sorbet garnished with a sprig
>   of mint. Paul had the.... In Copenhagen we went on a bus to
>   Tivoli, there were two buses, we got on the second one, the buses
>   were waiting when we went ashore ... and then ...

—although some people tend towards the detail technique, and may encounter social disapproval as a result. If we don't eliminate details, the summary would be too long, and risk not being a summary at all. (Imagine if the traveller told every detail—then the answer to the question might be longer than the cruise itself!) Yet, still, some details seem to be important, since they give specific examples of more abstract ideas—a chance to grasp those ideas.

Abstraction

Cutting across the high levels of generality are planes of abstraction. "Prohibition," for example, is an **abstraction**—a word for an idea or concept. Mention of the stop sign at the bottom of a lane, prohibiting drivers from rolling down the lane and directly out into the road, is a concrete reference. We can touch the sign, and locate it in the physical world, the way we cannot "touch" *prohibition*, although we experience the abstract phenomenon *prohibition* each time we encounter stop signs. (On the plane of *generality*, the stop sign would be a "detail," or "specific.")

At a very *general level*, the first paragraph of the Calhoun passage is about something like *the heterosexualization of desire* through *sex/gender dimorphism*—what *is that*? At a less general level, we encounter "prohibitions against gender crossing" ... and "gender crossing" would be ... *what*? At a still less general and more specific level, we get the answer, finding prohibitions "against cross-dressing" as an example. Now we have a grasp on "sex-gender dimorphism" (probably).

The second paragraph begins at a high level, too—"Children and especially adolescents are carefully prepared for heterosexual interaction"—and then *goes down* to the level of specifics: dating, dances, and so on.

We could create a diagram of the gists that traces the process of reading, the up and down shifts in **levels of generality**. Such a diagram would show the levels in action, descending and rising. Or we could create a **tree diagram** that deliberately ignores the process of reading the passage, and that just shows the overall organization of generality and detail (see Figure 3.1).

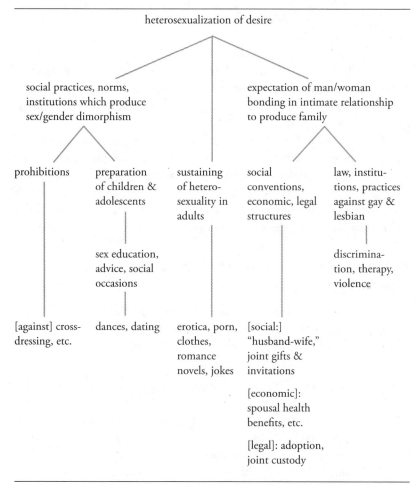

Figure 3.1. Diagram of the levels of generality in the Calhoun passage. Read from top to bottom, the diagram shows high to low levels of generality. The columns show how mid-level generalizations provide a context for higher-level abstractions, and how they are in turn supported by low-level details. The diagram, like a snapshot or a portrait, captures an analysis of Calhoun's reasoning in the passage.

What might we learn from this pattern? As readers, if we find the beginning claims of a scholarly paragraph difficult (what is "dimorphism"?), we might be patient, and wait to see if these high-level claims are demonstrated with examples or instances that might link the general claim to our concrete experience; as writers, we might anticipate that our readers will look for these lower levels, so they can get a firmer grasp of what we're talking about. Notice how the diagram in Figure 3.1 shows how higher-level generalizations relate to one another, and how certain details are significant.

Selecting some of the details for a summary helps a summary reader to grasp what the abstractions mean. Calhoun's persuasiveness depends at least partly on the way she summons so many examples of the practices and norms which heterosexualize desire: the summary preserves this quality of the original.

While noting for gist is a means of recording compactly—or "remembering"—a spread of details which might otherwise escape your recollection, you might also think of it as a "forgetting": once the high-level gist is transferred to the summary, it "forgets" the details which accompanied it. By reintroducing select details, you can help generalities "remember" their origins, and show them to your reader.

3C Using Gist and Levels of Generality to Write Summary

Taking the clusters of gist produced by reading-and-noting Calhoun's passage, and keeping an eye on the structure of generality and detail, we can write a short summary of these four paragraphs.

> Calhoun (1994) explains how heterosexual society makes heterosexuality seem natural and creates a "negative social reality" for lesbians and gay men. She identifies social practices like dating, sex education, and erotica that construct sex/gender dimorphism. She also catalogues social conventions (e.g., joint invitations to husband-and-wife) and legal and economic structures (e.g., adoption procedures, spousal health benefits) which produce the "single unit" of man and woman.

As well as representing content, the summary

- attributes these statements as originating with another writer ("Calhoun (1994)");

- characterizes the action of the original (Calhoun "explains" how society has come to view heterosexuality as natural); and
- describes the development of the discussion (it "identifies" practices and "catalogues" examples).

With each of these moves—attributing statements to the speaker-who-is-not-me, characterizing the action of the original, and describing its development—a writer takes a position in relation to the original.

The writer's position might be developed by saying what larger phenomenon this one is part of; for example,

> Calhoun's discussion reminds us that what we view as "natural" can often be traced not to nature but to social custom. She takes a social constructionist view of ...

The position could also be developed by estimating the commonness or uncommonness of the claims made by the original. For example, saying

> Summoning arguments that are established by feminist reasoning, Calhoun ...

locates Calhoun in current, and fairly common, claims about the social construction of gender.

This estimation also secures a position for the writer of the summary and makes this an independent version by not sticking to the order of the original. By beginning with points from the last paragraph—heterosexuality produced as "natural," "negative social reality" for gays and lesbians—the summary takes a reader to this element of the original first, thereby emphasizing this aspect of Calhoun's discussion. This is not to say that it would always be best to do so, only that for the purpose of *this* summary—perhaps an emphasis on the naturalizing effects of social norms—this order is good. With *other* intentions, or another perspective on the topic, a writer might have started at another point—for example:

> Calhoun (1994) describes legal and institutional discrimination against gays and lesbians (adoption and custody laws, for example, spousal benefits in the workplace), but also brings to light the array of social habits that extend such discrimination: we learn what is "natural" and expected—and what is "unnatural"—not only from laws and policy but also from everyday practice: routines of socializing like dating and dances among adolescents, for instance, and, among adults, social invitations to the man–woman couple.

Other summaries might arrange for still other emphases by selecting another point at which to begin, and another order to follow.

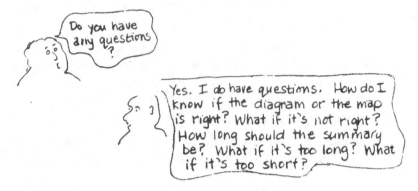

While there are no rules for recording and manipulating these gists, it can be a good idea to arrange them on a single page or to write them on separate slips of paper and rearrange them in different patterns so you can see them all at once. In the same way, creating a diagram of the levels of generality clarifies relations between abstractions and the details that they organize. That way, you can escape the order of the original, and design your own. And by arranging gists in a non-linear way, you can induce them to make new connections with one another. By making new connections amongst claims, you offer new perspectives on the original. That is, *even if* the reader of the summary had already read the original, the summarized version is *new*: it is reconfigured for the present purposes. Your arrangement of the materials of the original is an expression of your position *vis-à-vis* the original, and, however familiar readers are with the original, the summary will be new to them.

Exercise 2
The following passage examines the relationship between stress and disease. Create a tree diagram that maps out the levels of generality connecting different types of stress and effects with particular examples. Write a 50-word summary of the passage.

Generally, stressful events are thought to influence the pathogenesis of physical disease by causing negative affective states (e.g., feelings of anxiety and depression), which in turn exert direct effects on biological processes or behavioral patterns that influence disease risk.[1] Exposures to chronic stress are considered the most toxic because they are most likely to result in long-term or permanent changes in the emotional, physiological, and behavioral responses that influence susceptibility to and course of disease.[1-2] This includes stressful events that persist over an extended duration (eg, caring for a spouse with dementia) or brief focal events that continue to be experienced as overwhelming long after they have ended (eg, experiencing a sexual assault).[3]

Behavioral changes occurring as adaptations or coping responses to stressors such as increased smoking, decreased exercise and sleep, and poorer adherence to medical regimens provide an important pathway through which stressors influence disease risk. Stressor-elicited endocrine response provides another key pathway. Two endocrine response systems are particularly reactive to psychological stress: the hypothalamic-pituitary-adrenocortical axis (HPA) and the sympathetic-adrenal-medullary (SAM) system. Cortisol, the primary effector of HPA activation in humans, regulates a broad range of physiological processes, including anti-inflammatory responses; metabolism of carbohydrates, fats, and proteins; and gluconeogenesis. Similarly, catecholamines, which are released in response to SAM activation, work in concert with the autonomic nervous system to exert regulatory effects on the cardiovascular, pulmonary, hepatic, skeletal muscle, and immune systems. Prolonged or repeated activation of the HPA and SAM systems can interfere with their control of other physiological systems, resulting in increased risk for physical and psychiatric disorders.[1-2]

Notes

1 Cohen S, Kessler RC, Gordon UL. Strategies for measuring stress in studies of psychiatric and physical disorder. In: Cohen S, Kessler RC, Gordon UL, eds. *Measuring Stress: A Guide for Health and Social Scientists.* New York, NY: Oxford University Press; 1995: 3–26.

2   McEwen BS. Protective and damaging effects of stress mediators. *N Engl Med.* 1998:338(3): 171–179.

3   Baum A, Cohen L, Hall M. Control and intrusive memories as possible determinants of chronic stress. *Psychosom Med.* 1993:55(3): 274–286.

Sheldon Cohen, Denise Janicki-Deverts, and Gregory E. Miller 2007 "Psychological stress and disease." *JAMA* 298: 1685–87, 1685.

Exercise 3

Here is a passage from an article examining how clinical diagnosis might make the stigma of mental illness worse. We may think that psychiatric diagnoses lead to treatments and possible cures, but Corrigan examines how these diagnoses can increase how people see the mentally ill as a different group. In this passage, he outlines what he calls the "stigma process."

Use the reading-and-noting technique to capture the passage's gists, and the mapping technique to create a tree diagram displaying its range from generality to detail. It might help to focus first on the up-down relations between abstractions (e.g., "cues" and "discrimination") and details (e.g., "Jim Crow laws"). Then modify the diagram to reflect the causal process analyzed in the passage: e.g., how does believing a stereotype lead to a result different from the result of disbelieving it? You might use arrows to indicate how one abstraction leads to another. When you are satisfied with your tree diagram, write a two- or three-sentence summary of the passage.

Researchers working at the interface of social work and psychology have framed the stigma process in terms of four cognitive structures: cues, stereotypes, prejudice, and discrimination. This model [...] parallels a cognitive behavior model of action by specifying signal, cognitive mediator, and behavioral result (Corrigan, 2000). The process begins with stigmas, which are the cues that signal subsequent prejudice and discrimination.

Goffman (1963) adopted the term *stigma* from the Greeks who defined it as a mark meant to publicly and prominently represent immoral status. Stigmas are typically the marks that, when observed by a majority group member, may lead to prejudice. Goffman noted that some stigmas are readily apparent and based on a physical sign such as skin color (a cue for ethnicity) or body size (a cue for obesity). Other stigmas are relatively hidden; for example, the public cannot generally tell who among a group of people falls into such stigmatized groups as gay men, Catholics, undereducated people, and people with mental illness. Instead of an unequivocal physical cue, hidden stigma is signaled by label or association (Link, Cullen, Frank, & Wozniak, 1987; Penn & Martin, 1998). Labels may be self-promoted ("I am a gay male") or given by others ("That person is mentally ill"). Hidden stigma can also be ascertained based on association; for example, observation of someone leaving a psychiatric clinic might lead to the assumption that the person is mentally ill.

Theorists in this area of study view stereotypes as knowledge structures that are learned by most members of a cued social group (Augoustinos, Ahrens, & Innes, 1994; Judd & Park, 1993; Krueger, 1996). Stereotypes are especially efficient means of categorizing information about social groups. Just because most people have knowledge of a set of stereotypes does not imply that they agree with them (Devine, 1989; Jussim, Nelson, Manis, & Soffin, 1995). For example, many people can recall stereotypes about different racial groups but do not agree that the stereotypes are valid. People who are prejudiced, on the other hand, endorse these negative stereotypes ("That's right; all people with mental illness are violent") and generate negative emotional reactions as a result ("They all scare me") (Devine, 1995; Krueger, 1996). In contrast to stereotypes, which are beliefs, prejudicial attitudes involve an evaluative (generally negative) component (Eagly & Chaiken, 1993).

Prejudice, which is fundamentally a cognitive and affective response, leads to discrimination, the behavioral reaction (Crocker, Major, & Steele, 1998). Discriminatory behavior manifests itself as negative action against the out-group. Out-group discrimination includes outright violence (for example, lynching experienced by African Americans and assaults directed

> at gay men) and coercion (for example, laws that restrict the full rights of people in an ethnic or religious minority group, such as the Jim Crow laws of the late 1800s through the early 1960s). Out-group discrimination may also appear as avoidance, not associating with people from the out-group. This can be especially troublesome when employers decide not to hire and landlords decide not to rent to people from an ethnic or religious minority group to avoid them.
>
> Patrick W. Corrigan 2007 "How clinical diagnosis might exacerbate the stigma of mental illness." *Social Work* 52 (1): 31–39, 32–33.

3D Establishing the Summarizer's Position

We have identified several ways in which summarizers take a position in relation to the writer whose ideas they are representing.

They can use reporting expressions ("Calhoun explains"; "Corrigan argues"). By doing so, they characterize the action of the original—in this case, as an explanation or an argument. Or the original might be characterized as an analysis, or some observations, or a commentary on something, or a review of research on something, or an explanation.

Reporting expressions can also suggest the summarizer's assessment of the original. Consider the difference between what is implied by the verbs "argue" and "demonstrate," for example: do you hear a difference between "Singer argues that colonial history has been suppressed in public-school curriculum" and "Singer demonstrates that colonial history has been suppressed in public-school curriculum"?

Summary can also mention what kind of study produces the knowledge: field research, for example, or statistical analysis, or experimental or theoretical inquiry, or review of recent research, or extension of a research tradition.

Summarizers can also take a position by pointing to issues which are not mentioned in the original but whose wider applications the original suggests. By taking such a position, summarizers can estimate the generalizability (or limits) of the statements presented in the original. This is what the authors of the next passage do, as part of their article reporting an anthropological study of "RVers." RVers are people who spend much of their year in recreational vehicles: motorhomes, truck-campers, trailers. In the field work reported below, researchers found amongst RVers a sub-category, the "private-park RVers," who stay in organized, commercial facilities:

> When RVers select a place to park their rigs they are also making a choice about lifestyle and about identity. Some choose private resort parks where their personal space is limited but where they feel safe and comfortable. They seek the protection of walls and guards; they enjoy the luxury of water and sewer hookups, electricity and cable TV; their space is organized into streets and blocks where each RV has its own "pad"; and leisure activities are organized by professionals who encourage and promote contact among park residents. Many private resort parks have strictly enforced rules about how a rig may be parked, where dogs may be walked, the conditions under which residents may have guests, and for how long and under what circumstances children and grandchildren may visit. Many of the people who choose this lifestyle see themselves holding standards of affluence, respectability and orderliness and they particularly appreciate the fact that the other park residents are similar to themselves in age, social standing, consumption level and interests. In thinking about private parks one is reminded of the distinction made by Bellah et al. between "lifestyle enclaves" and communities. Lifestyle, they point out, "brings together those who are socially, economically, or culturally similar, and one of its chief aims is the enjoyment of being with those who 'share one's lifestyle'" (Bellah et al. 1985: 72). In their terms, groups such as retirement "communities," organized around a common lifestyle, are "lifestyle enclaves," not communities. A community is inclusive and focusses on the interdependence of private and public life while recognizing and tolerating the differences of those within it. In contrast, "lifestyle is fundamentally segmental and celebrates the narcissism of similarity. It usually explicitly involves a contrast with others who 'do not share one's lifestyle'" (Bellah et al. 1985: 72).

> Dorothy Ayers Counts and David R. Counts 1992 "'They're my family now': The creation of community among RVers." *Anthropologica* 34: 153–82, 169.

As summarizers, Counts and Counts take Bellah et al.'s distinction between "lifestyle enclaves" and communities and apply it to RVers, a group Bellah et al. do not consider in their original study. It's not difficult to see how another writer summarizing Bellah et al. could apply this distinction to still other groups of people living together, such as gated communities, kibbutzim, or residents of inner cities or new suburbs.

Alternatively, summarizers can estimate the limits of statements that appear in the original. A little later in their study of RVers, Counts and Counts argue that another category of RVers, the boondockers, "epitomize the values upon which America was founded." Someone summarizing Counts and Counts might identify a limitation to their discussion by suggesting difficulties that might arise in discussion of Canadian, British, or French RVers.

Exercise 4

Write a two- to three-sentence summary for each of the passages below. Practise the reading-and-noting technique, producing gists whose order you can arrange or rearrange according to the perspective you want to offer your reader. To get a feel for the structure of each passage, attempt a rough sketch of its levels: pick out the lowest level of detail, and the higher levels of generality. Use some of the techniques discussed above—choosing reporting expressions that characterize the action of the original, naming the kind of research being conducted, identifying the implications or limitations of the research—to establish your position as a summarizer.

a) In "Sickness as a resource," Mary Douglas applies an "anthropological approach" to the study of cultural difference in the medical disciplines.

SICKNESS AS A RESOURCE

[...] the sick Londoner who is choosing complementary medicine [is] equivalent to the African villager who is confronted by the reverse option. The choice is not between science or mumbo-jumbo, but choosing the traditional versus the exotic system, and in effect it means choosing between therapeutic communities. The African patient faced with the choice between the Christian missionary doctor with an exotic pharmacopoeia and the traditional diviner with his familiar repertoire is under the same sort of pressures as a Westerner choosing between traditional and exotic medicine. For minor ailments he can pick and choose separate remedial items without incurring censure, but if it is his own life or the life of his child that is at risk, his therapeutic community will take a strong line. He may have friends on either side of the divide, or choosing may involve him in a complete switch of loyalties. It is rather like religious conversion: if there is a strong political alignment dividing the two therapies, there will be political pressure not to convert to the other side. That is a good beginning for the anthropological approach.

The next step is to follow the monitoring that is going on in any community. Wherever there is illness, warnings are being issued, and informal penalties being threatened. Talcott Parsons founded medical sociology when he identified and named the "sick role." When a person defines himself as sick, he can escape censure for doing his work badly, being late, being bad-tempered, and so on, but the community which indulges the sick role also exacts a price: the sick person is excused his remiss behaviour on condition of accepting the role, eating the gruel or whatever is classified as invalid food, taking the medicine, and keeping to the sick room, out of other people's way.

Having adopted the sick role, a person cannot play his or her normally influential part. The patient is reproved for trying to go on working; if the patient complains of pain, the answer is that complaining is aggravating the condition and a more severely restricted diet may have to be prescribed; every complaint is met with potential criticism so that the patient ends by lying back and accepting the way others have defined the sick role. Dragging around looking tired, his friends ask if the doctor has been called in yet, and if so, they want to know who, and are free with advice as to who can be trusted. It is a matter of pride for them if their favourite doctor is called, and a threat of withdrawn sympathy if it is one of whom they disapprove. These friends interacting with the patient, listening to symptoms and offering advice, form what the anthropologist John Janzen (1978) calls the "therapeutic community."

At the early stages of illness, there is some choice: either behave as if you are well or admit to being sick and bear the consequences. If the illness worsens and the invalid refuses the advice of friends and family, it is going to be difficult to ask for the neighbourly services or the loans of money on which lying in bed depends. The rival merits of traditional and alternative medicines are put to the test, not according to the patient's recovery but according to the negotiating of the sick role. The outcome will depend on the therapeutic community. For the sick person, the power of the medical theory counts for less than issues of loyalty and mutual dependability, unless he or she is completely isolated.

The background assumption is that any society imposes normative standards on its members. That is what being in society involves. Living in a community means accepting its standards, which means either playing the roles that are approved, or negotiating the acceptability of new ones, or suffering from public disapproval. The option for spirituality is a form of negotiation. But of course communities differ in the amount of control they exert: some are quite lax and standardization is weak; others exert ferocious control. In this perspective it would be interesting to know whether the persons who have chosen alternative therapy have also chosen a therapeutic community to support them with friendship and counsel.

Mary Douglas 1996 "The choice between gross and spiritual: Some medical preferences." In *Thought Styles*. London: Sage, 33–35.

b) The following passage is an excerpt from James Clifford's book about travel.

TRAVELING CULTURES

What about all the travel that largely avoids the hotel, or motel, circuits? The travel encounters of someone moving from rural Guatemala or Mexico across the United States border are of a quite different order; and a West African can get to a Paris *banlieu [sic]* without ever staying in a hotel. What are the settings that could realistically configure the cultural relations of these "travelers"? As I abandon the bourgeois hotel setting for travel encounters, sites of intercultural knowledge, I struggle, never quite successfully, to free the related term "travel" from a history of European, literary, male, bourgeois, scientific, heroic, recreational meanings and practices (Wolff, 1993).

Victorian travelers, men and women, were usually accompanied by servants, many of whom were people of color. These individuals have never achieved the status of "travelers." Their experiences, the cross-cultural links they made, their different access to the societies visited—such encounters seldom find serious representation in the literature of travel. Racism certainly has a great deal to do with this. For in the dominant discourses of travel, a nonwhite person cannot figure as a heroic explorer, aesthetic interpreter, or scientific authority. A good example is provided by the long struggle to bring Matthew Henson, the black American explorer who reached the North Pole with Robert Peary, equally into the story of this famous feat of discovery—as it was constructed by Peary, a host of historians, newspaper writers, statesmen, bureaucrats, and interested institutions such as *National Geographic* magazine (Counter, 1988). And this is still to say nothing of the Eskimo travelers who made the trip possible![1] A host of servants, helpers, companions, guides, and bearers have been excluded from the role of proper travelers because of their race and class, and because theirs seemed to be a dependent status in relation to the supposed independence of the individualist, bourgeois voyager. The independence was, in varying degrees, a myth. As Europeans moved through unfamiliar places, their relative comfort and safety were ensured by a well-developed infrastructure of guides, assistants, suppliers, translators, and carriers (Fabian, 1986).

Note

1 Lisa Bloom (1993) has written insightfully on Peary, Henson, Eskimos, and the various efforts by *National Geographic* to retell a deeply contested story of discovery.

James Clifford 1997 *Routes: Travel and translation in the late twentieth century.* Cambridge, MA: Harvard UP, 33–34.

3E Reporting Reporting

Since scholarly writers so often cite the words of others, summarizers of scholarly writing can find themselves citing others' citations—**reporting reporting**.

Writing about the experience of undocumented immigrants in the southwestern US, and analyzing that experience for evidence of "community," Leo R. Chavez cites another's ideas:

> Suffice it to say that despite all the work that has been carried out on communities, the question still remains: What underlies a sense of community? Anderson (1983) examined this question and suggested that communities are "imagined." Members of modern nations cannot possibly know all their fellow-members, and yet "in the minds of each lives the image of their communion [....] It is imagined as a *community* because, regardless of the actual inequality and exploitation that may prevail in each, the nation is always conceived as a deep, horizontal comradeship" (Anderson 1983: 15–16). In this view, members of a community internalize an image of the community not as a group of anomic individuals but as inter-connected members who share equally in their fundamental membership in the community.
>
> Leo R. Chavez 1994 "The power of the imagined community: The settlement of undocumented Mexicans and Central Americans in the United States." *American Anthropologist* 96 (1): 52–73, 54.

A careful summary of this passage would account for Chavez's own summarizing activity:

> In his study of the settlement patterns of undocumented immigrants in the US southwest, Chavez (1994) cites Anderson's notion of community as "imagined": a subjective sensation of being connected with others, despite inequality and the absence of face-to-face contact, an "image of [...] communion with others" (Anderson cited in Chavez, p. 54).

This sort of **double reporting** identifies the source's position with respect to the studies he cites. The summary is not saying that people imagine communities, nor is it saying that Chavez says people imagine communities. What it *is* saying is that Chavez says that Anderson says that people imagine communities.

Here, part of the summarizer's contribution to the scholarly conversation lies in tracing the history of a statement. In the summarized version, "imagined community" starts with Anderson, then steps over to Chavez, and then steps again—into the summary. This summary records the idea's journey: its point of departure, its use in another location, its arrival into a new piece of writing, trailing behind it mementos of its journey.

Sometimes, in our activity as summarizers, we need to recognize that ideas undergo significant transformations as they move from study to study. In the following passage, sociologists Irvine, Kahl, and Smith expand upon research conducted by two earlier sociologists, Anderson and Snow, into the ways in which the homeless protect themselves against the stigma of homelessness:

> Our research contributes to the discussion begun by Snow and Anderson about how the homeless seek to "salvage the self" when cast into stigmatizing social identities. Whereas Snow and Anderson focused on identity talk, particularly the forms of distancing and embracement, we introduce redefining as another form that helps minimize stigmatizing affronts. Although some homeless pet owners responded to such affronts with open or contained defiance, we found that the majority redefined pet ownership so that the meanings ascribed to it reflected the activities that characterized their relationships with their animals. They pointed out that they could provide what other dogs lacked and that their way of caring for an animal surpassed the typical standards, which require a house. They asserted their ability to provide food for their animals, even at personal sacrifice, and to offer enhanced quality of life through constant companionship, an outdoor environment, and freedom. Redefining differs from distancing, which would involve disassociating oneself from the roles of pet owner or homeless person. It also differs from embracement, which would involve the avowal of the negative social identity of irresponsible pet owner. If homeless pet owners simply agreed with the accusation that they could not provide for their companion animals, then they would accept the social identities imputed to them, which cast them as incapable of caring for themselves, and therefore unworthy of animal companionship. Instead, redefining is an attempt to challenge the basis of the affront. By redefining pet

ownership, the homeless pet owner can assert that he or she may be homeless but not helpless.

Leslie Irvine, Kristina N. Kahl, and Jesse Smith 2012 "Confrontations and donations: Encounters between homeless pet owners and the public." *Sociological Quarterly* 53(1): 25–43, 38–39.

Clearly, the work of Snow and Anderson is important here, and a summary of this passage would need to refer to this previous research, but it would have to do more than that: it would have to capture the significant ways in which Irvine et al. build upon the work of their predecessors. A summary of the passage might begin: "Expanding upon research by Snow and Anderson on the strategies used by the homeless to resist 'stigmatizing social identities,' Irvine et al. note that the homeless redefine their identity as pet owners. Their analysis suggests that redefining differs significantly from both 'distancing' and 'embracement,' the main strategies Snow and Anderson identify."

3F Experts and Non-Experts

In the cases above, the researchers are citing other scholars. But sometimes, in some kinds of scholarly writing, the cited voice belongs not to a scholar but to a **research subject**: someone who has been interviewed, or whose voice has been otherwise captured for study. In this next passage, researchers have studied racist and anti-racist attitudes in an inner-city neighbourhood in Rotterdam.

The existence of discrimination is not denied by the participants who hold more racist views. Dutch people "haven't always been angels themselves, that's for sure, because they've completely discriminated against people," and "foreigners are certainly discriminated against, if only because their skin's a different colour" (participants "K" and "L" respectively). Several times during the discussions, however, it is pointed out that it is not so much ethnic minorities who are discriminated against, but Dutch local residents (K: "I feel now like I'm discriminated against instead of them"). Community and social workers, housing corporations, schools, and also municipality officials were accused of favouring ethnic minorities and of only standing up for minority groups. It was held, for instance, that

Dutch children would receive less attention in schools and might even be left behind.

Maykel Verkuyten, Wiebe de Jong, and Kees Masson 1994 "Similarities in anti-racist and racist discourse: Dutch local residents talking about ethnic minorities." *New Community* 20 (2): 253–67, 257.

Whereas Chavez appears to agree with Anderson's notion of "imagined community" (or at least to take a position very near Anderson's) and Irvine et al. build upon research they largely accept, the writers of the passage above probably do not agree with some of what they cite from their research subjects. But, in a way, whether they agree or disagree is not the point. They are not arguing for or against the idea that ethnic minorities are favoured by official policy, and their study provides no evidence to support either position. Instead, Verkuyten et al. cite the words of others as indications of social phenomena. If we summarize the passage above as—

> In their research into attitudes toward ethnic minorities in an inner-city neighbourhood in Rotterdam, Verkuyten et al. (1994) discovered not only a generally shared acknowledgement of racism but also a perception of a kind of reverse discrimination: some informants expressed the view that ethnic minorities were favoured by official policy and institutional practice.

—we are not saying that racism exists or that ethnic minorities are officially favoured; nor are we saying that Verkuyten et al. say that racism exists or that ethnic minorities are favoured. Rather we are saying that Verkuyten et al. say that *some people say* that racism exists and that minorities are favoured. If we were to summarize the passage as—

> Verkuyten et al. report that, in the inner-city neighbourhood of Rotterdam they studied, ethnic minorities were favoured by official policy and institutional practice.

—we would be misrepresenting the original.

We could say that when Chavez cites Anderson, or Irvine et al. cite Snow and Anderson, they are citing fellow experts, and joining them in conversation. And when Verkuyten et al. cite "K," they are reporting the words of a person who is a non-specialist, not involved in the research conversation. But the categories **expert** and **non-expert** are not airtight, and the boundary between them can be contested. Below is an example where experts—"scientific circles"—and non-experts are cited, both groups providing examples of attitudes toward creole languages.

> Today, even in scientific circles, a persistent stigma is attached to creole languages.[1] Because their formative period was relatively recent, the 17th and 18th centuries, they are often seen as not yet fully formed complex languages. The descriptions of creole languages in some linguistic circles are similar to the attitudes of many creole speakers toward their languages. These languages are described as "reduced," simple, and easy to learn; lacking in abstract terms, they are inadequate for scientific, philosophical, and logical operations. For most of their histories, creole languages have not been considered adequate for government, schooling or Western religious services.
>
> The effect of pseudoscientific arguments or preconceived emotional ideas are evident in the negative attitudes lay persons generally hold toward creole languages and their speakers, and are revealed by the many pejorative terms used by both native and non-native speakers alike. Folk terminologies describe the French lexicon creoles as "broken French," "patois," "dialects," or "jargons," and many assume that creole languages are "diminished," "reduced," "deformed," "impoverished," "vitiated," "bastard" forms of the European standard languages that contributed to their birth.[2] Many educated and middle-class Haitians, members of the petite-bourgeoisie, as well as Haitian élites, view kreyòl [creole] as a simplified form of French at best. Many claim it is not a real language at all, but a mixture of languages without a grammar. The different varieties of kreyòl are viewed by Haitians of these social categories with a great deal of ambivalence. *Kreyòl rèk* [rough creole] and *gwo kreyòl* [vulgar creole] are often associated with pejorative connotations regarding the sounds (harsh, not harmonious, guttural, deformed), the grammatical features (debased, corrupted, elementary, lacking complexity), the social origin of speakers (rural, lower class), and defects usually attributed to the speakers themselves (coarse, clumsy, stupid, illiterate, uneducated). On the positive side, the same varieties have been associated with national identity, authenticity, independence, sincerity, and trustworthiness. Much of this is connected to romantic notions about rural people—rough, coarse, but also authentic, real.

Notes

1 Diamond's (1991) article in *Natural History* titled "Reinventions of Human Language: Children Forced to Reevolve Grammar Thereby Reveal Our Brain's Blueprint for Language" includes the following:

> Between human languages and the vocalizations of any animal lies a seemingly unbridgeable gulf [....] One approach to bridging this gulf is to ask whether some people, deprived of the opportunity to hear any of our fully evolved modern languages, ever spontaneously invented a primitive language [....] Children placed in a situation comparable to that of the wolf-boy [...] hearing adults around them speaking a grossly simplified and variable form of language somewhat similar to what children themselves usually speak around the age of two [...] proceeded unconsciously to evolve their own language, far advanced over vervet communication but simpler than *normal* languages. These new languages were the ones commonly known as creoles. [p. 23, emphasis added]

2 August Brun, a French scholar writing in the early part of the 20th century, claimed that "une langue est un dialecte qui a réussi. Un patois est une langue qui s'est dégradée" (quoted in Pressoir 1958: 27). (A language is a dialect that has been successful. A patois is a language that has deteriorated.) Such a view is still held by some educated Haitians today.

Bambi B. Shieffelin and Rachelle Charlier Doucet 1994 "The 'real' Haitian creole: Ideology, metalinguistics, and orthographic choice." *American Ethnologist* 21 (1): 176–200, 181–82.

An account of what these people say can be analyzed for levels, with the lowest levels (in the analysis below) being named speakers quoted directly (Figure 3.2).

(Notice that in this passage only the specialist speakers are specifically identified. What do you make of that?) The analysis incorporates a higher level than appears in the original, naming the larger phenomenon to which this situation belongs. (Higher still could be *social distinction, ranking*.) The analysis also diagrams a *conflict*, a *complication* or *ambivalence* the passage presents: the co-occurrence of negative and positive attitudes toward Haitian Creole. The following summary assigns statements to this company of speakers:

Shieffelin and Doucet's (1994) survey of attitudes toward creoles reminds us of the persistent social habit of evaluating and ranking speech and speakers. In their descriptions of creoles, even linguists have tended to stigmatize these languages, referring to them as incomplete, and insufficient for use in government or schooling. Lay people also stigmatize creoles, characterizing these languages as illegitimate, "deformed," "impoverished": middle-class Haitians, for example, according to Shieffelin and Doucet, judge the sounds of Haitian Creole and the origins of its speakers pejoratively, yet, at the same time, celebrate an ideal notion of the rural classes.

Think of what the summary would be like without reporting expressions—something like "Haitian Creole is a reduced, simple language unfit for use in government or education; its sounds are coarse...." This would be a radical misrepresentation of the original.

While the distinction between experts and non-experts may seem pretty clear when one considers professional ethnographers and their research subjects, it's not so clear in the next passage, which comes from

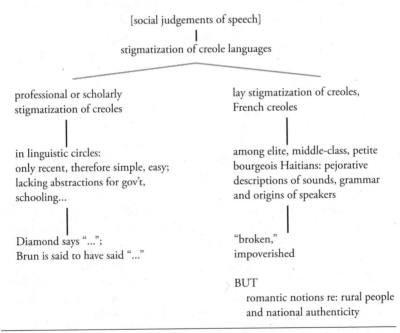

Figure 3.2. Levels of generality for Shieffelin and Doucet (1994).

an article analyzing the historical circumstances of open admissions in the US in the 1970s, when large numbers of "non-traditional" students entered university: members of minority and marginalized groups joined members of the groups which had traditionally comprised university populations. Here Lu cites Geoffrey Wagner (Professor of English at City College, New York) and author of *The End of Education*. Wagner is one of the gatekeepers whose reaction to open admissions Lu analyzes. Notice also the scholarly technique for indicating added emphasis: "(emphasis mine)." Sometimes you will see "(emphasis added)" or "(italics added)." Sometimes the technique affirms the original, though in the following passage it seems to encourage skepticism on the part of the reader toward the source being quoted.

> To Wagner, open admissions students are the inhabitants of the "world" outside the sort of scholarly "community" which he claims existed at Oxford and City College. They are dunces (43), misfits (129), hostile mental children (247), and the most sluggish of animals (163). He describes a group of Panamanian "girls" taking a Basic Writing course as "abusive, stupid, and hostile" (128). [...] Wagner predicts "the end of education" because of the "*arrival* in urban academe of *large*, indeed *overwhelming, numbers* of *hostile* mental children" (247; emphasis mine).
>
> Min-Zhan Lu 1992 "Conflict and struggle: The enemies or preconditions of basic writing?" *College English* 54 (8): 891–913, 893–94.

Originally, Wagner might have considered himself an "expert," but Lu's citation seems to have the effect of undermining that status, of transforming his words into indications of social attitudes, or earmarks of a political phenomenon. Just as Verkuyten et al. do not enter into scholarly conversation with the Rotterdam residents whom they cite, Lu captures Wagner as a social type rather than a fellow scholar. In this passage, for example, Lu cites isolated patches ("dunces (43), misfits (129)"); commandeers verbatim wordings ("'girls,'" "'abusive, stupid, and hostile'") to exemplify the original; adds emphasis by using italics where none appear in the original—in all, forcefully *re-accents* the original.

Let's take one more look at this process of contextualizing reported statements. The next passage comes from an elderly woman's memoir (recorded as oral history) of her childhood experiences 60 years before in a Catholic boarding school for aboriginal children in Canada.

> ... oh my was I ever homesick. You know home wasn't much, in fact the nuns didn't call it home, they called it our *camp*. And that used to hurt me. It still does when I think about it. When we'd talk about going home, they'd say, "You're not going home you're going back to your camp." That was their impression of the reserve. Well in a way they were right because the homes we had in those days were made out of great big log houses.
>
> Mary Englund 1981 "An Indian remembers." In *Now You Are My Brother*, ed. Margaret Whitehead. Victoria, BC: Provincial Archives, 59.

An accurate summary would *not* be:

> The children's homes were only camps.

At the very least, quotation marks would show that the writer is *not* vouching for this word:

> The children's homes were only "camps."

More explicitly, the word can be attributed to its original speakers:

> The nuns at the school referred to the children's homes as "camps."

But still we are missing aspects of context, which we can retrieve by adding another layer of citation—

> Mary Englund remembers that the nuns at the school referred to the children's homes as "camps."

—and another layer of context:

> Sixty years later, Mary Englund remembers that the nuns at the school referred to the children's homes as "camps."

Now the citation process includes a record of the survival of that word "camp"—enduring a lifetime in Englund's recollection, uttered once more on the occasion of the oral historian's research.

Exercise 5

The following passage comes from an essay by Raymond A. Anselment on seventeenth-century responses to smallpox. Write a three- or four-sentence summary of this excerpt, making sure you maintain the distinction between the positions occupied by

Anselment, the professional historians Anselment discusses, and Anselment's seventeenth-century sources. Of particular importance here is Anselment's assessment of the expert historians who preceded him.

Seventeenth-century letters, memoirs, and diaries personalize the mounting figures in the Mortality Bills [weekly records of deaths occurring in London]. Not all families were as fortunate as that of Ralph Josselin, four of whose children survived the smallpox. John Chamberlain's letter to Sir Dudley Carlton informed him that viscount Lisle "hath lost his eldest sonne [i.e. son] Sir William Sidney of the small pockes, which were well come out and yet he went away on the sodain [i.e. suddenly]; he hath now but one sonne left."... In his autobiography, William Stout described the sorrow that overwhelmed his mother when her two youngest sons died of smallpox soon after their father:

> The loss of these two children, so near together and so soon after their father, was so [great an] affliction to my mother that she continued in much sorrow for a long time; as was also my sister, which added to her other bodily infirmities, reduced her very low.[1]

... Neither these reactions nor the moving responses of Mary, Countess of Warwick and Ann, Lady Fanshawe support the widely accepted modern belief that the high mortality rate among infants and children in the seventeenth century inured parents to their children's deaths. When "it pleased God to take" her only son just before he came of age and despite her efforts to save him, the Countess of Warwick wrote that her "sad and afflicted husband ... cried out so terribly that his cry was heard a great way; and he was the saddest afflicted person could possibly be." Her own actions left her sorrow unstated yet obvious: she "instantly" left her house in Lincoln's Inn Field "and never more did I enter that house; but prevailed with my Lord to sell it."[2] ...

None of these poignant expressions of grief confirms Philippe Ariès's influential suggestion that parents sought refuge from pain and sorrow in a deliberate indifference to the danger of death so commonplace among their children.[3] The grief of both mothers and fathers, on the contrary, suggests an emotion only partly accountable by Lawrence Stone's controversial view of the period's gradual transition from the "Restricted Patriarchal Nuclear Family" to the "Closed Domesticated Nuclear Family."[4] In their understated eloquence, the sufferings of these parents are as heartfelt as any Stone found for the later years of allegedly growing family importance. Perhaps, as he and others have suggested, the economic, humanistic, and religious forces of the Renaissance helped to shape the sensibilities that gave new importance to the value of the family as well as the individual. But perhaps the grief is instinctive.

Notes

1 William Stout, *The autobiography of William Stout of Lancaster, 1665–1752*, ed. J.D. Marshall, Manchester, Chetham Society, 1967, p. 76.

2 Warwick, op. cit. pp. 30–31.

3 Philippe Ariès contended in *Centuries of Childhood* that "People could not allow themselves to become too attached to something that was regarded as a possible loss" (p. 38). Dr. W.F. Bynum kindly called my attention to Michael MacDonald's criticism of Ariès's position: in *Mystical Bedlam*, Cambridge University Press, 1981, particularly 75–85, MacDonald questioned the prevalence in the seventeenth century of "emotional austerity and indifference to members of the immediate family."

4 Lawrence Stone, *The family, sex and marriage in England, 1500–1800*, New York, Harper & Row, 1977.

Raymond A. Anselment 1989 "Small pox in seventeenth-century English literature: Reality and the metamorphosis of wit." *Medical History* 33 (1): 72–95, 81–83.

Challenging Situations for Summarizers

So far, we've looked at passages from scholarly articles that contain a wide range of generality. We've considered strategies that help summarizers record gists and reproduce the sense of the original in their summary, and we've used tree diagrams to examine patterns of generality. We've seen that, in composing a summary, the summarizer establishes a position and creates something new—a compact piece of writing, ready to be used in new contexts.

Passages that offer only high-level generalities or, at the opposite extreme, only low-level details can prove particularly challenging for the summarizer. This circumstance presents itself not only in scholarly writing but also in everyday situations—for instance, when taking minutes at a meeting, reviewing a movie, conducting an interview, or telling a story.

In this chapter we begin by looking at passages that remain at high levels; that is, they omit the low-level examples that demonstrate the abstract ideas at work. Then we'll look at passages that remain at low levels, those that tend to omit high-level abstractions. As we shall see, our summarizing strategies can be adapted to fit diverse circumstances.

4A High-Level Passages

Some passages (and even whole articles and books) remain at high levels of generality. The following passage, for example, presents no details, no specifics—only high-level abstractions.

According to commemorative rhetoric, the past makes the present. Commemoration is a way of claiming that the past has something to offer the present, be it a warning or a model. In times of rampant change, the past provides a necessary point of reference for identity and action (Shils 1981). In contrast, the literature on social memory often emphasizes the importance of contextual factors in shaping commemorative practices and symbolism (Olick and Robbins 1998). Images of the past are malleable. Traditions are "invented" and memories are altered for instrumental reasons in the present (Hobsbawm and Ranger 1983). Social memories are subject to, and are products of, production conflict and purposeful memory entrepreneurship (Wagner-Pacifici and Schwartz 1991). Producers, moreover, cannot control the ways in which images of the past are perceived (Savage 1994). Scholars therefore look at how people use memory to create identities and at how dominant narratives suppress alternative ones, and view the past as a terrain on which competing groups struggle for position (Bodnar 1992; Foucault 1977). These accounts emphasize that commemoration is explainable in terms of its contemporary circumstances: the present, from this perspective, makes the past.

Jeffrey K. Olick 1999 "Genre memories and memory genres: A dialogical analysis of May 8, 1945, commemorations in the Federal Republic of Germany." *American Sociological Review* 64: 381–402, 381.

An analysis of this passage for levels of generality produces something like Figure 4.1:

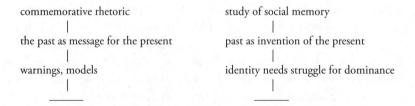

Figure 4.1. Diagram of high levels of generality in the Olick passage.

As you can see, the lower levels on our diagram are empty—and if, in summarizing this passage, you wanted to put your reader in closer touch with these ideas, you would have to come up with supporting details or specific examples. In the example below, the details supplied by the summarizer are emphasized.

> Public commemorations of the past include **monuments, ceremonies, speeches, symbols, and anthems**. Describing scholarly approaches to such commemorations, Olick (1999) points to contrasting schools of thought. One of these schools studies "commemorative rhetoric," and treats commemoration as a message from the past for the present (p. 381). So, the public ways of commemorating **a national tragedy or a social movement, for example**, would be seen as a message from the past to the present: an example to avoid or to follow. On the other hand, theories of "social memory" analyze commemoration as a story about the past invented in the present to advance some present interests over others (p. 381). **We could think of yearly commemorations of the 9/11 tragedy in the US as an example: these reminders might be seen as promoting ideas which benefit some groups rather than others, years after the event occurred. We could apply Olick's distinction to the ways, in Canada, that accounts of the "birth" of national health care in the 1960s are repeated years later.** We can speculate that commemorative rhetoricians would analyze these accounts as a "warning or a model" (p. 381), while sociologists of public memory would analyze them as strategies in a current struggle to control the culture and economy of health care.

It's hard work summarizing a passage that is composed at a very high level of abstraction. And risky—perhaps these specific mentions are not the best illustrations of the phenomenon under examination. But by coming up with examples, summarizers can measure their understanding of the passage and also offer readers handholds as they make their way across

High-level generality ... low-level details

these high-level ideas. The specific mentions provided by the summarizer show the **summarizer's position**—his or her perspective on the material summarized—without attributing that position to Olick. Notice, however, that this summary is nearly as long as the original. This may be a tendency of summary that attempts to represent a passage that remains at the higher "levels."

Exercise 1

In his much-cited analysis of modernity in the late twentieth century, Anthony Giddens explains "trustworthiness." In the following passage, he distinguishes two types of trust: trust in persons and trust in systems. He also talks about "access points," which are "points of connection between lay individuals or collectivities and the representatives of abstract systems. These are places of vulnerability for abstract systems, but also junctions at which trust can be maintained or built up" (p. 88). This passage stays at high levels, which presents a challenge for both summarizer and reader. Adding details would locate Giddens's distinctions within current conditions and thus secure a position for the summarizer and guide a reader's understanding. Try to come up with some specifics that illustrate these high-level ideas. Then write a two- or three-sentence summary that includes this lower-level material.

TRUST IN ABSTRACT SYSTEMS

Trustworthiness is of two sorts. There is that established between individuals who are well known to one another and who, on the basis of long-term acquaintance, have substantiated the credentials which render each reliable in the eyes of the other. Trustworthiness in respect of the disembedding mechanisms is different, although reliability is still central and credentials are certainly involved. In some circumstances, trust in abstract systems does not presuppose any encounters at all with the individuals or groups who are in some way "responsible" for them. But in the large majority of instances such individuals or groups are involved, and I shall refer to encounters with them on the part of lay actors as the *access points* of abstract systems. The access points of abstract systems are the meeting ground of face-work and faceless commitments. It will be a basic part of my argument that *the nature of modern institutions is deeply bound up with the mechanisms of trust in abstract systems*, especially trust in expert systems.

Anthony Giddens 1990 *The Consequences of Modernity*. Stanford, CA: Stanford UP, 83 (emphasis in original).

Exercise 2

In the following passage from their book *In Search of Hospitality*, Conrad Lashley and Alison Morrison examine how the media, especially "the television personality food programme," goes beyond obvious messaging about food, such as recipes, to influence people's ideas of food and hospitality. However, they don't mention a specific food show or provide any details about the "social attitudes, social relations, and consumer motivations" that are influenced by such programmes. Drawing on your own knowledge of TV or internet shows about food that feature a prominent host "personality," identify examples of attitudes, relations, and consumer motivations that might be affected by the show. What might be an example of the "obvious messages"? What is involved in "hospitality"? What is it about? Write a summary that is about the same length as the original, but which includes these examples to illustrate how such influence might work.

In the modern world, a wide spectrum of media produce messages about food and hospitality. Of these, television food programmes will impact upon the greatest number of consumers at any one time. At first sight, one might think that these programmes simply offer some obvious messages about food and hospitality: cooking instruction for the recycling of traditional recipes and the presentation of new dishes. However, a semiotic examination of one particular segment of the media, the television personality food programme, reveals that such programmes offer much more complex and potentially more powerful influences about hospitality that involve social attitudes, social relations, and consumer motivations.

Conrad Lashley and Alison Morrison 2013 In *Search of Hospitality*. Hoboken: Taylor and Francis, 130.

Exercise 3

In the following passage from his article "Harry Potter and the Functions of Popular Culture," Dustin Kidd considers the role that popular culture plays in "defining and distributing the norms of society." The title, of course, lets you know that Kidd is mainly concerned with J.K. Rowling's *Harry Potter* series. Create a tree diagram representing levels of generality in the passage and then build lower levels with specific social norms and details drawn from your own knowledge of *Harry Potter* (including the novels, films, games, costumes, and whatever else you identify). Write a summary of Kidd and use the norms that you identify and the details from *Harry Potter* to speculate on how Kidd's argument might work. (Try imagining yourself saying "in other words." For example, "Kidd draws on the suggestion of Durkheim's work on suicide and Merton's on crime that 'adherence to social norms increases one's sense of social importance and responsibility': in other words, adherence to norms does..." *what?*)

Social norms, as guides to social behavior, are important mechanisms in social cohesion. Durkheim's study of suicide and Robert Merton's study of crime reveal that anomic communities experience higher suicide and crime rates, suggesting that adherence to social norms increases one's sense of social importance and responsibility. Popular culture is not the only source of norm production in advanced capitalist societies, but it is perhaps the most important because of its wide distribution. To compare popular culture and crime as sources of social norms, it is important to recognize that many Americans are not aware of all of the laws of their country, state, or community, but they are enormously aware of popular culture. Most crimes never become truly public events; only the major crimes make the news, and few Americans attend trials. So, crime has a very limited role as a means by which norms are produced and distributed.

The role of popular culture, in contrast, is quite large. Although no American consumes all of American popular culture, most Americans consume quite a lot of it. In their book *The Dominant Ideology Thesis*, Nicholas Abercrombie,

> Stephen Hill, and Bryan Turner identify popular culture, in the form of mass media, as the key means by which the ideas of the dominant classes might be transmitted to the whole of society in the era of late capitalism. Although the authors ultimately argue that no dominant ideology is in place in late capitalism—because the dominant class is too fragmented—the study nevertheless highlights the fact that popular culture is the most centralized and effective means for defining and distributing the norms of society.
>
> Dustin Kidd 2007 "Harry Potter and the Functions of Popular Culture." *The Journal of Popular Culture* 40(1): 69–89, 75.

4B Low-Level Passages

The next passage presents information at a much lower level than the readings above about "commemorative rhetoric" and "trustworthiness."

BRIAN

Brian is 14; his behaviour at school troubles staff and other students; he has become aggressive at home and at school; he sniffs glue. He is referred to a counselling clinic, and a schedule is arranged for him.

Brian is escorted each day to and from school either by family or by social services personnel. At school he is given "jobs" in the classroom during breaks. Two evenings weekly he is taken to a voluntary youth club run by some police officers in their spare time, and at weekends he joins a church youth centre for youngsters like himself, for outings and organized games. Once a week he also goes to an intermediate treatment centre, and one morning weekly he attends the clinic for group counselling and activities like painting and building models.

Adapted from Denis O'Connor 1987 "Glue sniffers with special needs." *British Journal of Special Education* 14 (3): 94–97, 96–97.

The preference for low-level detail in the O'Connor passage is represented by Figure 4.2:

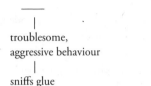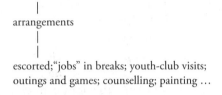

Figure 4.2. Diagram of low levels of generality in the O'Connor passage.

If you were to summarize this passage, you might find it hard to get free of the details or to make the summary any shorter than the original. But to summarize this low, "flat" passage for a scholarly context, you need to construct the higher levels—find words that name and condense these details. That is, you need to interpret the details as *meaning* something. So, for example, the high-level abstractions *deviance* and *surveillance* might be used to identify patterns in the details. From this, an even higher level can be constructed: *social control* (Figure 4.3).

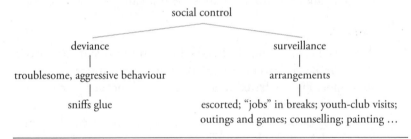

Figure 4.3. Diagram of reconstructed levels of generality for the O'Connor passage.

It's hard work summarizing a passage that is composed at extremely low levels. And risky—perhaps these abstractions are not right. Maybe *deviance* is a rather negative interpretation of Brian's behaviour. A summarizer might take a more positive view and might interpret Brian's behaviour as *resistance*, to school and family impositions, for example. Or *surveillance* might fail to capture the arrangements for Brian as good for him. A summarizer might interpret the details as evidence of *therapy* and *healing*. Or his troublesomeness might be interpreted as *dysfunction*. Each of these high-level abstractions is an interpretation of the details, and the summary which uses them will express the summarizer's point of view. One person might summarize the passage this way:

The case of Brian, reported in O'Connor (1987), illustrates institutional practices of therapeutic surveillance. The 14-year-old's deviant behaviour is identified, and then managed through a series of monitoring activities, mechanisms of social control executed at the level of daily life.

Another person might summarize the passage as illustrating various means of attending humanely to dysfunction and incorporating the troubled boy into supportive social networks. As interpretations, such high-level abstractions show the summarizer's position: his or her perspective on the material summarized.

Exercise 4

The following passage is from Amit-Talai's research into adolescent friendships. Here we see the writer's abstractions working alongside the words of a student interviewed at a Montreal high school. High-level abstractions, such as friendship, sociability, disclosure, and concealment, enable the researcher to examine adolescent relationships in the context of institutional structures. Identify the abstractions that the researcher uses to interpret the interview data. (What is she calling "discontinuity"?) Then come up with alternative abstractions. Using the abstract terms you have generated, write a two- to three-sentence summary reporting Mike's situation.

DISJUNCTION

As graduation approached some students tried to reassure themselves and each other that their high school friendships would persevere [...].

Most of the friends, however, didn't believe that such continuity was possible. As much as they dreaded yet another institutional dislocation, they expected high school friendships to give way before the new affiliations of college or work. Mike was sure that once summer ended and college began, his friends would no longer see each other. Everything would be different in college.

> Well, college is where you will find everyone from all different schools and they get together and you see how they are different from each other. You get to see how

they act and everything. And in that way, you are seeing a totally new change, you know. Everything that you do is going to change. Your social life is going to change. Your behaviour is going to change. It is all going to change once you go to college, that's what I think.

Discontinuity of peer relations might be resented and feared, but by the end of high school it had come to be seen as an inevitable and natural outcome of institutional passages.

Vered Amit-Talai 1995 "The waltz of sociability: Intimacy, dislocation and friendship in a Quebec high school." In *Youth Cultures: A Cross-Cultural Perspective*, ed. Vered Amit-Talai and Helena Wulff. London: Routledge, 161.

Exercise 5

Find abstract words to construct higher levels of meaning in the following passage, a report from sociological research on attitudes toward crime. In a two- or three-sentence summary, report Mae's situation, using the abstract terms you have come up with. (It's possible that not all the terms you propose will come into play in your summary.)

INTERVIEW WITH MAE

Mae is 68 years old, Australian-born of British ancestry; she lives alone in a small country town in New South Wales. She lives in her home behind multiply-deadlocked front and back doors and windows, afraid of "home invasion." The only time Mae has had to contact the police was when a neighbour threw a firework on her roof. Mae is not poor—living in her own home in retirement—and is reasonably fit and well. Eighteen months ago, her husband died of natural causes. Since then, Mae has stopped watching any crime series on television—even series she had watched comfortably with her husband before he died. Indeed, the same shows seem to have changed for her since then: "That's the trouble, they're getting too much like what's happening out on the streets ... like what you read in the paper."

While she avoids all crime on television because "You see these things happening and I think you imagine that it's going to happen to you," Mae has taken to reading the local and national newspapers far more since her husband died. Her knowledge of crime comes almost entirely from this media source, since she does not go out much and has never experienced a criminal incident. It is in these newspapers that Mae has "become far more aware of the drug problem now." In the local paper she scrupulously reads the court cases, finding here the accounts of "home invasions" which she fears so much. Her reading of the paper tells her that nine out of ten cases are "about drugs"; and Mae is thus quite able to construct a causal narrative of crime, where youth unemployment leads to drug-taking and thus to "home invasions." As a result, she has "only recently" begun worrying about her grandchildren and drugs. This is also something she "sees so much of on TV, where people are dying from taking drugs. Peer pressure and all those sorts of things. It doesn't matter how good a child is—they can be turned around, can't they?"

Adapted from Deborah Lupton and John Tulloch 1999 "Theorizing fear of crime: Beyond the rational/irrational oppositions." *British Journal of Sociology* 50 (3): 507–23, 516–17.

4C Summarizing Narrative

In many disciplines, most notably history and literary studies, scholarly writers are likely to encounter **narratives**. These are organized chronologically: things, people, places are mentioned according to the order in which events occurred. When we look at narrative from a summarizer's point of view, we find conditions something like those we have just been investigating in anecdotal reports and research interviews. Narratives typically remain at a low level: particular people and things, particular actions and events. As is the case with other writing dominated by low-level detail, summarizers may find it useful to use abstractions to identify the significance of the details. Consider, for example, the narrative passage below, to which we have added gists and abstractions. It is the beginning of the well-known fairy tale "Little Thumb."

There was once upon a time a man and his wife, fagot-makers by trade, who had seven children, all boys. The eldest was but ten years old and the youngest only seven.

many children, close in age → *fertility*
8 males → *masculine dominance*

They were very poor, and their seven children incommoded them greatly, because not one of them was able to earn his bread. That which gave them yet more uneasiness was that the youngest was of a very puny constitution, and scarce ever spoke a word, which made them take that for stupidity which was a sign of good sense. He was very little, and when born no bigger than one's thumb, which made him be called Little Thumb.

poor → *poverty*
needy children → *dependency*

very small → *diminutiveness*
LT stays quiet → *reticence*

people are wrong about him → *misjudgement*

The poor child bore the blame of whatsoever was done amiss in that house, and, guilty or not, was always in the wrong; he was, notwithstanding, more cunning and had far greater share of wisdom than all his brothers put together; and if he spake little he heard and thought the more.

always blamed → *injustice*

wiser, alert → *intelligence, attentiveness*

There happened now to come a very bad year, and the famine was so great that these poor people resolved to rid themselves of their children. One evening, when they were all in bed and the fagot-maker was sitting with his wife at the fire, he said to her, with all his heart ready to burst with grief:

"Thou seest plainly that we are not able to keep our children, and I cannot face to see them starve to death before my face; I am resolved to lose them in the wood tomorrow, which

they get even poorer → *hardship, scarcity*

decide to get rid of children

father is sad → *sentiment, love*

but he plans to leave them → *trickery, conspiracy, ambivalence* will be very easily done; for while they are tying up fagots, we may run away and leave them without their taking any notice."

"Ah!" cried the wife, "and canst thou thyself have the heart to take thy children out along with thee on purpose to lose them?"

mother loves the boys, protests → *love, sentiment, conflict*

In vain did her husband represent to her their extreme poverty: she would not consent to it; she was indeed poor, but she was their mother. However having considered, what a grief it would be to her to see them perish with hunger, she at last consented, and went to bed all in tears.

mother resists, father persuades → *dispute, conflict, persuasion*

mother agrees but weeps → *grief, regret*

Little Thumb heard every word that had been spoken; for observing, as he lay in his bed, that they were talking very busily, he got up softly and hid himself under his father's stool that he might hear what they said without being seen.

LT notices the talk → *attentiveness*

hides & listens → *concealment, cunning*

Charles Perrault 1969 "Little Thumb." *In The Blue Fairy Book*, ed. Andrew Lang. New York: Airmont, 266–67.

Figure 4.4 illustrates how readers of this narrative may pay attention to details, actions, and conditions to the exclusion of any abstractions these details may imply:

man and wife	7 children, ages 7-10,			a decision
	puny youngest	blaming of youngest, who is silent	no food	"… to lose them in the wood tomorrow"

Figure 4.4. Analysis of low-level information in the "Little Thumb" passage.

A summary could be written from this analysis:

> Having seven sons between the ages of seven and ten, and no food, a man and wife decide to abandon their offspring in the forest. The youngest child is puny, and gets unfairly blamed for everything.

However, such an analysis might raise questions as to the significance of these events and conditions—the connections between blame and abandonment, for example. And some aspects of the story which are evident in the original—the father's ambivalent sentiments, the smallest boy's intelligent silence—are lost in condensation. Telling details vanish. By using the techniques suggested in Chapter 3 and the last section (4B), you can write a more conceptual summary—one suitable for scholarly purposes—which supplies the higher-level concepts that the original text doesn't provide *and* preserves the effect of these details. You can also give names to the story's episodes and build the higher levels by reading for abstractions which interpret the lower-level details.

This reading for abstraction provides materials for a more conceptual, interpretive summary:

> In a situation of great **scarcity**, Little Thumb's parents resolve to abandon their seven hungry sons in the forest. But **scarcity** and **abandonment** are complicated by **injustice** in the family—Little Thumb is unfairly blamed for everything—and by **misjudgement**— he is reckoned as dull, when in fact his **intelligence** of the world is sharper than others': he overhears the parents' **conspiracy**. This is a story not only of **hardship** and **scarcity** but also of **concealments** lurking in **abandonment**, hidden **virtue**, and secret **intentions**.

Other summarizers might come up with different abstractions to interpret the story's details, and still others might have different focuses, for example, *fertility* (the abundance of children amidst this scarcity) or *grief* and *ambivalence* (the complexity of the father's sentiments) or *masculine dominance* (the mother is outnumbered by males, and the father overcomes the mother's objections). The choice of which abstractions to use depends very much on the reasons for summarizing the passage.

In literature courses, students are often warned not to retell the story; their papers may be penalized for what their readers call "plot summary," that is, a list-like account of events in the original work. Yet professional scholars often summarize plot. Here, a literary scholar, publishing in a major journal in the field, briefly summarizes the plot of two novels for younger readers, M.T. Anderson's *Feed* and Nancy Farmer's *House of the Scorpion*:

Feed details the experiences of Titus, a teenager of the late twenty-first century, after his body/computer chip integration system is exposed to a virus from a rogue revolutionary group. His girlfriend Violet is also exposed to this virus and uses the experience to express to Titus the dehumanizing nature of consumer technology, a point neither can truly grasp nor eradicate. *The House of the Scorpion* refigures adolescence as yet another physical extension of capital, with Matt, the biological clone of a drug lord, existing for the sole purpose of organ harvesting. As Matt realizes that his potential and the advancements of science have designed him as living commodity, he finds himself questioning his own subjectivity, as well as confronting the possibility of destroying the global drug trade.

Abbie Ventura 2011 "Predicting a better situation? Three Young Adult speculative fiction texts and the possibilities for social change." *Children's Literature Association Quarterly* 36: 89–103, 91–92.

What makes "plot summary" like this acceptable? Its generalizing, interpretive abstractions seem to be the features that distinguish it from the kind of "plot summary" that literature teachers object to. For example, Ventura notes that in the first novel Violet and Titus contend with "the dehumanizing nature of consumer technology" and that in the second Matt, the protagonist, is reduced to a "living commodity." These interpretive abstractions bring the stories within range of the **research question** Ventura is asking: how does recent dystopian writing for young adults represent adolescents as agents of social change? For someone else summarizing *Feed* or *The House of the Scorpion*—someone with a different research perspective—the interpretive abstractions would be different.

Exercise 6

"School" is from Mary Englund's memoir, a transcribed oral history collected in 1980, late in Englund's life (we encountered another passage from her memoir in Chapter 3). Here Englund is answering an historian's questions about her experience in a religious residential school at Mission, British Columbia, during the second decade of the twentieth century. As Englund reports at the beginning of this memoir, children of school age were gathered from First Nations villages and settlements by priests, and transported to boarding schools. Using note-taking for abstractions, introduced earlier in this chapter, write a three- to four-sentence interpretive summary of the narrative fragment below.

SCHOOL

We weren't allowed to speak our language in school. We had to speak English right from day one. [...] It was a difficult situation. See they had different Indian dialects. Along the Fraser Valley they had the Stalo and the Thompson and us here was the Chelhalis. We talked very differently than they did. So if we talked to them it was all English. Even if we could talk with one another, the nuns wouldn't allow it. Of course, there was a lot of us that could talk the same language; you take from Fountain to Pavillion down to Mount Currie we all talked the same language. When we were alone in some corner we did talk our own language and if the Sisters caught us it was, "You talk English!" That's where a lot of girls kind of forgot their language. If you're there, stayed there a certain length of time, you forget certain words in Indian. You couldn't explain yourself too much in Indian as you would in English. They said it was better for us to speak English because we could learn English and read and write better if we kept our English, if we spoke English instead of talking Indian.

When the principal came over—Father Rohr, he was French—they'd sit and talk French and we knew very well they were talking about us, all of us, they could talk French. We used to tell them that, "How come you can talk French in front of us, and you wouldn't allow us to talk Indian in front of you?" And of course they got after us for that. You weren't allowed to question. Oh yes, they weren't very nice in that respect.

Of course all the parents thought that was great you see, that we should talk English and be able to write so that we'd be able to write letters when we got home, to do things for the Indian people. You were something great when you come home, "Oh she can write now." They were kind of proud of us in a way once you were able to write your name, your mother's name, your father's name and whoever was in the family. We were doing all right. They were proud of you then. I remember my grandmother—I don't know how old she was but she was partly blind and she was all crippled with arthritis—she'd pat us on the head because we can write.

We were not to tell our parents what went on in the school. That was another rule. We were not allowed to discuss what goes on in school when we go home. We never got sugar at school, no sugar in our porridge or in our tea so when we went home I guess this one girl was telling her parents how she never got sugar at school. When she got back to school she was really reprimanded by the principal Father Rohr. And he didn't go about it in a nice way. He went about it in a way very insulting, telling you what you did in your *camp* and what you told your father and mother and the tattletales. And your parents never had anything to say of what you were doing in the school because they didn't know. [...]

Englund 1981: 63–64.

Exercise 7

"Alert Bay," excerpted from *An Error in Judgement*, provides an historical account of conditions in a small, isolated community on Vancouver Island, British Columbia. In this section of her book, Culhane Speck focuses on the effect of the residential schools on the Alert Bay community. This passage is written for a scholarly context, and it proceeds at a much higher level of generality than the passage in Exercise 6. Using reading-and-noting techniques, write a three- to four-sentence interpretive summary of this passage.

ALERT BAY

An Anglican-administered industrial residential school, St. Michael's, which housed upwards of 200 students, was established in Alert Bay in 1929. Attendance was compulsory, and the Indian Act provided for a variety of punishments which could be levied against uncooperative parents, including fines and jail sentences. Students were prohibited from speaking their own language, and along with training in Christian scriptures and a basic academic program up to a grade 8 level, boys were taught carpentry, mechanics, farming, and animal husbandry, while girls received instruction in cooking, sewing and homemaking.

The explicit goal of the residential school system was to break the bonds between generations, thus "freeing" the young from the shackles of tradition and the influence of their families. Native parents, of course, made every effort to thwart this estrangement from their children and more and more people migrated from the smaller, more isolated Kwakwaka'wakw villages to Alert Bay in order to be able, at least, to visit with their children regularly. For the most part graduates of the residential schools did not assimilate into Canadian society. Many had no desire to, and others who tried found the doors closed to them. At the same time, when they returned to their home villages they often found they had lost both the ability to communicate fluently with parents and grandparents, and the practical, as well as social, skills necessary to fit into village life.[1]

While rank and social status determined by the potlatch system continued to function within Kwakwaka'wakw society, new divisions rooted in colonial relations arose and either over-lapped with the aboriginal hierarchy or co-existed beside it. The terms and conditions for survival and opportunities for upward mobility—often synonymous terms in this context—were now defined by the dominant non-Native society and were therefore most available to Native people who possessed one or more of the following attributes: conversion to Christianity, mission or residential school education, at least formal denunciation of potlatching and other elements of aboriginal culture, mixed blood, and residence in Alert Bay rather than in one of the outlying villages. Some Indians did become successful skippers or boat owners in the commercial fishing industry and a few found steady work in logging. Others owned and ran small stores on the reserves. The majority, however, worked when work was available and/or received government relief. [...]

By the end of the 1930s, most of the Kwakwaka'wakw living in Alert Bay had converted to Christianity, and education, rather than being resisted, began to be encouraged for the young.

"We had to think about what will be best for the kids," a Kwakwaka'wakw elder would later explain.[2]

Notes

1   Ernest Willie, presentation to *The Goldthorpe Inquiry*, (1980), Transcript. Vol. 1, pp. 94–113.

2   Jack Peters, presentation to *The Goldthorpe Inquiry*, (1980), Transcript. Vol. 1, p. 48.

Dara Culhane Speck 1987 *An error in judgement: The politics of medical care in an Indian/ white Community*. Vancouver, BC: Talonbooks, 84–85.

5

Readers Reading I

Handbooks for writing recommend knowing your audience. This seems like sound advice. But who is your audience when you write at college or university? In Chapter 1, we noted that the university is a research institution that includes very different types of readers involved in their own disciplines. How do you get to know these sorts of readers? What causes these readers to react negatively or positively to a student's writing? To answer these questions, we need to learn more about academic readers—their reading practices, values, and expectations. This chapter will help us begin to think about our readers by learning how to practise the **think-aloud protocol**. This technique can be used to engage with academic writing that you are assigned to read; it can also be used to better understand how a reader experiences your writing. But before we begin our examination of readers and their reactions, let's consider a few ways that *social context* or *circumstance* affects how we use language and how people respond to us.

5A Who Do You Think You're Talking To?

In everyday conversation, we have a good idea of our listener: it's the person in front of us. Sometimes the person is a family member or a friend, and conversation is easy. Sometimes the person is a stranger, and this can make conversation more difficult. But usually we have some legitimate, acknowledged reason for addressing the stranger: they're a receptionist in a doctor's office; a retail clerk; a person enrolled in the same fitness class—we have information that enables us to address them usefully in the situation. In any case, once we get going, we check the listener's response; we make inferences, and adjust our emphases, our themes, and the ways we address people.

Still, even face-to-face, we can sometimes struggle with inferences about our audience. Language and cognitive specialists study these efforts: Herbert Clark's work on "audience design" (1992), for example, investigates people's habits of inference in addressing others. Clark finds that conversation keeps us busy at various levels of consciousness as we estimate the frame of mind of our co-conversationalists and others who might overhear us. We estimate others' knowledge of the world, calculating the extent of **mutual knowledge**—what can be safely assumed and what needs to be explained. Some studies by Wallace Chafe (1994) discover, in addition to these calculations, our ongoing estimates of **listeners' centre of attention**: what is in the spotlight for them, what has slipped into the shadows.

When we are writing, we can't see our audience in front of us, to watch their reactions, but often we know so much about them that we don't need to see them. For example, working in genres like the postcard or the personal letter, we normally have a reliable picture of our reader. Also, we have received postcards and letters ourselves, so we have experience of our own responses to certain forms, and also of the social occasions and expectations which call for postcards and letters.

On the other hand, when we are working in genres like the letter of complaint (e.g., to request compensation for a defective product) or the job application letter, we have, generally, much less information about our audience—except, probably, as a social type: a corporate employee handling public relations, or a human-resources director. If we have not ourselves received many complaints or applications, we can't rely on our own response to such documents when we make decisions about what to include, what to leave out, how to word things, and what order they should take. If, however, we are dedicated complainers or job applicants, we may be familiar with typical outcomes of our writing—redress or silence, offers or brush-offs. From these responses, we infer aspects of the situation and alter our approach for the next time. Of course, if we could eavesdrop on a director of human resources as she talked about job applications, we would probably become much better at understanding how mutual knowledge and the listener's centre of attention work while reading job application letters.

How do student writers of university essays learn to position themselves in relation to their readers? How do student writers infer aspects of this situation? The exercises which follow can help you and your instructor talk about how you interpret your situation as a student writer.

Exercise 1

In groups of three or four, compare your answers to the questions below. If you haven't yet had writing returned to you at college or university, then use your experience of high-school assignments and then guess at or estimate university-level expectations and response. Make notes of the answers and your discussion. You will need them for Exercise 2.

- What do you do and how do you feel when you get marked essays returned? For example, do you look at the grade, read the instructor's comments, throw the assignment out, reread it, tear it to bits, show it to your friends?
- What do you consider typical marking commentary on essays? What kinds of things do markers say about your essays in particular?

Collaborate with other members of your group to compose a 300- to 400-word summary of your findings, accounting for differences and similarities in your habits and perceptions. Try to make a connection between your habits and attitudes upon having a marked essay returned to you and your ideas of markers' typical remarks. For example, if you celebrate the return of the essay, this may be directly related to teachers' typically expressing delight at particular aspects of your essays.

Exercise 2

Using the information you have gathered in Exercise 1, and sharing your findings with other members of the class, locate the student writer's distance from or closeness to her or his markers: in what sense do student writers "know" those who read and mark their work—as friends, acquaintances, strangers, social types? Is the student writer's experience of the academic genres like that of the writer of the postcard or that of the writer of the job application? How does it compare to writing essays in high school? From the information you have collected in Exercise 1, what inferences would you make about the situation, and about academic readers? How do you picture readers of your essays? How do these readers read? What do you know about them, so far?

5B Traditions of Commentary on Student Writing

One obstacle to "knowing your audience" in the university context are **unitary views of language**: the idea that a single set of standards can be applied to all forms of writing or speech. Unitary views of language often manifest themselves in set rules (e.g., never end a paragraph with a quotation; don't use the first person; never begin a sentence with "and"). "Good" writing is then determined by whether these rules are followed or not. Many elements of the typical commentary that students get on their work (e.g., their writing is "sloppy," "careless," or "awkward") are motivated by ideas about there being a single, unitary ideal writing (e.g., "precise," "careful," "flowing"). Such feedback might have value as an indirect indicator that problems with grammar, usage, and punctuation are interfering with the reader's understanding. But it can also be vague or ambiguous, and it may overshadow more practical information about readers' expectations of scholarly writing, what information they need, and to what extent they are (or aren't) paying attention.

As we saw in Chapter 1, genre theory—the idea, that is, that typical ways of speaking and writing enable particular social activities—suggests that different writing situations will call for different forms of expression. The research genres display features which are not necessarily unique to them but which are arranged in ways that distinguish research writing from other kinds of writing. And the research genres differ amongst themselves: marine biology has things in common with archaeology but also has ways of speaking that it doesn't share with archaeology; anthropology resembles psychology in some ways but not in others. Diverse ways of doing research tend toward diverse ways of using language.

Standardized usage, on the other hand, tends to assume that there is only *one* correct form. These unitary views of language produce their own genres: handbooks of usage, for example ("Improve your English with this handy and authoritative reference text!"). We could also call the marker commentary on student essays a "genre," one traditionally supported by unitary views of language. Composition textbooks often provide their users (students and teachers alike) with marking symbol guides: *run-on*, *gr*, *awk*, *logic*, *vague*, *ww* (= "wrong word"), *org* (= organization), *evidence*. Designed to operate universally across genres, the symbols can suggest that "[lack of] logic" or "vagueness" is identifiable regardless of reader or situation. Traditional advice given to students on their essays often mentions "argument" (you need one) and "evidence" or "details" (you need these to support your argument). But these all-purpose terms can be misleading. In her study of writing in history, Sharon Stockton (1995) found that

> "[a]ll faculty agreed ... that *argument* is the key word for good writing and that the absence of argument constitutes the central problem in students' written work" (50), but that expectations differed depending on students' level, and "[i]n fact, faculty assignments, grades, and comments on student papers seem to imply that explicit argument as such was not the central issue of concern" (51). Despite professors' calls for *argument*, "[u]ltimately, assignments and evaluations show that written sophistication in student writing was in this department [History] a function of *narrative* complexity"—"a certain specialized form of narrative" (52). When professors said "argument," they had a variety of other things in mind.

> Janet Giltrow 2000 "'Argument' as a term in talk about student writing." In *Learning to Argue in Higher Education*, ed. S. Mitchell and R. Andrews. Portsmouth, NH: Boynton Cook/ Heinemann, 132–33.

In this case, unitary views of language led to traditional advice on student writing that was misleading. In other situations, traditional commentary can usefully represent a reader's uneasiness and yet fail to point to the particular conditions which would satisfy the reader's expectations. For example, a literature professor, reading a student's essay for a Shakespeare class, wrote "evidence?" in the margin next to the writer's claim: "In the absence of the romantic bond, Othello's life would lose much of its meaning, and he would revert to his role as a 'soldier for pay'." When asked to explain his comment, the professor elaborated:

There are a number of problems there; I asked for evidence. I am asking for evidence as to whether [Othello] was ever spoken of in those terms by anyone including himself as a "soldier for pay" because that has certain connotations to it and he is a general after all. Is "soldier for pay" a formulation which matches someone's view of Othello in the play? Is there any evidence that he loses the romantic bond? That this would happen? That he would go back to being a general?

Giltrow 2000: 134.

Here the traditional comment "evidence?" unfortunately obscures a particular marker's more complete and informative response: a reader of a literature essay needed to hear some voice from the play corroborating the student writer's prediction about Othello. Using general terms like "evidence," marginal commentary can fail to express the reader's **genre-specific expectations**—in this case, the literary-critical expectation that the student writer's statements will be woven with wordings from the original text. In a different research genre, "evidence" would mean something else.

Sometimes traditional notations can appear contradictory. For example, an academic reader sometimes asks for "specifics" in the presence of specifics: a student writes in a paper for a course in the sociology of the environment, "our water comes from a metal tap and flows down a metal drain ... we drive over concrete roads and highways"; and the professor responds, "This is the point at which I wonder when it's going to get more specific" (reported in Giltrow 2000: 136). In this case, the "specifics" the student has already offered fail to impress the reader of a sociology paper: the professor anticipates something more focused about the research that will be reported, not just any concrete references to everyday life. But if used in another genre—for example, in an essay question on a language-proficiency examination—these very specifics about taps and roads might have inspired a positive response. It may be true enough to say that an essay should have "specifics"—but that won't be much help to writers. Questions remain: *what kind of specifics? specifics of what? what do you mean, "specific"? what are the specifics for?*

It is therefore possible that traditional marking commentary can go on at *too high a level of **abstraction*** (see Chapter 3 for an introduction to abstraction) to be entirely informative to student writers; as the above examples show, traditional notations can transmit misleading, incomplete, or contradictory information. This high level of abstraction and generality no doubt has its own social function: it suggests unanimity, a consensus about what "good" writing is (it is "clear," "coherent," "logical"; it has an "argument"), a solidarity amongst authoritative readers. The idea that "good" writing can be identified and characterized in these ways is no doubt comforting to markers. Yet student writers often remain puzzled by these responses in the margins of their papers.

We can see, then, that traditional commentary has its shortcomings. Taking traditional commentary to heart, writers might come to think of writing mainly as a struggle to reach an inaccessible ideal: their sentences will never be good enough. But more important perhaps is the generality of commentary, suggesting a timeless and universal standard for expression, when, in fact, even in the research disciplines, diversity and change prevail.

Rather than give up on feedback altogether, we can work on developing techniques for giving and getting useful responses to writing. The techniques we concentrate on in the following sections focus on *the reader's experience of using the text*: how the reader understands, anticipates, and makes meaning. We find out about how readers behave when they meet words, sentences, paragraphs. From this information, we draw a portrait of the reader.

5C An Alternative to Traditional Commentary: The Think-Aloud Protocol

People studying readers' behaviour try to find out about reading comprehension: how do readers get messages from texts? What kind of writing makes the message obscure? What kind makes it clear? You can probably imagine that this kind of research is not easy. If we want to find out about how people obey traffic signals, we can put ourselves at an intersection and watch cars speeding up, slowing down, stopping, and then going again. But how can we watch people read?

To catch readers in the act, researchers have devised ways of measuring physical signs of reading, like eye movement. Other measures try to get at comprehension itself by asking readers questions about what they have read, or asking them to do other tasks connected with their reading.

Another technique for researching the reading process is the think-aloud protocol. The think-aloud method (Waern 1988) asks subjects to report the ideas that are going through their heads as they perform a task, like writing an essay or reading one. Think-aloud reports are like eyewitness testimony of events that researchers can't witness themselves. Rather than using typical marking expressions, such as "wrong word" or "faulty diction," readers simply report what is going through their heads as they come to an understanding of what they are reading. With this kind of report available, writers can decide what revisions might benefit readers.

The think-aloud protocol resembles forms of usability testing of documents. In the process of composing manuals, instructions, information bulletins, and other genres, technical writers sometimes test their documents' efficiency by having them read out loud—by people who might purchase software, for example, or citizens who might seek information about a government program, or car owners who might need to know about a vehicle recall. As they read aloud, the subjects report their understanding and their difficulties. In light of these reports, and informed about where other readers are likely to have trouble, writers then revise (or not). The think-aloud protocol is thus both an instrument of research and a tool for professional writers.

It can also contribute to students' conceptions of their readers, as research conducted by Karen Schriver (1994 [1992]) has shown. Gathering her subjects from senior writing classes and dividing them into experimental and control groups, Schriver provided the experimental group with ten transcripts, over a six-week period, of readers using written instructions for aspects of operating a computing system. In the meantime, the control group was taught audience analysis and text design by more traditional methods.

In the following excerpt from a transcript, a reader reports his thoughts (italics) while reading (bold type):

> *OK, now I'm going to try ...* **Commands for English Text. EMACS enables you to manipulate words, sentences, or paragraphs of text.** *These commands sound like the ones I'd use all the time—good.* **In addition, there are commands to fill text, and convert case.** *I don't know what it means to fill text. I guess it means putting data from one text into another ... that is, filling the text with what you want in it. Well, I guess I'll soon find out.*
>
> **Editing files of text in a human language** *human language? Boy that sounds strange, what could they be distinguishing here? Maybe computer language or machine language from human language?* **ought**

to be done using Text mode rather than Fundamental mode. *Well, I don't know what text mode or fundamental mode is, so how will I know which I'm in? Let's see* ... **Invoke M-X Text Mode to enter Text mode.** *I won't do that because I do not have time to see the other section. That's terrible to tell me to* ... **See section 20.1 [Major Modes], p. 85.**

Karen Schriver 1994 (1992) "What document designers can learn from usability testing." *Technostyle* 19 (3/4): 22 (emphasis added).

Testing at the beginning of the study showed that the two groups of students were equivalent in their ability to predict when readers would have trouble with what they were reading. Testing after six weeks of instruction found that, while the control group had not changed in their ability to predict readers' difficulties, the experimental group's ability to identify where actual readers had in fact had trouble understanding what they were reading improved by 62 per cent. Improving dramatically in the accuracy of their analyses, these students also changed in the way they talked about problems: their remarks became more reader-centred ("readers might not see the connection here," "I don't understand this word") and less text-centred ("this paragraph is too long"). The control group changed much less in this dimension of analysis.

5D Adapting the Think-Aloud Protocol in the Writing Classroom

Think-aloud can be practised on any piece of writing, for any piece of writing is a document to be used, in some way, and readers can report their experience of making use of it. This method can be adapted for use in the academic writing classroom.

Like technical writers observing a person working with a draft of a software manual, we observe a reader working with an instance of scholarly writing—a summary, a proposal, a research paper. From these observations, we learn where potential readers may have problems with a particular piece of writing. But we also learn about more than just particular sentences in particular writings. As Schriver's research shows, writers can also learn from think-aloud when the text being read is not their own: overhearing a reader working on someone else's writing, they gain experience which they can use to sketch their portrait of the reader. Schriver's research suggests that this kind of close-up experience of readers' behaviour can be generalized—to anticipate readers' responses to our own work-in-progress, to explain responses to previous work, to help us plan future work.

Thinking out loud while reading doesn't necessarily come naturally. For one thing, most thinkers-aloud have long experience of traditional marking commentary and, in their first attempts, are liable to reproduce its sounds ("this is well organized," "there should be a thesis statement," "this flows"). And, face-to-face with the writer, thinkers-aloud may be tempted to praise, contracting perhaps for praise in return. It's also tempting just to read, and not to comment.

Recognizing that readers may not be sure of how to respond to texts without trying to revise them, we have developed models and guidelines for thinking aloud. The model below has been used in research studies. Here an instructor is thinking aloud as she reads (original text in bold; reader thinking aloud in italics):

The purpose of this paper will be to show how the representation of Africans can be extended to the representation of women in *Heart of Darkness* written by Joseph Conrad. *This sounds like the essay question to me. That's not terrible, but I find I don't really pay attention when I hear the sound of an essay question. "The Heart of Darkness written by Joseph Conrad"—that sounds as if I don't know Conrad wrote* Heart of Darkness. *I'd prefer something like "Conrad's* Heart of Darkness." **This will be accomplished by the analysis of the inhuman role of women in the story,** *"the inhuman role of women"—I stop there—the women behave in a non-human way? that doesn't seem to be right—oh, maybe. I'm thinking of Kurtz's "Intended" ... "inhuman"? oh well* **... the supremacy imposed upon them, and their physical attributes which emit a darker figure of**

the human woman. *"Supremacy"? in what sense? I think I see what he's getting at, but it's hard work getting through this sentence: what does "supremacy" have to do with "inhuman" and then "darker figure"? "human woman"? Maybe the body ... there could be something here in the disparity between dark interpretations of the body and interpretations of woman as supreme ideal, but this whole first paragraph reminds me of the introduction to a five-paragraph essay: thesis statement, three points.*

Generalizing from observations and transcripts of successful think-aloud sessions, we can provide explicit guidelines for those who will be responding in instructional situations—students, teaching assistants, professors.

Guidelines for Readers

You are not a marker/evaluator; you are a person *using* a document. You make *no judgements*; you only report what's going on in your mind. As you read, report moments when you're working inefficiently—not understanding.

But rather than saying ...	*aim for ...*
this is ungrammatical	*I'm having trouble with this sentence. There's something about it that makes me stop. I've read this sentence twice. Now I'm going on but I'm still not sure....*
this is the wrong word	*This word makes me stop. Why do you say "social" agenda? That's a positive term to me, but you seem to be using it in a negative way. I don't really know what "peer review" means. I have no idea.*
there's no thesis statement	*OK, I'm through the first paragraph, but I can't really say what you're going to focus on. Is it the public perception, or the corporate model? I'm through the first paragraph, and I figure you see a connection between the "back-to-basics" idea and the "standardization" Zieber mentions. I think you're going to talk about that.*

repetition

I think you already said this—or did I get it wrong? Is there something different here and I missed it?

no transition

I'm having a hard time making a connection between this paragraph and this one—this is about the university's "service agenda" and this one is about "depersonalization." Is the connection that they're both individualistic? That's my guess but I don't know if that's what you intend. It's hard work here.

the main point should be at the start

Oh now I see what you're saying. I'm going to go back and re-read to see if I missed something.

As you read, also report moments when you're working efficiently—understanding, getting new ideas of your own:

who learns and why *yes I see that—the "who" is about access, and that's a question of social class and the distribution of wealth, and the "why" is about the role of knowledge in the society, or in the economy. I'm thinking it's also "what"—if you put the who and the why together you start to go towards the answer to the "what"—what should be taught?*

Offer frequent reports of the **gist** of what you're reading:

OK so far I have this main idea in mind: the Zieber article might seem more radical but it's actually more traditional. That's what I'm getting from this.

If you notice what appear to you to be errors in spelling or grammar, say so. It's part of your experience of using the piece of writing, and useful information for the writer. If spelling and grammar turn out to be tremendous obstacles to your appreciation of the writer's intentions, then you need to report this circumstance. But you might also try to report the degree to which missing apostrophes or odd spellings are confounding your efforts to find meaning:

I notice that "is" comes after "institution and government"—that should be "are," I think, but it's not stopping me ...

I've lost this sentence, I thought it was ending. Now I see a comma, so I'm going back to reread ...

By giving the writer the measure of difficulty—"it's minor, so fixing this isn't going to make much difference overall"; or "it's a big block, so it had better be attended to"—you make "grammar" a matter of the *reader's experience* of the text, rather than a matter of living up to the rules for correctness.

And to these suggestions for readers, we add guidelines for writers, encouraging them to take advantage of this opportunity to see what happens when their writing is out in the world, on its own, without their justifications or apologies.

Guidelines for Writers

You don't need to explain or justify what you've done. Instead, value the chance to watch someone making meaning from what you've written. Listen carefully to your reader's comments. Take notes, and feel free to ask the reader to repeat herself if you miss something or pause for a moment while you complete a note. Your reader's response will guide your revision strategies.

Earlier in this chapter, we said that think-aloud can be practised on any piece of writing. Here is an example of an experienced academic reader thinking aloud as she reads a passage from Ian Hunter's 1988 book, *Culture and Government*:

> **Unlike classical education** *I guess I have a general idea of what this is, although I'm not sure how he sees it in this context,* **Romantic aesthetic education** *I'm stopping here, "Romantic aesthetic education," does that mean that "Romantic education" was aesthetic? or that "aesthetics" was one branch of Romantic education? I think it's the latter* **was directed at the individual's aesthetico-ethical organisation** *"aesthetico-ethical," I don't like "o" suffixes, but lots of people use them; so this would be moral development going along with learning to appreciate beauty*—**at producing** *here is an explanation* **a synthesis out of the divided "ethical substance"** *I stop there, what is that? I'm just going back, maybe I missed something, no ... ;* **and this practice of ethical reconciliation has indeed passed into the modern teaching of English.** *I don't understand the "divided substance" but I have a hunch about*

reconciliation—not that I could explain this to anyone, so far. **Unlike the latter, however,** *OK the romantic idea is different from the modern one* **the Romantic aesthetics of self-cultivation was for most of the nineteenth century a more or less voluntary "practice of the self"** *"practice of the self," not sure what that is but I like the sound of it, I guess it's equivalent to "self-cultivation," improving yourself, something you do on your own initiative,* **confined to caste groupings at one remove from the emerging machinery of popular education** *it was something the elite did, I think that's it, although "one remove" sounds not very far away and the elite would be very far away from the classes served by "popular education," maybe I don't use "at one remove" the proper way. OK it was elite practice, I think that's it, but I wish there were a specific—what groups of people did this, what did they do? Maybe it doesn't matter that I don't know what "divided substance" is; I'm not sure what it has to do with the elite being separate from the masses. But I get the general idea that ...*

What should the writer do with the reader's commentary? Well, he doesn't have to do anything: his book is published, and he is well known. But when we overhear this commentary, we learn about the difficulties a reader can have when she encounters many complicated abstractions without examples or details.

Exercise 3

While the topic of the reality TV show *American Idol* may seem familiar, the way of discussing it in Passage 1 below is probably not. Guided by the suggestions and models above, practise think-aloud: read Katherine Meizel's text aloud, stopping and reporting those moments when you experience an unusual effort to understand (after a word, phrase, sentence, end of paragraph), including places where you need to reread, question and speculate, or want to offer ideas of your own. Do this exercise with a partner, who will record your observations; remember to read and report aloud.

PASSAGE 1

Though rooted in earlier American religious-political doctrines, the mores of Manifest Destiny and the "spirit of capitalism" (Weber 2), the phrase "American Dream" entered popular discourse from the "melting-pot" crucible of the Great Depression—as Sandage observes, the nation's archetypal expression of success, emerging from the tremendous national failure of the 1929 stock market crash. In his 1931 book *The Epic of America*, James Truslow Adams described an "American dream, that dream of a land in which life should be better and richer and fuller for every man, with opportunity for each according to his ability or achievement" (415). Ability or achievement. This subtle distinction has proven to be key, not only in *American Idol*, but over the long history of American music. It has been significant in the discursive genres of camp and of outsider music, in which artists who deviate severely from expected aesthetic and/or social parameters may nevertheless be received as embodiments of a certain kind of individualistic authenticity.

Katherine Meizel 2009 "Making the dream a reality (show): The celebration of failure in American Idol." *Popular Music and Society* 32 (4): 475.

Passage 2 below is the opening section of a literary narrative, written in a fairly traditional "realist" style. It provides a vivid contrast to the scholarly style of Meizel. As you did with passage one, work with a partner with one of you reading the passage aloud while stopping to think aloud to report gists and difficulties, especially where you need to reread.

PASSAGE 2

The morning express bloated with passengers slowed to a crawl, then lurched forward suddenly, as though to resume full speed. The train's brief deception jolted its riders. The bulge of humans hanging out of the doorway distended perilously, like a soap bubble at its limit.

Inside the compartment, Maneck Kohlah held on to the overhead railing, propped up securely within the crush. He felt someone's elbow knock his textbooks from his hand. In the seats nearby, a thin fellow was catapulted into the arms of the man opposite him. Maneck's textbooks fell upon them.

"Ow!" said the young fellow, as volume one slammed out of his lap and back onto the seat. "Everything all right, Om?"

"Apart from the dent in my back, everything is all right," said Omprakash Darji, picking up the two books covered in brown paper. He hefted them in his slender hands and looked around to find who had dropped them.

Maneck acknowledged ownership. The thought of his heavy textbooks thumping that frail spine made him shudder. He remembered the sparrow he had killed with a stone, years ago; afterwards, it had made him sick.

His apology was frantic. "Very sorry, the books slipped and —"

"Not to worry," said Ishvar. "Wasn't your fault." To his nephew he added, "Good thing it didn't happen in reverse, hahn? If I fell in your lap, my weight would crack your bones." They laughed again, Maneck too, to supplement his apology.

Ishvar Darji was not a stout man; it was the contrast with Omprakash's skinny limbs that gave rise to their little jokes about his size. The wisecracks originated sometimes with one and sometimes the other. When they had their evening meal, Ishvar would be sure to spoon out a larger portion onto his nephew's enamel plate; at a roadside dhaba, he would wait till Omprakash went for water, or to the latrine, then swiftly scoop some of his own food onto the other leaf.

If Omprakash protested, Ishvar would say, "What will they think in our village when we return? That I starved my nephew in the city and ate all the food myself? Eat, eat! Only way to save my honour is by fattening you!"

Rohinton Mistry 1995 "Prologue: 1975." *A Fine Balance*. Toronto: McClelland & Stewart, 3–4.

Exercise 4

After reading and thinking aloud about the passages in Exercise 3, answer the following questions:

- What have I learned about my own reading practices?
- What expectations do I have when reading literary narratives as opposed to reading scholarly work?
- What have I learned about the reading practices of others?

Exercise 5

Think-aloud protocol takes practice. Reading and thinking aloud demands highly active engagement. It may take courage to create gists out loud while someone listens. It takes even more courage to be candid about what you don't understand. And, until you get used to think-aloud, you may find it annoying to pause so often to talk out your experience.

The following passages provide opportunities to practise think-aloud with a partner. Take turns reading and thinking aloud.

Passage 3 below is the opening section of an article about Jamaican Creole, and attitudes toward that language.

PASSAGE 3

Recent discussion among both Jamaican scholars and laypeople suggests that Jamaicans' attitudes toward Jamaican Creole (hereafter JC) are changing.[1] This change, some suggest, has accompanied the increased popularity of Dancehall culture and nationalistic "consciousness raising" efforts (Christie 1995, Shields-Brodber 1997).[2] Concurrent with these revisionist efforts, there came a call in 1989 by the (Jamaican) National Association of Teachers of English (NATE) to validate JC in the schools. This event reflected movement at an institutional, policy-making level, while the rise of Dancehall operated at the level of popular culture. Such a shift in attitudes toward "things Jamaican" marks a significant conceptual reorientation, in light of the high esteem that historically has been given to British culture, and more recently to American culture.

A history of low prestige

It has been said that language is the theater for the enacting of the social, political, and cultural life of a people, as well as the embodiment of that drama (Alleyne 1993). After roughly 150 years of Spanish occupation, Jamaica came under British control in 1655. English became the language of prestige and power on the island, reflecting the social status of its users, while the emergent Creole was regarded as the fragmented language of a fragmented people.[3] One theory of creole genesis holds that, because slaves were transported to the West Indies from a number of different ethnic groups along the western coast of Africa, they shared no common language; thus, in the new colony, they acquired a simplified variety of English in order to communicate with their British rulers and one another, while retaining no West African forms (Turner 1949; Alleyne 1984, Chap 6; Holm 1989: 471–2). Historically, then, the speech of the slaves has been regarded as infantile by laypeople and linguists alike (Turner 1949)—as language that was not fully formed. It was not "proper" English; but then, because many of its lexical items resembled English ones, there was no reason to think it might be anything other than English.[4]

Language-internal clues also corroborate the low-prestige of JC. The language-internal phenomenon of pejoration, which has accompanied the emergence of many creole languages, has also figured into the history of Jamaican Creole "Patois." Lexical items from West African sources have taken on negative connotations, particularly in communities with large acrolect- or standard English-speaking populations. An example of one such pejoratized word is *nyam* "to eat," which has come to suggest an animal's way of eating rather than eating in a general sense. When used to describe human eating, *nyam* connotes sloppy or uncultivated devouring of food, as in "Don't *nyam* your dinner" (Alleyne 1976), or, "He had to *nyam* and scram!"

In a socio-linguistic investigation of attitudes toward a language variety that arose out of contact among groups of people coexisting under conditions of unequal power, it must be recognized that such social conditions affected the context of development of the new language. Research has shown that attitudes toward language can be markedly polarized and tightly held—both institutionally and personally, openly and internally.

Notes

1 Linguists tend to refer to this language as "Jamaican Creole," but it is widely referred to as "Patois" by native speakers. The two terms will be used interchangeably in this paper, particularly because the

term "Patois" was widely used by respondents in the interviews reported.

2 Briefly, "Dancehall" is a largely urban working-class phenomenon in vernacular Jamaican culture, associated with styles of dance, music, clothing—and (important in this context) lyrics that strongly favor Jamaican Creole (Cooper 1993).

3 Interested readers are directed to Lepage 1960 and Cassidy 1961 for introductions to the history of the island which discuss issues of linguistic development.

4 Taylor (1963: 804) gives an example of how lexical correspondence and similar phonological form have mistakenly been taken as adequate grounds for assuming that the grammatical categories of one language (French) operate in another (Martinican Creole).

Alicia Beckford Wassink 1999 "Historic low prestige and seeds of change: Attitudes toward Jamaican Creole." *Language in Society* 28: 57–92, 57–58.

Passage 4 is taken from the introduction to an article published in the journal _Social Work_.

PASSAGE 4

Autistic children never play normally with other children. They often do not respond normally to their mothers' affections or to any tenderness. (Freedman, Kaplan, & Sadock, 1976, p. 449)

The sociopath persistently violates the rights of others, shows indifference to commitments, and encounters conflict with the law. (Rathus, 1984, p. 451)

These quotes are two examples of how the use of diagnostic terms can sometimes worsen the stigma of mental illness. Stigma can significantly undermine the quality of life of people with mental illness. The social opprobrium that results from stigma can rob people labelled mentally ill of a variety of work, housing, and other life opportunities commonly enjoyed by adults in the United States. It can also prevent some people who might otherwise benefit from clinical services from pursuing treatment in an effort to avoid the label. One important part of the system of care—clinical diagnosis—may strengthen the stereotypes that lead to stigma. Diagnosis may intensify both the "groupness" and the "differentness," aspects governing public perceptions of people with mental illness.

Corrigan 2007: 31.

The passage above is taken from the introduction to Corrigan's article. The following passage is taken from the conclusion. Practise think-aloud on the passage. What stylistic features of the passage seem to belong to conclusions? Compare your reading experience of the introduction and the conclusion.

PASSAGE 5

Diagnostic classifications augment public perceptions of the groupness and differentness of people with mental illness. These classifications are perceived as homogeneous, and composite traits are seen as stable. As a result, individual members of a diagnostic class tend to be seen in terms of their diagnosis instead of the idiosyncratic nature of their problems. One way to change this kind of stigma is to challenge the very foundation on which it rests. Changing to a dimensional perspective of diagnosis undermines the sense of difference perpetuated by diagnosis and replaces psychiatric classification with a continuum that includes normal life. Stressing the evidence that supports recovery will diminish the stigma related to diagnosis. Facilitating interactions between professionals and people in recovery will also challenge the stigma.

Corrigan 2007: 37.

5E Reading on Behalf of Others

Classroom situations bring to light some special conditions of think-aloud response. Readers who are fellow students or the instructor share with the writer certain knowledge of the immediate scholarly situation: readings, assignments, circumstances exclusive to that course. Consider the following first sentence of an essay, and two possible comments on the part of the marker:

> The four articles have in common a focus on the experience of marginalized identities in times of social change.

TRADITIONAL COMMENTARY: *What articles?*

THINK-ALOUD COMMENTARY: *I know which articles you're referring to, but others wouldn't.*

For the student writer, the traditional remark "what articles?" can seem odd. After all, the marker *knows* about the articles. A reader who is trying to avoid traditional commentary may choose to keep quiet at points like those exemplified by the passage above. After all, she *does* know which articles the writer is referring to. But readers are also reading on behalf of other readers: people who have not been in this class and are unfamiliar with the reading list. So think-aloud includes one's own reactions and the reactions of readers whose difficulty in understanding is predictable. Similarly, in reading the following sentence, a marker encounters a specialist term which has been thoroughly discussed in class:

> Chavez's work (1994) on undocumented immigrants offers new perspectives on **transnational communities**.

The instructor marking the essay might respond with a traditional instruction: "Define." Since the marker was present during discussion, and has read the materials being discussed, this too can seem odd. By contrast, a thinker-aloud might stop and report at this point, not because they don't know the meaning of "transnational community" but because they anticipate the difficulty faced by another reader—another participant in scholarly discussion—coming across this specialist term. They want the meaning of the specialist term to be established to accommodate readers who were not privy to the classroom discussion.

What does this attention to other readers say specifically about student writing in the university? It suggests an awareness of the way in which academic writing does not just respond to the immediate concerns of a given course, but bridges the gap between the classroom and a broader research situation: the instructor-reader needs to see the writing relating to the larger conversation that the course intersects with—needs to see it anticipating a broader audience. The audience is still not "general," like the audience of, say, the print or digital news. But it extends beyond the classroom (and a particular context) and into a wider world.

Above, we saw how traditional commentary taking the form of a question—"what articles?"—might confuse a student writer. In fact, markers often respond with questions, a habit that appears prone to causing confusion. A study conducted with five writers responding online to one another's work showed the ambiguity of reader questions (Cowan et al. 1998). As the researchers worked on analyzing responses and measuring the revisions which resulted, they found that the meaning of the questions could be ambiguous.

> TEXT: According to Kabeer, following Giddens, community membership is made up of both rules *and* resources.

> MARKER: *What's the difference?*

In this example, does the question mean that the reader *doesn't know* what the difference is between "rules" and "resources"?

> *What's the difference?* meaning: I don't know what the difference is.

Or is the question really an instruction to do something?

> *What's the difference?* meaning: You should define these terms and explain the difference.

Or is the question a sign of the reader engaging with the point?

> *What's the difference?* meaning: I'm thinking that the *difference* is complicated. Maybe a "rule" can be a "resource" in some circumstances. I wonder if the "rule" about female seclusion could be a "resource" contributing to ethnic identity.

To minimize the possibility of such misunderstandings, when reporting a question in think-aloud protocols, try to specify your intentions:
* I don't know what this is.
* I can imagine readers appreciating seeing this briefly discussed.
* You've made me think about this, and now I wonder....

5F Reliability of Readers

How far can you count on your thinking-aloud reader? What if your reader is not particularly experienced in the genre in which you are writing? What if you are inexperienced and the reader is as inexperienced as you are? What if you are asked to think aloud on a paper for a social geography course, and you have never seen a paper or taken a course in social geography before?

If you are the reader, declare your position: *"I don't even know what social geography is.... I don't know anything about social geography, but still I'd say that it's hard to see how this paragraph relates to what you say in your introduction ... now this seems to repeat what you've said before ... OK what you're saying is...."*

If you are the writer, consider the source: this is a novice's effort to understand what you have written. The novice will have some experience of scholarly writing, and, assuming that they are engaged in the process, their responses will still be valuable.

All think-aloud responses to a piece of writing are inevitably formed by the reader's particular position in the world, a position that includes personal experiences, interests, degree of engagement, disciplinary affiliation, political leanings, and many other factors.

We might wonder, then, how idiosyncratic responses are, overall. In the study mentioned above (Cowan et al. 1998), the researchers were particularly interested in the degree to which readers' independent responses agree. They found that, during the four-month period of the study, agreement amongst readers increased. It seems that being in earshot of readers reading, thinkers-aloud developed a sense of a larger audience and became spokespersons for that audience, which included them but also went beyond them. Without explicit coaching to do so, readers began to read on behalf of others, or their ways of expressing their responses made them more representative of others' reactions. This is a limited finding, but enough to encourage the practice of listening in on other writers getting feedback.

Exercise 6
The excerpt below is from the beginning of a student paper. Working with a partner, who will record your observations, practise think-aloud protocol while reading the passage.

Dance, an expression of emotion the mind captures and then portrays through the body. North American "society has implemented a prejudgment on [male dancers] ... that participate in a form of expression that has been imbedded in our civilization," (Smih) resulting in a limited number of male dancers. Boys have shied away from dance because North American society has taught them it is not masculine enough. It is this assumption that has affected dance and the male dancers based on the prejudgment society has made through popular culture. A prejudgment that dance is considered to be a too feminine of an activity, and only homosexual men would be attracted to dance because it is 'girly,' and allows you to express emotion through various dance moves. Men who love dance often drop out of dance by the time they reach high school because of the teasing.

Here is the citation entry for Smih in the Works Cited of the paper:

Smih, Laura. "Gender Discrimination." What Can You Do for Dance? Blog. N.p. April 2011. Web. 14 August 2013.

Now, compare your think-aloud results with those of a professor doing think-aloud with the same passage.

Dance, an expression of emotion the mind captures and then portrays through the body. *I expected this sentence to continue, just a sec, I'll reread.* **Dance, an expression of emotion the mind captures and then portrays through the body.** *I thought everything after "Dance" was an aside, but I see it's the main point, so is it that "Dance is an expression of emotion that the mind captures and then portrays through the body."* **North American "society has implemented a prejudgment on [male dancers] ... that participate in a form of expression that has been imbedded in our civilization," (Smih) resulting in a limited number of male dancers.** *Okay, so society prejudges male dancers, and this discourages males from dancing. Is Smih a researcher? Is it Smith? I wonder if this is a study. Let me look at the Works Cited. Oh, it is Smih. I see this is a blog. Hmm. Not sure what to do with that. Smih is making a claim of fact, and the citation makes me think there's research informing this claim, but when I look at the blog I don't think so. Okay, so this is Smih's opinion. I'll carry on.* **Boys have shied away from dance because North American society has taught them it is not masculine enough. It is this assumption**

that has affected dance and the male dancers based on the prejudgment society has made through popular culture. A prejudgment that dance is considered to be a too feminine of an activity, and only homosexual men would be attracted to dance because it is 'girly,' and allows you to express emotion through various dance moves. *I understand what the basic claim is here. I wonder how popular culture has done this, but I assume this will be shown later. When I think of pop culture and male dancers, I think of many examples where dance is portrayed positively. So, I wonder what particular examples of pop culture have done this.* Men who love dance often drop out of dance by the time they reach high school because of the teasing. *If this is true, it is very unfortunate. This is a claim of fact, so I hope evidence (statistics?) will be provided later. I think even a testimonial or example would help me accept this.*

Exercise 7

The excerpt below is the beginning section of a student paper. Practise thinking aloud with a partner, using the suggestions and model above: read out loud, stop and report your thinking. When you experience difficulty in understanding, stop and report this difficulty; when you are reading efficiently, report this experience.

Everyone has their own definition of community. For some people it is the place they grew up. For others it is the place they live and work in. Anderson says community is "imagined" (quoted in Chavez 1994). But what is community? Webster's (1987) defines community as "a unified body of individuals; ... the people with common interests living in a particular area; ... an interacting population of various kinds of individuals ... in a common location." What happens to a community when its original basis, the idea people have of its founding and its reason for existing, is threatened? In this paper I will investigate one such case: coastal communities where fishing has been a way of life and now the salmon stocks are greatly reduced and, in some cases the fishery has been closed.

> ### Exercise 8
> Using a draft of a work in progress or an exercise that you have completed, exchange your writing with a partner and take turns reading aloud and practising think-aloud protocol. (We encourage you to use think-aloud on an ongoing basis with the essays you write in this and other classes.)

5G Presupposing vs. Asserting

One of the central goals of the think-aloud protocol is to help us become better at estimating the knowledge we share (or don't share) with our readers. Another way to approach this goal is to analyze the way that writers sometimes provide explanations and at other times seem to assume that their readers already understand apparently obscure matters. Consider, in the following example, how the writer makes several assumptions about readers' knowledge of the topic through **definite expressions**—*the* or *this* phrases that are long, including several nouns that modify each other:

> Recent research in **the history of nineteenth-century psychiatry** has explored **the expanding powers of the medical profession** and **the proliferation of the asylum**, that "magic machine" for curing insanity. **This medicalization of madness** has been portrayed as a "top-down" process....
>
> Patricia E. Prestwich 1994 "Family strategies and medical power: 'Voluntary' committal in a Parisian asylum, 1876–1914." *Journal of Social History* 27 (4): 799.

An alternative version of these sentences shows just how much the original takes for granted and assumes as already known by the reader.

> Psychiatry was practised in the nineteenth century. In the nineteenth century, the powers of the medical profession expanded, and asylums proliferated. Madness was medicalized.

Whereas the original version **presupposes** this knowledge, the alternative version **asserts** it. Perhaps you can hear how the first version constructs the reader as *knowing*, and the second constructs the reader as *unknowing*, and needing to be told. In the original passage, presupposing the reader's familiarity with research findings allows the writer to draw the reader's attention to the research processes that constructed that knowledge. One might say that it is here, in the attention to research processes, that the passage asserts.

In any social situation, the choice between presupposing and asserting can be tricky, for, as we see, it conveys messages about the speaker's ideas of mutual knowledge, what the reader knows. It can also convey messages about the speaker: by always asserting, the speaker can seem naïve or can appear to have just learned something that is in fact well known. And it seems that students can sometimes make the mistake of starting too far back, explaining too much, and thereby offending their expert readers. John Swales (1990) reports a case study of just this situation, where a PhD student's dissertation in the biological sciences explained too much, presupposed too little, and excited sarcastic and impatient comments from her readers. At the same time, however, readers can react negatively to a writer's offhand mention of a complicated concept and can appreciate an explanatory account of it. In the sample above, for example, what does it mean, exactly, for something to be "medicalized"? These days, lots of people are finding instances of "medicalization" here or there, but we may have been neglecting the concept itself, taking too much for granted.

Presupposing expressions can take many forms: proper nouns, for example. (To say simply "Chomsky" rather than "Noam Chomsky is a transformational linguist" presupposes that readers know who Chomsky is, and can identify him for themselves. And the second version, while asserting rather than presupposing, still assumes that we know what a transformational linguist is.) We will not go into all these forms here. Nor can we come to any conclusions about what kinds of knowledge students should presuppose and what kinds they should assert, for, at this point, we don't know a lot about this aspect of the style of the research genres—or any other genres. What we do know, however, is that readers are sensitive to patterns of **presupposition**.

Exercise 9

To develop your awareness of the effect of presupposition and assertion, rewrite each passage below, turning presupposing expressions, which are shown in bold-face type, into assertions. To do this, you may find yourself resorting to *there* expressions (e.g., "the three aspects of readability" becomes "*there are* three aspects of read-ability"), which seem specially designed in English to assert new information.

PASSAGE 6

Scholars have long noted, often with disapproval, **the tardiness of the introduction of printing to the Muslim world**, but **the consequences of that introduction on the production, repro-duction, and transmission of knowledge in Muslim societies** are now only beginning to be understood.

Adeeb Khalid 1994 "Printing, publishing, and reform in Tsarist Central Asia." *International Journal of Middle East Studies* 26: 187–200 (emphasis added).

PASSAGE 7

When Margaret Fuller's *Woman in the Nineteenth Century* first appeared in the winter of 1845, few readers were prepared to accept **her uncompromising proposition** that **"inward and outward freedom for woman as for man shall be as a right, not yielded as a concession."**

Annette Kolodny 1994 "Inventing a feminist discourse: Rhetoric and resistance in Margaret Fuller's *Woman in the Nineteenth Century.*" *New Literary History* 25 (2): 355–82 (emphasis added).

PASSAGE 8

During the 1980s and 1990s a number of factors emerged in various countries of western Europe to raise anew questions about **the meanings of national identity. The finally acknowledged presence of settled immigrant populations** (as opposed to transient-worker populations), **the arrival in western Europe of large numbers of asylum-seekers from southern and eastern Europe and from the Third World** and, most recently, debates in the countries of the European community about some of **the provisions of the Maastricht Treaty** have been among the most significant factors that have fuelled controversies about national identity.

Christopher T. Husbands 1994 "Crises of national identity as the 'new moral panics': Political agenda-setting about definitions of nationhood." *New Community* 20 (2): 191–206 (emphasis added).

6

Orchestrating Voices

In the last chapter, we examined some reading practices of scholars and explored the think-aloud protocol as a way to help writers anticipate their readers' responses. In this chapter we return to citation and summary to consider how scholars arrange multiple—sometimes numerous—summaries in ways their readers can understand. We will also look at a common genre of research writing, the **research proposal**, in which this practice is particularly prominent.

Up to this point, each of your summaries has brought one writer (or one partnership of writers, in the case of co-authored work) to the page. You have concentrated on making arrangements for this speaker, those arrangements also indicating the **position** you are taking. But it is unusual for scholarly writers to enter into dialogue with only one other writer. As a rule, they convene the scholarly conversation by bringing several or many other voices to the page, and arrange for these speakers to talk to one another. You may already be familiar with the activity of developing an essay by using two or more writers. You may have been asked to write comparison essays or you may have written research essays citing your sources. Or you may have been told to consult a certain number of sources—three, or five, say—in writing a research paper.

Here we see this gathering of voices as a conversation, and we use the term **orchestration** to emphasize that you as a summarizer are arranging this conversation.

6A Making Speakers Visible: Writing as Conversation

While in some disciplines (particularly the sciences), the speakers in a conversation may remain nearly invisible (appearing only as superscripted numbers until the reader turns to the reference list), in this chapter we will focus on more prominent appearances of speakers—on using the techniques of reporting and summarizing that we practised in Chapters 2 through 4. So, as we integrate our summaries of various writers, we will make these writers visible as speakers joining a developing conversation.

In Chapter 2C, we encountered examples of orchestration when we looked at why scholars use citation. Orchestration is a particularly striking feature in **introductions**, which give scholars an opportunity to construct a **state of knowledge** in which the key voices speak briefly, providing a snapshot of research on a given subject. But orchestration can also figure prominently as a way to develop entire articles or essays, to structure the larger practices of summary and reporting of research. Indeed, the **review article**, a high-prestige genre which surveys scholarship to find limitations and new directions for research, proceeds almost entirely through orchestration. And orchestration can be especially important when non-scholarly voices are introduced—when scholars construct examples or include the voices of research subjects.

Let's begin by listening to some of the ways that scholarly writers incorporate other researchers as they convene a scholarly conversation.

Sometimes the guest speakers are arranged into distinct groups, and the shared concerns of their writings are presented one after another. To emphasize this, in the following passage we've put the words that identify the research subjects in bold. Most of these precede large clusters of citations:

> Recognition of the benefits associated with music for human well-being has prompted recent research into the value of auditory stimulation as a means of enriching the environment of captive animals. The value of auditory enrichment has been studied in a variety of species, including **birds** (Gvaryahu et al., 1989; Ladd et al., 1992; Nicol, 1992; Reed et al., 1993), **cattle** (Evans, 1990; Uetake et al., 1997; Wisniewski, 1977), **horses** (Houpt et al., 2000) and **primates** (Brent and Weaver, 1996; Hanson et al., 1976; Markowitz and Line, 1989; Novak and Drewson, 1989; Ogden et al., 1994; O'Neill, 1989; Shepherdson et al., 1989). Many of these studies report changes

in the behaviour and/or physiology of animals exposed to music recordings, radio broadcasts or ecologically relevant sounds.

Very recently, it has been discovered that **kennelled dogs** also react to their auditory environment (Wells et al., 2002b). Specifically, dogs housed in a rescue shelter were found to spend more of their time showing behaviours suggestive of relaxation (i.e. decreased barking, increased resting) upon exposure to classical music and more of their time displaying behaviours suggestive of agitation (i.e. increased barking) upon exposure to heavy metal music.

Deborah Wells 2004 "A review of environmental enrichment for kennelled dogs, *Canis familiaris*." *Applied Animal Behaviour Science* 85: 307–17, 312.

Orchestration of this kind is relatively straightforward. Wells briefly surveys the research on the effect of music on various animal species before reporting at length findings from her own research on kennelled dogs, the subject of this article. Grouping similar studies together, treating most of them very briefly, proves an efficient way for Wells to survey the state of knowledge before she moves on to her particular research interest. You might notice that others' research is reported at a very general level: we don't really know what was found out, even broadly, about horses and "auditory stimulation," or cattle or birds.

Often, however, orchestration works in more complex ways, allowing the writer to engage much more directly with previous research and even to move beyond simply establishing a state of knowledge. Here is an example of orchestration taken from a study of parents' perceptions of the dangers posed to their children who use computers to go online. Valentine and Holloway speak directly about their position—"We argue that ..."—but then introduce a series of speakers who develop the argument for them. Note how they introduce a group of these speakers and then let one of them (Canon 1987) speak directly at length. Notice also how the last sentence of the passage is begun by one speaker (Wenger 1987) and completed by another group of speakers (Bingham, Holloway, and Valentine 1999b).

We argue that, counter to parents' anxieties, technology does not simply impinge on society from outside or follow a predetermined course. Rather, activities such as playing and learning are shaped by shifting associations (and disassociations) between humans and nonhuman entities in which the properties of technology are not inherent but emerge in practice (Law 1994). In doing so, we draw upon an approach—Actor Network Theory—that is well developed within the sociology of science and technology (Canon 1987; Latour 1993; Star 1995). Canon (1987, 93) explains that:

> The actor network can be distinguished from the traditional actors of sociology, a category generally excluding any non-human component and whose internal structure is rarely assimilated to that of a network. But the actor network should not, on the other hand, be confused with a network linking in some predictable fashion elements that are perfectly well defined and stable, for the entities it is composed of, whether natural or social, could at any moment redefine their identity and mutual relationships in some new way and bring new elements into the network.

Thus, computers cannot be viewed as invariant objects, nor as impacting on social relations in fixed ways producing a predictable set of effects. Rather, they must be seen as "things" that materialise for people as diverse social practices and that may vary as much as the contexts in which they are used (Law 1994; Bingham, Holloway and Valentine 1999b). Indeed, technology may play very different roles within different "communities of practice" (Wenger 1987) and so may emerge as a very different tool within them (Bingham, Holloway, and Valentine 1999b).

Gill Valentine and Sarah Holloway 2001 "On-line dangers?: Geographies of parents' fears for children's safety in cyberspace." *Professional Geographer* 53 (1): 71–83, 75.

Occurring well into the second section of this article, this passage shows Valentine and Holloway using orchestration to develop a particular way of seeing computers rather than to establish an initial state of knowledge. They introduce a specific sociological approach—Actor Network Theory—and the group of researchers who adopt this approach. In doing so, they align themselves with these researchers and speak as part of a group.

It takes some skill to make hospitable arrangements for speakers—to introduce strangers to one another, to renew acquaintances. The following sections offer you a chance to develop this know-how by focusing on different types of speakers.

Exercise 1

Passage 1 is taken from an article by Ronnie Hawkins that examines how our relatively recent self-identification as primates helps us understand and possibly modify our behaviour. In this excerpt, Hawkins surveys research looking at identification with groups and the implications of this identification.

Passage 2 is from a famous study on obedience conducted by Stanley Milgram in the early 1960s. In this experiment, subjects were told they were playing the role of a teacher in a learning study. The "teachers" asked "learners" questions and administered electric shocks when the learners answered incorrectly, increasing the shock for every wrong answer. The "learners" were actually actors who pretended to be shocked and complained as the experiment proceeded. The aim of the experiment was to see whether the "teachers" would obey orders from the researcher and continue to apply the electric shock, even when it was obviously unsafe. The passage is taken from the end of the article, where Milgram discusses the findings.

Write a summary of Hawkins that expands upon the mention of Milgram. Introduce and directly summarize Milgram. Conclude by explaining the implication of this emphasis on Milgram for Hawkins.

PASSAGE 1

While some researchers emphasize rational factors such as material rewards or maintaining self-esteem in identifying with and overvaluing one's own ingroup, others point out that the dynamic underlying our "groupness" is far less "rational" than emotional—a fact that is clearly borne out by the phenomena that emerge from crowds or mobs. [...] In reviewing different theories regarding group identification, Judith Harris recognizes "the immense power of group behavior" stemming from its place in our evolutionary history and points out the intense peer pressure that forces children to become part of a group and the severe penalties that are imposed for not "fitting in" (Harris 1998, 138–39, 168–71). A tendency for individuals to adopt the most common cultural beliefs and practices in a human population, termed "conformist transmission," has been found to be of adaptive value in computer simulation studies, and thus potentially to be a major factor in maintaining within-group similarities and between-group differences (Henrich and Boyd 1998). [...] Social pressure to conform within human groups, however, can cause individuals to doubt their own perceptual judgments (Asch [1952] 1987), to forego giving aid to others who seem to be in need (Latane and Darley 1970), and even to deliberately produce what is believed to be severe pain in others under instruction from an authority figure (Milgram 1963). Individuals immersed in an ingroup may lose the ability to assess situations realistically in their intense desire for group cohesion, a phenomenon noted to interfere with intelligent decision making in the international arena that has been termed "groupthink" (Janis 1972). Such "groupthink" may, in fact, figure large in our tendency to believe we are being "rational" by destroying the natural world to amass "capital" or by continuing to develop weapons for nuclear, chemical, and biological warfare.

Ronnie Zoe Hawkins 2002 "Seeing ourselves as primates." *Ethics & the Environment* 7 (2): 60–103, 88–89.

PASSAGE 2

Of the 40 subjects, 26 obeyed the orders of the experimenter to the end, proceeding to punish the victim until they reached the most potent shock available on the shock generator. At that point, the experimenter called a halt to the session. (The maximum shock is labeled 450 volts, and is two steps beyond the designation: Danger: Severe Shock.) Although obedient subjects continued to administer shocks, they often did so under extreme stress. Some expressed reluctance to administer shocks beyond the 300-volt level, and displayed fears similar to those who defied the experimenter; yet they obeyed.

The experiment yielded two findings that were surprising. The first finding concerns the sheer strength of obedient tendencies manifested in this situation. Subjects have learned from childhood that it is a fundamental breach of moral conduct to hurt another person against his will. Yet, 26 subjects abandon this tenet in following the instructions of an authority who has no special powers to enforce his commands. To disobey would bring no

> material loss to the subject; no punishment would ensue. It is
> clear from the remarks and outward behavior of many participants
> that in punishing the victim they are often acting against their
> own values.
>
> Stanley Milgram 1963 "Behavioral study of obedience." *Journal of Abnormal and Social Psychology* 67 (4): 371–78, 376.

6B Orchestrating Scholarly Voices

In this section, we will continue to focus on orchestration of scholarly voices. Orchestrating these voices is relatively straightforward because they have much in common: they come from researchers publishing their findings for other researchers. That said, there are different types of speakers that pose their own particular difficulties: speakers already in dialogue, speakers with similar research situations who have never referred to one another's work, and speakers with different research situations who use the same abstractions.

Summary of more than one speaker can sometimes reproduce a discussion that has taken place face-to-face—or "page-to-page": *A* wrote something, and *B* responded to what *A* wrote. *A* and *B* know each other—or, at least, *B* has read what *A* wrote—and the summarizer reproduces this part of the conversation. For example, in 1973 David Rosenhan published an article entitled "Being Sane in Insane Places" which reports on a study that involved sending pseudopatients—healthy people feigning certain symptoms—to a number of psychiatric hospitals in the United States. In 1994 Jim Schnabel published an article on scientific hoaxes in which he introduces Rosenhan's study and discusses it at length. Here is an excerpt from Schnabel's article in which the author summarizes Rosenhan's study:

> Rosenhan published a description of these experiments, and descriptions of the rather depressing environments within psychiatric hospitals, in *Science*, concluding: "It is clear that we cannot distinguish the sane from the insane in psychiatric hospitals. The hospital itself imposes a special environment in which the meaning of behavior can easily be misunderstood" (Rosenhan 1973, 257).
>
> Jim Schnabel 1994 "Puck in the laboratory: The construction and deconstruction of hoaxlike deception in science." *Science, Technology, & Human Values* 19 (4): 459–92, 466.

Schnabel considers Rosenhan's study a "hoax" because it involved active deception of the psychiatrists and staff in the target hospitals, but he argues that it was an ineffective hoax "because the hypotheses and institutions targeted still seem to be intact." Orchestrating Rosenhan and Schnabel is relatively easy to do because Schnabel has already established the conversation. If we are summarizing Schnabel, we can easily introduce Rosenhan as an example of an attempted (and unsuccessful) scientific hoax: e.g., "Schnabel (1994) argues that Rosenhan's pseudopatient study is an unsuccessful hoax because it didn't create much change in psychiatric practice." This activity involves the reporting reporting (or double reporting) activities we looked at in Chapter 3E.

But just as scholars rarely create a dialogue with just one speaker, they rarely orchestrate a discussion of writers they haven't read directly. The obvious limitation with recreating such "page-to-page" dialogue is that the orchestration of speakers is largely set by *B*: Schnabel allows Rosenhan to speak only in brief excerpts, and it is difficult to start a new conversation. So our summary will tend to agree with Schnabel's assessment of Rosenhan. One way around this limitation is to read Rosenhan for ourselves. This might provide an occasion to let Rosenhan speak directly, and to disagree with Schnabel's assessment:

> Rosenhan (1973) reports eight pseudopatients' experiences within twelve hospitals in order to emphasize the depersonalization that they experienced, which he attributes to the hierarchical organization of the hospital, attitudes toward mental illness, and a tendency to see patients in terms of their diagnosis (255–257). In this sense, the pseudopatients' sanity is less about deceptive access to the hospital—what Schnabel calls a "hoax"—than documenting their depersonalization. Rosenhan concludes, "The consequences to patients hospitalized in such an environment—the powerlessness, depersonalization, segregation, mortification, and self-labeling—seem undoubtedly counter-therapeutic" (257).

Here, the direct summary of Rosenhan clarifies that he does not see his study as a hoax; and it draws attention to what was left out of Schnabel's summary—namely extensive descriptions of the depersonalizing environment of the psychiatric hospitals. By summarizing Rosenhan directly, we could create controversy or debate. We could object to Schnabel labelling Rosenhan's "experiment" a "hoax" and then deeming it a failure because it did not produce sufficient change.

In other cases, the speakers' relationship is not so immediate. It's not so much that one wrote in reaction to another, but that they are in earshot of one another. They research similar objects, address similar questions. So here a researcher (Hyland 1999) who is investigating citation itself cites two writers (or a single and a pair) in the same paragraph, weaving their findings together, representing them in shared sentences (and also providing direct contact with each of the sources):

> Myers (1990) and Berkenkotter and Huckin (1995) have traced the passage of research articles through the review procedure and see the process as one of essentially locating the writer's claims within a wider disciplinary framework. This is achieved partly by modifying claims and providing propositional warrants, but mainly by establishing a narrative context for the work through citation. One of Myers's case study subjects, for example, increased the number of references from 57 to 195 in a resubmission to *Science* (Myers 1990: 91). Both Myers and Berkenkotter and Huckin see academic writing as a tension between originality and humility in the community, rhetorically accommodating laboratory activity to the discipline. So while Berkenkotter and Huckin's scientist subject sought to gain acceptance for original, and therefore significant, work, the reviewers insisted "that to be science her report had to include an intertextual framework for her local knowledge" (Berkenkotter and Huckin 1995: 59).
>
> Ken Hyland 1999 "Academic attribution: Citation and the construction of disciplinary knowledge." *Applied Linguistics* 20 (3): 341–67, 342–43.

While Berkenkotter and Huckin do not mention Myers—and so, the relationship is not exactly "face-to-face"—the similarity of their studies (how researchers revise their work to get it published) is similar enough for Hyland to let them speak one after the other on the same topic. Differences between the cited writers are set aside, in the interests of establishing common ground: a finding confirmed by at least two studies. This common ground is mapped by the summarizer. (For another occasion, though, the *differences* might be the theme of the summary.)

The examples above involve writers who directly summarize other writers or who share a common research situation with them. The similarity of the research situation, or of the fact that their publications directly responded to one another, makes orchestrating the different writers relatively straightforward. Sometimes, however, writers seem to have something in common because they use the same terms or abstractions;

but because they research different things, orchestrating them is more difficult. The two passages below both involve a technical term and its acronym—"traditional ecological knowledge" (TEK)—but the use of the term issues from different research situations. In the first passage, Henry Huntington and his co-authors briefly define TEK in the context of their study of beluga whales.

> Beluga whales (*Delphinapterus leucas*) are circumpolar in distribution and are hunted by indigenous peoples throughout the Arctic (Kleinberg et al., 1964). While some previous biological research on belugas has used the expertise of local hunters to plan the research and to add to data gathered from scientific observations (e.g., Frost and Lowry, 1990), a practice which continues through the work of the Alaska Beluga Whale Committee (Adams et al., 1993), little has been done to document systematically such local expertise, also known as traditional ecological knowledge (TEK). The primary purpose of this research was to capture TEK data in order to (1) describe beluga ecology as seen by indigenous hunters and elders and (2) identify specific contributions such data can make to scientific understanding of beluga ecology.
>
> Henry Huntington and the Communities of Buckland, Elim, Koyuk, Point Lay, and Shaktoolik 1999 "Traditional knowledge of the ecology of beluga whales (*Delphinapterus leucas*) in the Eastern Chukchi and Northern Bering Seas, Alaska." *Arctic* 52 (1): 49–61, 69.

In the next passage, which is taken from the beginning of another article, George W. Wenzel focuses on different **definitions** of TEK.

> [TEK is] knowledge and values which have been acquired through experience, observation, from the land or from spiritual teachings, and handed down from one generation to another. (Definition of TEK in GNWT policy statement, as quoted in Abele, 1997: iii)
>
> TEK is *knowledge*. (Hunn, 1988: 14, italics in original)
>
> In recent years, scientists have come to Nunavut in search of Inuit traditional ecological knowledge.... [W]hen Inuit knowledge is collected ... it is almost always taken out of context, misinterpreted or given meaning different than it had in the first place. (Stevenson, 1996a: 3)
>
> The first of the above statements constitutes the formal definitions of traditional knowledge as defined by the Government of the Northwest Territories. The second and third, both by anthropologists,

encapsulated two important contemporary, if not necessarily harmonious, views of traditional ecological knowledge that together intimate not only why TEK has become an important intellectual issue, but also an increasingly political topic in the contemporary North.

George W. Wenzel 1999 "Traditional ecological knowledge and Inuit: Reflections on TEK research and ethics." *Arctic* 52 (2): 113–24, 113.

These writers obviously have something in common: TEK. They work in the same scholarly area, and there is good reason for them to get to know one another. An online search of databases would find them both, maybe side by side. But their claims about TEK issue from different kinds of research situations—differences the search results would not display conspicuously. Whereas Huntington et al. *use* TEK in their research on the migrations and movements and other behaviours of beluga whales in Alaska, Wenzel *reflects on* TEK itself. Arranging for these two researchers to speak to each other, we would need to explain the different circumstances from which their statements issue—an important occasion for putting to use your practice in characterizing the discussion you are citing. Huntington et al. (1999) is an instance of research in marine biology; Wenzel (1999) is an instance of review of and reflection on research methodology.

Exercise 2

Write a summary of the passage from Huntington et al. (above, p. 118) that focuses on the term "traditional ecological knowledge" (TEK). Then develop it by bringing Huntington et al. into conversation with Wenzel (above). In doing so, you might consider Huntington et al. as an example of how TEK is used, rather than putting Huntington et al. up against Wenzel all by themselves (for this could somewhat misrepresent the case: Huntington et al. and Wenzel are not in direct dialogue with one another).

Exercise 3

Choose two related scholarly sources from your course readings. Preferably, these authors will research similar objects or address similar questions. Paying careful attention to their research context, orchestrate a discussion of about 200 words using the techniques introduced above.

6C The Challenges of Non-Scholarly Voices

The previous section involves writers who have things in common: they are relatively contemporaneous and they are scholars. However, there are occasions when older scholarship or non-scholarly writings need to be introduced. These writers may hold different, problematic views on certain subjects, or they may not be researchers at all—they may represent genres or situations not primarily focused on research.

The next passage appears in an archaeologist's study of the role of alcohol in legitimating authority in Celtic societies: chief-sponsored drinking and feasting in the Iron Age. Some of her data are archaeological: material artefacts recovered in physical investigation. Some of her evidence, however, is documentary: contemporary written accounts of feasting in Iron Age societies. So you will see her bringing together speakers whose statements issue from radically different contexts: she cites "Classical authors" on Celtic societies and a modern author describing Tlingit (North American West Coast) society.

You will notice that to bring these two types of speakers together she makes special arrangements: research in *"many ethnographic contexts ... [provides] additional* information" (emphasis added) on preindustrial societies. You will also notice that the Classical authors are introduced with great care, and with attention to their peculiarities. It's almost as if difficult writers wait in an anteroom while the summarizer explains and anticipates their odd behaviour: in this case, they fail to take account of what modern scholars would be interested in, and have a tendency to obsess over the "bizarre" and to "romanticize or demonize 'exotic' peoples" (which the Celts would have been to these Classical authors). Moreover, they can be unreliable reporters, from a modern point of view: when they lack data on one group of exotic people, they just repeat what has been said about some other group. In effect, the summarizer says, "Now, I've got some people I want you to meet. You can't believe everything they say, and I've heard them dwell on some things that might not interest you. But, even though they're kind of strange, I think they've got some valuable information. Here they are. Let's all be polite."

> The general formula followed by most Classical authors describing the alien cultures on their peripheries was modelled on Herodotus and consisted of several categories of information: 1) population; 2) antiquity and ancient history; 3) way of life; 4) customs (Tierney

1960, 190). Unfortunately for modern scholars the unusual and bizarre aspects of the last two categories were generally recounted in some detail, while information considered mundane, common knowledge or uninteresting was less frequently recorded. Two pitfalls facing the modern scholar attempting to derive "facts" from these accounts are "Randvölkeridealisierung" (Tierney 1960, 214) and "ethnographische Wandermotive" (Tierney 1960, 201). The first is the tendency of Classical ethnographers to romanticize or demonize "exotic" peoples. The second refers to the borrowing of descriptions of customs from accounts of one culture and transposing them wholesale or only slightly modified to a completely different group of people, whenever hard facts were lacking or could benefit from being fleshed out in a more dramatic way [....]

Despite these potential difficulties, several significant themes related to Celtic drinking and feasting behaviour (both insular and continental) recur in Classical sources. Some of these themes, particularly those also found in the later insular Celtic texts, may result from similarities between geographically and temporally different groups of the Celts (Nash 1976, 116). One such theme is that of the king's or hero's portion at a banquet, described as early as Phylarchus (Tierney 1960, 197). Another is the concept of guest-friendship, mentioned by Diodorus Siculus (Tierney 1960, 250) and again by Caesar (Tierney 1960, 274); both accounts stress the Celtic emphasis on open-handedness and generosity as important virtues.

Generosity as the defining characteristic of a good chieftain or king is a common theme in both Classical and insular texts, but also in many ethnographically recorded societies at a chiefdom level of organization. Athenaeus' account of Lavernius' banquet is a good example (Tierney, 1960, 248). The Celtic chieftain Lavernius, pleased by the praise of a poet at his feast, scatters gold along the plain behind his chariot, and "the poet picked it up and sang another song saying that the very tracks made by his chariot on the earth gave gold and largesse to mankind" (Tierney 1960, 248).

Athenaeus' verbatim transcription of four of the nine surviving extracts of Book 23 of Poseidonius' *History*, the recognized "Bible" on the Celts, describes food, drink, and heroic feasting and combat, and bardic display at great length. In fact, the passage on food and drink is the longest surviving portion of Poseidonius' Celtic ethnography. This may reflect the special emphasis on food and drink in the Celtic world observed by Poseidonius.

The symbolic as well as functional significance of feasting is documented in many ethnographic contexts (Chapman 1980, 66); such sources provide additional preindustrial configurations for modelling prehistoric social organization. The Tlingit potlatch is a good example of a society in which feasting acts as an institutionalized form of social regulation. As described by Kan, "the unity and solidarity of clan relatives were emphasized by the obligatory sharing of property and food that characterized their relationships" (1989, 65–66). The status of a Tlingit aristocrat depended on the rank and wealth of his parents (especially his mother), marriage to a person of equal or greater rank, the number and scale of potlatches sponsored by his parents in his honour, and accomplishments in activities which generated wealth and enabled him to give his own potlatch(es) or actively participate in those given by his matrikin (Kan 1989, 82).[1]

Note

1 Note the key role played by feasting in establishing and maintaining status in this society.

Bettina Arnold 1999 "'Drinking the feast': Alcohol and the legitimation of power in Celtic Europe." *Cambridge Archaeological Review* 9 (1): 71–93, 72–73.

Exercise 4

In the exercises at the end of Chapter 4, you summarized passages from Mary Englund's "An Indian Remembers" and Dara Culhane Speck on Alert Bay. Using the techniques in Chapter 5 for generating high-level names or abstractions, orchestrate the passages from Englund and Speck (pp. 78–80). In doing so, keep in mind that the passage from Englund is a transcript of a recorded interview with Mary Englund in which she recalls aspects of her life at a residential school in Mission, BC, in the early twentieth century.

6D Orchestrating Academic Textbooks and Popular Writing

We don't have to go as far afield as the archaeologist we just read to find difficult speakers. In many undergraduate courses, reading assignments include (or sometimes focus exclusively on) textbooks: academic genres composed by specialists for non-specialists. Rather than make new knowledge, or take another step along a line of inquiry, or interrogate the accumulation of knowledge in a field, textbooks synthesize and report what is known so far.

Of course, many textbooks provide an historical view of knowledge in a discipline, or subfield of a discipline, and bring to light the social dimension of knowledge as a product of interaction amongst researchers. In this respect, they resemble the research genres. And many textbooks offer a critical overview of knowledge in a field, implying directions for further inquiry. In this respect too they resemble the research genres.

But their position vis-à-vis their readers differs from that of the research genres. First, they construct readers as "not knowing": if anyone has a question, it's the student/reader; if anyone has the answer, it's the textbook. (In the research genres, as we have seen, writers represent themselves as sharing questions with their readers.) Second, they construct readers as listeners rather than co-conversationalists (although many textbooks will provide exercises and assignments which direct their readers to a limited role as participants in scholarly discussion).

The academic textbook genres and the research genres each have their place, and many scholars end up writing textbooks. Writers in the research genres can hear the difference between research article and textbook. When reading the following passage from a textbook, try to identify what features of the research genres are missing.

> One of the direct benefits of the end of the 45-year cold war between the United States and the Soviet Union has been a substantial decline in foreign military and political presence in the Third World. An indirect cost of this withdrawal, however, has been the acceleration of ethnic, tribal, and religious conflict. Although ethnic and religious tensions and occasional violence have always existed in LDCs [Less Developed Countries], the waning of superpower influence triggered a revival of these internal conflicts and may even have accelerated the incidence of political and economic discrimination. Ethnicity and

> religion often play a major role in the success or failure of develop-
> ment efforts. Clearly, the greater the ethnic and religious diversity
> in a country, the more likely it is that there will be internal strife
> and political instability. It is not surprising, therefore, that some of
> the most successful recent development experiences—South Korea,
> Taiwan, Singapore, and Hong Kong—have occurred in culturally
> homogeneous societies.
>
> Michael P. Todaro 1997 *Economic Development.* New York: Longman, 34.

Students may learn to recognize the different styles that indicate the
circumstances under which statements are produced in textbooks and
research articles: the first acting to inform, the second acting to inquire.
However, the differing purposes of the textbook and research genres can
put students in a difficult position when gathering materials for a paper
in an undergraduate course: they consult research articles, chapters, and
books—but they also still hear the informative voice of the textbook
on similar topics. If they repeat the statements of the textbook without
attributing them, taking them as common knowledge and public truth,
they fail to observe the scholarly requirement of providing the traces of
statements, the footprints that statements leave in their history of use.
Yet even if they do attribute the statements to their authors, they can
still interrupt a scholarly conversation by bringing in a speaker who had
prepared for a different kind of discussion. How can this speaker be
accommodated?

Just as Bettina Arnold made special arrangements for "Classical
authors" (pp. 120–22), you can introduce the textbook speakers with an
ac-count of their origins and intentions. For example, consider this passage:

> *Prejudice* is defined as a positive or negative attitude based on infor-
> mation or knowledge which is either illogical, unrelated to reality,
> or is a distortion of fact, and which is unjustifiably generalized to all
> members of a group. Although prejudice can be either favourable
> or unfavourable, psychologists use the term most frequently in the
> negative sense.
>
> J.E. Alcock, D.W. Carment, and S.W. Sadava 1994 *A textbook of social psychology*, 3rd ed.
> Scarborough, ON: Prentice Hall, 222.

Alcock et al. might be introduced to a research conversation by contextualizing their discussion:

> In their introductory book on social psychology, Alcock et al. (1994) offer a general definition of *prejudice*: [...] This definition suggests that prejudice could be corrected by referring to external reality or logic.

In this case, the special arrangement identifies the writing situation: an introductory course in social psychology. A reader might expect that researchers in the field of social psychology would test this definition. As the passages on TEK and the civilizing process in Section 6B indicate, different researchers often develop specific definitions that are applicable to what they are studying (e.g., Huntington et al. use the term TEK with specific reference to beluga whales) or they may even make the term itself part of what they are studying (e.g., Wenzel reflects directly on how TEK has been defined). Each of these definitions has its own context, one the summarizer must represent. So too the summarizer here represents the context for the definition of prejudice: a context addressing undergraduates rather than researchers.

Another case, popular writing, may initially seem to present an obvious non-research situation. Consider consumer publications like newspapers or magazines that are funded by advertisement or subscription through mass distribution to a general audience or specific non-research interests (e.g., hobbies, sports, fashion). Some of these special interests may be extremely useful to researchers. Similarly, research in education might benefit from professional publications read by teachers: such publications could be studied for current themes in the profession's self-image, for example, or could provide evidence for changes in professional practices—ways of doing things in the classroom. Or a study of political rhetoric might take recourse to opinion-editorials published in newspapers or political magazines. In all of these cases, the writing situation will be relatively easy to identify, and the speaker can be introduced accordingly, not as a voice that brings a scholarly perspective, but as one that reflects the subject matter under investigation.

However, there are situations that are more difficult to identify. The writers of books written for a popular audience may be researchers, but they are not addressing other scholars or even students. Whereas the situation of an article can be identified by looking at the publication (e.g., is it a consumer magazine or an academic journal?), a book can be harder to place, because books are published by all sorts of publishers.

Here is a passage from a book on demographic trends, written by experts but addressed to a broad audience distributed beyond the scholarly community.

> A country filled with young people is one whose retailers compete predominantly on price. In such a country, anything that can lower the average cost of production and reduce the price to the consumer is important. A young Canada during the 1960s and 1970s enabled the big retail mall to be born and thrive, making it possible for stores to lower costs and pass the savings on to customers. The malls won't disappear but their glory days are over. In the 20 years to come, the demographic shift will favour a revival of neighbourhood specialty stores supported by local customers for whom price is no longer the most important factor in a purchase decision.
>
> David K. Foot and Daniel Stoffman 1996 *Boom, bust & echo: How to profit from the coming demographic shift.* Toronto: Macfarlane Walter & Ross, 82–83.

And here is a linguist well known in scholarly circles but on this occasion writing for an audience as broad as that addressed by Foot and Stoffman above.

> Many women feel it is natural to consult with their partners at every turn, while many men automatically make more decisions without consulting their partners. This may reflect a broad difference in conceptions of decision making. Women expect decisions to be discussed first and made by consensus. They appreciate the discussion itself as evidence of involvement and communication. But many men feel oppressed by lengthy discussions about what they see as minor decisions, and they feel hemmed in if they can't just act without talking first. When women try to initiate a free-wheeling discussion by asking, "What do you think?" men often think they are being asked to decide.
>
> Communication is a continual balancing act, juggling the conflicting needs for intimacy and independence. To survive in the world, we have to act in concert with others, but to survive as ourselves, rather than simply as cogs in a wheel, we have to act alone.
>
> Deborah Tannen 1990 *You just don't understand: Women and men in conversation.* New York: Ballantine Books, 27–28.

What features of scholarly style are missing from these two passages? If these were research publications, what would be different about them? By analyzing the style of the writing, you can make guesses at the situation. Foot and Stoffman, for example, make bold assertions and prognostications: e.g., "In the 20 years to come, the demographic shift *will* favour a revival of neighbourhood specialty stores ..." (emphasis added). Tannen expresses similar certainty and makes unqualified generalizations: e.g., "*Women expect* decisions to be discussed first and made by consensus" (emphasis added). Neither writer seems concerned with what others have to say or with research on their topics. At least they don't summon other voices: there is no citation and little in the way of reporting expressions in these passages. Both writers are experts, but here they do not seem to be speaking to other experts. Will these outgoing, friendly speakers fit into the scholarly conversation you have arranged? Will they pay attention to the qualifications, abstractions, and uncertainties of the other guests? Or will they try to dominate? Chances are, these popular speakers won't fit in. Their statements will not interact with others'—and the conversation will be difficult to continue.

If you feel committed to including the popular speaker, you can take some measures to introduce the new arrival to the other guests: "Writing for a general audience and addressing such-and-such, x simplifies ..."; "While x's claims overlook the uncertainty of evidence in this area, they do represent/speak to widely held interest in/concerns about...."

Watch out for books whose covers list "PhD" after the author's name. This doesn't mean that the PhD is a hoax or not a good one, but that the authority of the book is being recommended to a non-scholarly audience. In the scholarly community, advertising that one has a PhD is not likely to impress, since most writers participating in scholarly discussions have one. One notable exception pertains to medicine, a discipline in which most of the research appears in scholarly journals rather than books: research articles in medicine tend to include the credentials of the researchers, possibly research teams may draw on a range of expertise that is both professional (researchers with an MD or an MHSA—a Master's in Health Science Administration) and academic (those with a PhD or a ScD—a Doctor of Sciences).

Exercise 5
The following passage comes from an undergraduate textbook. What features of style distinguish it from a research publication? If you wanted to use this information in an inquiry into Western conceptions of health, how would you represent your source?

Smith correctly concluded that the lack of dental decay and tooth loss observed in the tribal peoples was due to increased tooth wear, which kept the teeth clean and polished. He attributed the increased wear to the consumption of less cooked and less refined food and the absence of knives and forks, which meant that more chewing was required, as well as the presence of grit or "dirt" in the food. It was later learned that the absence of refined carbohydrates also contributed to healthy tribal teeth. The reduced tooth wear of contemporary peoples who eat industrially processed foods is likely related to the common problem of impacted molars, as Grover Krantz (1978) has observed. People eating coarse foods wear down the grinding surfaces of their teeth, which creates enough jaw space to accommodate the third molars when they erupt. When there is no significant wear, these "wisdom teeth" often must be extracted.

The association between traditional dietary patterns and healthy teeth was documented more systematically in a series of field studies conducted by American dentist Weston Price (1945), between 1931 and 1936. Price visited some of the most traditional peoples in Amazonia, East Africa, Australia, and throughout the Pacific and found that tooth decay and periodontal disease were virtually absent among self-sufficient peoples but steadily increased as they adopted the food patterns of industrial societies.

In 1956, shortly after Price's dental research, T.L. Cleave, a doctor in the British Royal Navy, used medical data on tribal peoples to isolate a single feature in the diets of industrialized people that caused what he called the "saccharine disease," a wide-ranging complex of conditions including tooth decay, ulcers, appendicitis, obesity, diabetes, constipation, and varicose veins. Like both Smith and Price before him, Cleave (1974) was impressed by the fact that tribal peoples did not suffer from many of the common ailments of civilization, and he attempted to find the special conditions that made the tribal peoples healthier. His primary finding was that the traditional foods of tribal groups were consistently much higher in dietary fiber than the highly refined complex carbohydrates consumed by industrialized peoples. Higher-fiber diets speed the transit time of food through the digestive system, thereby reducing many common diseases of civilization. It took many years for his findings to be incorporated into popular nutritional wisdom in the industrialized world, but now high fiber, along with low fat and low salt, is widely accepted as an important component of a healthy diet.

John H. Bodley 1997 *Cultural anthropology: Tribes, states, and the global system,* 2nd ed. Mountain View, CA: Mayfield, 147–48.

6E The Internet

Finally, let's consider the internet, a special case that can make it difficult to identify the writing situation. The internet is a benefit to researchers. At the very least, it offers efficient access to library catalogues and easy access to indexes that allow discipline-specific searches for publications on a topic. Increasingly, articles and whole scholarly journals and books are available in electronic form, either directly through index searches or on their own servers. In these cases, you should be especially careful to note the address or Uniform Resource Locator (URL) of the index or article (most indexes offer permanent URLs for articles, while some generate temporary URLs). Because libraries subscribe to index licences, a research librarian can help you understand the appropriate citation protocol for your library.

There are some complications, though, mainly arising from the operation of browsers and search engines. These technologies can lead you to domains where research publications mingle with popular publications, and both of these find themselves in the company of organizations sponsoring more or less viable points of view (e.g. anti-vaccine or anti-evolution websites masquerading as the publications of scientific organizations), and individuals promoting their own interests or ambitions for publicity. Recent amalgamations of online periodical indexes have, as well, tended to blur the distinction between peer-reviewed research publications and general-audience journalism. And even when you do find yourself on firm scholarly ground, in a peer-reviewed journal, searches can lead you first and predominantly to reviews of newly published scholarly books, rather than to the original publications themselves. Often, these book reviews can usefully introduce you to a new contribution to research. But, if you decide to bring a book-reviewer into the conversation, you will need to notify your reader that the voice they are about to hear is from the review genre.

How can you tell if you are finding speakers suitable for introduction into scholarly conversation? Online research journals will include the circumstances of publication: names and affiliations of members of the editorial board; procedures for submission and review of articles. Look for these indications. Stand-alone publications may be harder to evaluate. But your experience in identifying the characteristic sounds of scholarly voices should be a reliable guide for you by now.

Making arrangements for scholarly conversation is a challenge for undergraduates: as newcomers to research communities, they can find it hard to prepare an appropriate list of guest speakers. But it's also a challenge for graduate students, and sometimes for professional scholars, too.

Exercise 6

Sometimes course books are not textbooks designed to introduce newcomers to a discipline but comprehensive and informative representations of a point of view. The next passage comes from such a book. What features distinguish it from a research publication? How might you introduce this writer to a scholarly conversation?

> It may seem incredible that anyone in the Americas should perceive the continents' impoverished, largely marginalized indigenous peoples as a threat, but individuals and states are products of their history, even if they deny it. In countries where indigenous people form the majority or a substantial minority, the white, Western elite and the governments they dominate show the classic psychology of rich exploiters who have grown paranoid through fear or greed. "They know only too well what they have done to the Indian, and are paranoid that the Indian might one day do the same to them," says one Bolivian aid worker.

A complex racism was part of the institutionalization of the conquest, providing the historic rationale for human rights abuse. Medieval Hispanic concepts of "purity of blood" (*limpieza de sangre*) were transferred to the Indies, and American Spaniards became obsessed with classifying the various permutations of race. Racism, including cultural discrimination, became the ideological framework that justified the domination of the invaders and the subordination of the conquered.

Phillip Wearne 1996 *Return of the Indian: Conquest and revival in the Americas.* London: Cassell, 64.

Exercise 7

You now have means of inviting different speakers—both scholarly and non-scholarly—into the conversation you are arranging. All of the sources we have discussed have appeared in print media, and most have been transferred to digital media. Online, you will find scholarly voices and popular ones, but you will also find brand-new categories: new ways of speaking, new contexts, new genres. Currently, one of the most conspicuous of these is Wikipedia. Knowing about the conditions for successfully orchestrating a scholarly conversation, how would you estimate the possibilities for bringing a Wikipedia entry into the conversation? Devise guidelines for scholarly use of Wikipedia. In doing so, consult Wikipedia's own description of its editorial processes. How do these resemble or differ from those of scholarly publication?

6F Research Proposals

We have already noted that orchestration takes place in a variety of contexts, including introductions and review articles. Let's briefly consider another place where orchestration plays a crucial role—the research proposal.

Research proposals are a widely used genre in academic communities, but because proposals are rarely published, students—and most established scholars for that matter—write more of them than they encounter in the course of their reading. Undergraduate students are routinely asked to write brief proposals (often just a paragraph or two) as they prepare to undertake term papers and honours theses. Students applying to graduate school may be asked to submit proposals as part of their application or in order to be considered for scholarships, and graduate programs demand extensive proposals (which may be as long as articles or book chapters) from students preparing to write a thesis or dissertation.

For scholars, proposals are a routine fact of professional life. Seeking a place in a conference program or a spot in a collection of essays that will be published on a particular topic, they answer "Calls for Papers" with a proposal or (if the research has already been completed), an **abstract**. Conference organizers and the editors of collections evaluate the submissions they receive on bases we have become familiar with. They look for topics that excite interest in the research community. They look for evidence that the author of a proposal is in touch with established positions on a topic: statements reported from recognized sources. They look for the mention of a knowledge deficit: an estimate of the limitations of what has been said so far. They look for an account of the method: how knowledge will be constructed on this topic. Chairs of conferences and editors of collections also try to estimate the proposal's feasibility: can the researcher actually accomplish what she or he promises? Is the research site appropriate and manageable? Will it yield relevant data that can be usefully interpreted?

A medical historian interested in the issue of how particular diseases have been seen in gendered terms—as either essentially masculine or feminine—might compose a conference proposal which began by identifying the issue and some previous research on the topic:

> The role of early eighteenth-century medical theory in promoting contemporary beliefs about gender has been well established in both general studies (notably, Laqueur, 1990 and Jordanova, 1999) and accounts of particular physiological conditions (Lord, 1999), and diseases, including gout (Porter and G.S. Rousseau, 1998) and sexually transmitted infections (e.g. Stewart, 1996; Anselment 1999; McAllister, 2000).

Note the role of orchestration. The proposal begins by identifying and emphasizing important general studies (the two figures the writer identifies are, as the wording "notably" suggests, big names in their field, or at least scholars who have produced important studies). It then proceeds to identify more limited research studies on two research areas, "physiological conditions" and "diseases." Here the state of knowledge is partial rather than exhaustive: proposals for conferences and edited collections tend to be brief because the scholarship they lead to—the twenty-minute presentation, the twenty-five-page book chapter—is limited in scope.

The state of knowledge that orchestration establishes leads to a knowledge deficit—something research has not yet adequately addressed—and a research question (which may take the form of an actual question ending in a question mark, but in this case doesn't):

> As yet, however, there have been no studies of prevailing beliefs about the association of dropsy (the preferred contemporary term for edema, the abnormal accumulation of watery fluids in the body) and gender.

It is all very well to wonder about this, and the reader (who is also likely a medical historian) might feel a spark of interest, but he or she—as someone responsible for the success of a conference or volume of collected papers—would need to know more before accepting the proposal. What is the writer proposing to do? The reader might accept the claim—

> I propose therefore to examine late seventeenth- and early eighteenth-century discussions of dropsy ...

—but still not accept the proposal, having no idea how the researcher will find appropriate material in the vast research site made up by "late seventeenth- and early eighteenth-century discussions" (there were, after all, *a lot* of things written in those years). But if the researcher were to specify the research site more precisely, showing that it's relevant to the topic and explaining how it will be used to construct knowledge, the reader may feel more confident that the project is feasible. And so the proposal proceeds like this:

> ... published in *Philosophical Transactions and Collections of the Royal Society* as well as monographs by eminent physicians of the time, including Thomas Sydenham, Donald Monro, and Richard Blackmore. I'll begin by identifying eighteenth-century classifications of dropsy and then look at Sydenham's role in defining dropsy as a primarily feminine disease, before examining the problems of diagnosis, and the condition's ambiguous relationship to fertility (in particular, the difficulty of reconciling its association with infertility

with its tendency to mimic the look of pregnancy). This paper will conclude by briefly examining how the eighteenth century's most famous dropsy sufferer, Henry Fielding, attributed what he saw as particularly "feminine" feelings to his condition.

By this point the conference organizer would likely be persuaded of the feasibility of the proposal and—unless there were more interesting proposals to choose from—offer the scholar a chance to present.

Proposals have many stylistic features in common with introductions, perhaps the most notable of which is orchestration. But they differ from introductions in that, in many disciplines, they describe work that has not yet been completed. Indeed, the work may only have been planned, or just barely begun. In the case above, the conference paper that was eventually delivered differed significantly from the proposal as the researcher's inquiries led to new study texts and new insights. Conference organizers and editors know this: they know that the work may not have been done yet, and that the actual paper may differ from the one predicted by the proposal. (So at scholarly conferences, you can observe a by-product of the operation of the proposal genre: people standing up to present their work and saying, "First I have to tell you that the title of my paper has changed....") But the proposal gives conference organizers and book editors confidence in the process: the researcher is aware of the relevant research in the area (hence the emphasis on constructing a state of knowledge through orchestration); has a specific research question in mind; has a manageable research site and productive techniques for constructing knowledge.

Exercise 8

Ask one of your instructors for a proposal he or she submitted to a conference or in response to a call for papers for a book or special issue of a journal. Describe the moves by which orchestration is used to establish the state of knowledge. Identify the knowledge deficit and how it relates to the state of knowledge (for example, does the writer say that previous research has overlooked something? Or has it got something wrong?). Finally, identify the research site and the specific methods or techniques the writer will use to construct new knowledge.

Exercise 9

Write a 200- to 300-word proposal for a paper you will write for this or another course. Your proposal should include a title, a brief introduction to the topic it addresses, an orchestrated state of knowledge, some gap in the state of knowledge (something the research hasn't yet established) that leads to a research question, and an indication of how you will answer the research question.

Exercise 10

This exercise assumes that you have already developed a research question for a paper you are writing for this or another course. It also assumes that you have identified at least three or four scholarly studies that are relevant to this paper. Begin by introducing your research question and then introduce each of your speakers as they join the conversation. Each introduction should help your reader understand the circumstances under which the source is joining the conversation. Use summary, paraphrase, or even quotation to allow each speaker to address the question or respond to previous speakers. When might they agree or disagree? When might they need to say more? Aim for at least 250 words.

Definition

Until now we have found writers taking a position in relation to other speakers, and this chapter continues to explore writers' opportunities to take a position.

However, it is not only the writers who occupy positions in the research community; readers also occupy positions—sometimes near the writer, sometimes further away. Scholarly writers routinely find they must take positions in relation to their readers, and one way they do so is by considering their readers' need to have key terms explained. But **definition** is by no means only for the purpose of informing the uninformed. For readers already familiar with a term, definitions confirm common ground: through them the writer encourages readers to identify with the spirit of the definition. In this case, definition has the goal of corroborating and engaging what the informed reader already knows, involving this established knowledge in developing a discussion.

In this chapter we look at some circumstances in which academic writers define terms through **apposition** and **sustained definition**. But before we examine these, let's look at a traditional source of definitions—the dictionary.

7A Dictionaries

People rely on dictionaries—either practically, by looking words up, or theoretically, by comforting themselves that, should any problem of meaning arise, a dictionary could settle it. Often associated with this reliance is an idea that dictionaries are responsible for meaning: they make meaning, or they make words mean what they do.

Actually, this idea is backwards. Writers of dictionaries describe meanings that already exist. Or, better said, they describe how people use a word. Some language specialists don't talk about definition at all. Rather, they say that the "meaning" of a word is the set of circumstances under which it can be efficiently used. Consider, for instance, the following statements:

> The brain is not the only expensive organ in the body. There are four other expensive organs, the heart, the kidneys, the liver and the gastrointestinal tract.

It is hard to imagine who might consider organs "expensive"—organ traffickers perhaps, but then again, it's hard to picture a market for brain transplants. This seems to be one of the circumstances where it is not efficient to use the word "expensive." A dictionary's definition of "expensive" would not include these circumstances among those in which people use the word.

However, if we adjust our view of dictionaries, and see them as following rather than preceding use, we see that the community of speakers who use the word is the source of its meaning. These speakers (and writers), through their interactions and routine activities, develop and negotiate word meanings: the conditions under which a word can be efficiently used. It is possible, then, that in the case above dictionaries have simply failed to capture this particular community's use of "expensive."

Indeed, we must acknowledge that there are so many communities that no dictionary can account for all the ways they use words. Within the larger society, people get together in different groups, following different routines, and these shared routines are sustained by shared interpretations of the world—and shared habits in the use of certain words, including among specialist communities. So, while it would be difficult to find a dictionary that would provide a definition of "expensive" that justifies "the brain is not the only expensive organ," a community of language users made up of evolutionary biologists, for whom "expense" is a matter of the body's energy requirements rather than money, might well find the use of the word "expensive" in this sentence appropriate and efficient. And indeed, the passage above is from an article in a genetics journal.

Once we accept, first, that dictionaries only describe uses of words rather than establish definitions, and, second, that those recorded uses are only the most general kind, we can see that there are still defining opportunities—terms to be captured and refined in the account of their possible uses. Indeed, we may see that definition is an ongoing activity, part of the negotiating of agreement that occurs in any given community. In a research community, a flurry of defining or redefining activity can be a sign that a new object of inquiry is emerging, or a new perspective on an established object of inquiry is developing.

7B Appositions

When scholars use terms in ways that elude dictionary definitions, they often define those terms either to confirm common understanding with members of their own disciplinary community or to communicate an unfamiliar term to researchers in other communities. Here a pair of scholars working at the crossroads between a number of disciplines, including social psychology and epidemiology (the study of patterns of health and illness in populations), conduct research into the relationship between happiness and social networks. Notice how they define their key terms:

> Social networks consist of two elements: individuals (nodes) and the relationships (social ties) between them. Once all the nodes and ties are known, one can draw pictures of the network and discern every person's position within it. Within a network, one can speak of the "distance" between two people (also known as the "degree of separation"), which is the shortest path in the network from one person to another.

James H. Fowler and Nicholas A. Christakis 2009 "Dynamic spread of happiness in a large social network: Longitudinal analysis of the Framingham Heart Study social network." *British Medical Journal* 338: 23–27, 24.

Three familiar terms—*individuals, relationships,* and *"distance"*—are redefined by being assigned more specialized, technical terms—*nodes, social ties,* and *"degree of separation"*—that appear in parentheses. In each case, Fowler and Christakis define their terms by using an **apposition (or appositive)**, a grammatical structure that puts an equivalent expression next to a term which the writer estimates as important but difficult for a reader. The fact that the writers begin with the familiar, less precise term before giving its technical counterpart suggests that at this moment they are primarily concerned with readers who are unfamiliar with social network theory, the field that uses these terms.

As instruments of definition, appositives can help the scholar develop a position by narrowing the application of an abstraction. Here's another passage that defines through apposition:

> Academic knowledge is now generally recognized to be a social accomplishment, the outcome of a cultural activity shaped by ideology and constituted by agreement between a writer and a potentially sceptical discourse community.

Hyland 1999: 341.

If we stop reading at the comma, we realize that "social accomplishment" could mean a lot of things. What does it mean for knowledge to be *social*? What is it about knowledge that makes it an *accomplishment*? Using an appositive, the writer specifies what "social" will mean in this case, and also unpacks terms hidden in "social accomplishment": *cultural activity, ideology, community*. Appositives are a relatively unobtrusive way of activating an abstraction or specialized term. While a more extensive definition might inappropriately suggest that the reader is ignorant, the appositive quickly enriches established understandings or improves uncertain ones. By doubling a mention, appositives intensify the atmosphere around an abstraction.

In formal terms, we can say that an appositive creates a structure with equivalent material on each side of it, for example:

> They left a mess: empty soft-drink cans, Styrofoam cups, fast-food wrappers.

a mess   empty soft-drink cans, Styrofoam cups,
                      fast-food wrappers

This example uses a colon; the previous example used a comma. Other structures can also open a sentence for an appositive definition. Dashes and parentheses can do this, and so can "or." Writers may even signal appositional definitions with term like "in other words" or "i.e." (an abbreviation for the Latin phrase "id est," meaning "it is"). At other times, nearly synonymous terms can accumulate to confirm the sense in which a term in being used.

The next passage shows some of these techniques. Here, an historian reports his study of the controversy in the 1920s surrounding the unsolved murder of a young Scottish nanny working for a well-to-do family on the west coast of Canada, a case in which the racist press and political figures accused the family's Asian butler. Kerwin interprets these events through a series of accumulating abstractions (all of which apply to patterns of belief in the 1920s). The abstractions have been emphasized in bold.

> **Contemporary knowledge (or "discourses") about racial biology**, the effects of race-mixing, and the ability of two races to live within the same nation limited the vocabulary of the major players in this story, setting the ground rules for the debate. **Scientific knowledge** of the day, which concluded that miscegenation between Europeans and Asians was biologically disastrous, was common sense to people like Victor Odlum and Mary Ellen Smith. **Dominant understandings of British Columbia's history**, constructed through various narratives, further shaped interpretations of the Janet Smith case and the **"problem" of miscegenation**.
>
> Scott Kerwin 1999 "The Janet Smith Bill of 1924 and the language of race and nation in British Columbia." *BC Studies* 121: 83–114, 104.

Notice that Kerwin places the more specialist abstraction "discourses" in parentheses, to elaborate on "contemporary knowledge." Doubling the two terms like this both (1) improves our sense of what "discourses" are, reminding us that a discourse is a form of knowledge and that it carries the signs of its historical period, and (2) attaches both "contemporary knowledge ... about racial biology" and "dominant understandings" relating to "miscegenation" to other research that inquires into the themes and preoccupations of public discussion—into "discourses," that is. The doubling also helps confirm for the reader the sense in which the term "discourses" is being used in this passage.

Although the definitions we have just considered lack explicit indications—in the form of citation—of the research traditions that give rise to them, it is fair to say that appositives often seek to capture the contributions of earlier scholars. Let's look more closely at how the summarizer can use apposition to report the meaning of previous researchers' abstractions. Consider this passage from the article on the experience of undocumented immigrants in the Southwestern US:

> Since it is imagined, a sense of community is not limited to a specific geographic locale (Gupta and Ferguson 1992). Immigrants are said

to live in "binational communities" (Baca and Bryan 1980), "extended communities" (Whiteford 1979), "transnational communities" in "hyperspace" (Rouse 1991), and "transnational families" (Chavez 1992). These concepts highlight the connections migrants maintain with life in their home communities; living dislocated on the other side of a political border does not necessarily mean withdrawing from community or membership.

Chavez 1994: 54.

A summary might keep the abstraction *transnational communities*:

Chavez's work (1994) on undocumented immigrants offers new perspectives on transnational communities.

But it's likely that not all readers are familiar with Chavez's work (or that of the scholars he cites), or familiar enough with the term "transnational communities" to be exactly sure of what the writer of the summary means to say that Chavez has said. So the summarizer can define the term by reporting the gist of the latter part of the passage in the form of an appositive:

Chavez's work (1994) on undocumented immigrants offers new perspectives on transnational communities: communities, that is, whose members leave their homes and settle in another country but nevertheless maintain important connections with those original homes.

By defining "transnational communities" with an appositive, the summary accomplishes a number of things. It recognizes the position of the readers, and their possible unfamiliarity with or uncertainty about the term. It implicitly acknowledges that the term is somewhat specialized and limited in its distribution—at least for the time being—to certain research genres. It also demonstrates a respect for the complexity of the term: its capacity to capture the cumulative reasoning of scholars researching issues in human migration. At the same time, by using new words, the summary develops a new position on the concept—a new emphasis, a new version.

As the examples above suggest, much of the activity surrounding definition in research writing centres on abstractions because of their importance in organizing and interpreting lower-level details. In Chapter 4, we found that sometimes—mainly in narrative—we have to make interpretive abstractions to build higher levels from some fairly concrete, lower-level foundations. Most passages you summarize, however, will already be built up to higher levels, and will present you with ready-made abstractions (which is not to say that you cannot then build a little higher still, or modify the higher levels with your own interpretive abstractions). Since these abstractions condense and interpret lower-level specifics, you will probably transfer them from the original to your summary.

Exercise 1

The following passage comes from the beginning of an article on subjective well-being (i.e., happiness) that proposes a national happiness index. Identify the instances of apposition.

People's moods and emotions reflect on-line reactions to events happening to them. Each individual also makes broader judgments about his or her life as a whole, as well as about domains such as marriage and work. Thus, there are a number of separable components of SWB: life satisfaction (global judgments of one's life), satisfaction with important domains (e.g., work satisfaction), positive affect (experiencing many pleasant emotions and moods), and low levels of negative affect (experiencing few unpleasant emotions and moods). In the early research on SWB, researchers studying the facets of happiness usually relied on only a single self-report item to measure each construct. For example, Andrews and Withey (1976) asked respondents, "How do you feel about your life as a whole?" Respondents were provided with a 7-point response scale ranging from *delighted* to *terrible.* Recent measures of SWB, however, contain multiple items. For example, the PANAS (Positive and Negative Affect Scale; Watson, Clark, & Tellegen, 1988) measures both positive and negative affect, each with 10 affect items, and the Satisfaction With Life Scale assesses life satisfaction with items such as "In most ways my life is close to my ideal" and "So far I have gotten the important things I want in life" (Pavot & Diener, 1993). Although the psychometric properties of these scales tend to be strong, they provide only one approach to assessing SWB.

Pamela E. Oliver and Daniel J. Myers 1999 "How events enter the public sphere." *American Journal of Sociology* 105 (1): 38–67, 40–41.

7C Sustained Definitions

Definition can be as short as a gesture—a brief delay in the discussion as an abstraction is glossed and readers make contact with its complexity—or it can command more sustained attention. In this section we approach **sustained definition**, beginning with techniques for **formal definition** first developed in classical rhetoric.

Formal definition uses a particular kind of sentence structure. Consider the following definition:

> Daycare is the institutional provision of caretaking services to young children, including feeding, supervision, shelter, and instruction.

The definition first isolates the term to be defined—*daycare*—for scrutiny by making it the grammatical subject of the sentence. It then uses the present-tense form of the verb "to be"—*is*—to establish a statement of equivalence: on one side is the term, *daycare*, and on the other side is the definition:

> *... the institutional provision of caretaking services to young children, including feeding, supervision, shelter, and instruction.*

The defining side of the statement proceeds in two steps. First it enlarges our view by identifying the larger class to which *daycare* belongs:

> *... the institutional provision of caretaking services ....*

It then narrows our view again by identifying the features which differentiate *daycare* from other "institutional" kinds of "caretaking services" (for example, *health care* and *education*):

> *... to young children, including feeding, supervision, shelter, and instruction.*

This is the classical pattern of formal sentence definition.

We could say that the focus of the formal definition is on the *ideal*. This definition ignores cases where it is hard to distinguish between babysitting and daycare, where children are not exactly fed but feed themselves (or refuse to eat, or bring their own snacks), where care is provided on so informal a basis it might not be called "institutional" at all.

The next definition shows the same pattern of enlarging to classify and reducing to differentiate, but it presents the phenomenon—*broadcasting*—not as an ideal, but as something at least potentially open to varying interpretations. In particular, the passage exemplifies one of the development options open to the writer: following formal definition, the writer can "double" the definition by saying what the phenomenon *does*.

> Broadcasting is a system of social control that, through the trans-mission of electronic signals, normalizes the diverse experiences of individuals. Broadcasting interprets events and life conditions in ways that confirm society's ideological centre.

Here the definition first expands our focus by identifying the class to which broadcasting belongs (systems of social control), and then differentiates it from other members of the class (laws or customs, for example). Moreo-ver, this passage shows that formal definition can be in itself a step in an argument. Someone else could have defined *broadcasting* differently—as a result of having interpreted data differently, or having different data to interpret, or having a different disciplinary perspective.

> Broadcasting is a system of communication that, through the transmission of electronic signals, illuminates public and private life alike. By linking widespread communities through a shared network of information, broadcasting ensures that citizens in democratic societies recognize common and crucial features of their experience, and enables them to respond to those features as issues.

The two definitions of *broadcasting* would serve different arguments. This disparity won't surprise you if you think of definition as the presentation of a high-level, interpretive abstraction which the writer assigns to lower-level observations or data. So the definition is bound to be an expression of the reasoning and insight that have led the writer to assign the name in the first place.

Whereas formal definition isolates the phenomenon for scrutiny, sus-tained definition expands by locating the phenomenon amongst other, related phenomena in the world. In the next passage, an economist leads up to and defines *revolution*. The definition presents this event not in the usual political or historical terms but in new economic or market ones: entrepreneurship, clients, employees, property transfer.

> The potential revolutionary leader is an entrepreneur who recruits, deploys, and compensates insurgents. The potential revolutionary leader maximizes the expected wealth of his clientele, which is an alternative set of property owners and/or an alternative parasitic

ruling class. A revolution in this theory is an attempt to depose the incumbent ruler and his clientele in favor of the revolutionary leader and his clientele. **In other words**, a revolution attempts either to establish new property rights, or to enthrone a new ruling class, or both.

Herschel I. Grossman 1999 "Kleptocracy and revolutions." *Oxford Economic Papers* 51: 267–83, 268 (emphasis added).

It is quite challenging and (to many readers) unusual to think about revolution in this way instead of in terms of oppression and liberation, or disorder and violence. Happily, Grossman doesn't rest with just one statement of the definition. He *doubles the definition*, and says it again— "[i]n other words."

Sometimes definition works on *how words are used* by communities, rather than committing the writer (and reader) to a particular use of the term. Here researchers studying the processes that turn occurrences into public events analyze how the terms *parade* and *march* are used by both lay people and other researchers.

Insiders may accept these forms [of public action] as natural categories of action, while detached observers can observe the ways in which the categories themselves are constructed and evolve over time. The "protest" is one such ritualized form that conveys roughly the same meaning to activists, police, news reporters, the general public, and social scientists alike. This shared meaning has blinded researchers to the constructed nature of "protest" and led them to assume an unproblematic isomorphism between form and content in their definitions of protest events. But, as Tilly (1978) first told us 20 years ago, the forms or repertoires of protest shift across time and space and new forms of protest are often created by adapting nonprotest forms to new purposes. Identical forms may carry very different content. "Parade" and "march" are two names for exactly the same form (McPhail and Wohlstein 1986), and the words can be used interchangeably even though in the United States in the 1990s the popular connotations of *parade* involve entertainment, while the word *march* popularly applies only to message events. Likewise, there are many kinds of rallies, from pep rallies to protest rallies: they share the form of a stationary gathering with speeches containing informational and emotional content, but vary greatly in the issue they may address. As protest repertoires evolve, message content is often added to event types created for other purposes. In the United States in the 1990s, ceremonies, musical performances, literature distribution, and amateur street theater are all event types that are typically "apolitical," but all have carried protest content in past times and places and can and do sometimes carry protest content in the 1990s.

Pamela E. Oliver and Daniel J. Myers 1999 "How events enter the public sphere." *American Journal of Sociology* 105 (1): 38–67, 40–41.

Clearly the sustained definitions that Oliver and Myers develop here have moved far beyond the constraints of the formal definition: the researchers' sensitivity to historical context and to the different communities of language users allow readers an understanding of the terms "parade" and "march" that not even the best dictionaries could hope to duplicate.

Exercise 2

Read the following passage by LaFollette on gun control. Write a two- or three-sentence definition of fundamental right: "In LaFollette's discussion (2000) of the elements of debate over gun control, a fundamental right is...." You may want to include in your definition what is not a fundamental right. You might also try to come up with an example of a fundamental right other than the one LaFollette uses (freedom of speech). And you might find that his definition still leaves some things unclear or uncertain. If so, you can include this uncertainty in your definition: "It is unclear from this part of LaFollette's discussion whether...."

Most defenders of private gun ownership claim we do have a moral right [to bear arms]—as well as a constitutional one—and this right is not an ordinary right but a fundamental one [....]

If they are correct, they would have the justificatory upper hand. Were this a fundamental right, it would not be enough to show that society would benefit from controlling access to guns.[1] The arguments for gun control would have to be overwhelming. Yet there is also a hefty cost in claiming that this is a fundamental right: the evidence for the right must meet especially rigorous standards.

What makes a right fundamental? A fundamental right is a non-derivative right protecting a *fundamental* interest. Not every interest we individually cherish is fundamental. Since most interests are prized by someone, such a notion of "fundamental interest" would be anemic, serving no special justificatory role. Fundamental interests are special; they are integrally related to a person's chance of living a good life, *whatever her particular interests, desires, and beliefs happen to be.* For example, living in a society that protects speech creates an environment within which each of us can pursue our particular interests, goals, needs, and development, whatever our interests happen to be. Is the purported right to bear arms like this paradigmatic fundamental right?

Note

1 Todd C. Hughes and Lester H. Hunt, "The Liberal Basis of the Right to Bear Arms," *Public Affairs Quarterly* (in press).

Hugh LaFollette 2000 "Gun control." *Ethics* 110: 263–81, 264.

Exercise 3

In *Verbal Hygiene* (1995), from which the next passage is excerpted, Deborah Cameron, a linguist, investigates attitudes towards language: people's tendency to associate certain features of speech and writing with decency and orderliness, and other features with slovenliness and defiance. Her analysis of a particular historical expression of such attitudes makes use of an abstraction—moral panic—which has been at work in other disciplines: social theory, criminology, and, as she says, "cultural [history]." In the passage below, she provides a long definition of moral panic.

Summarize this passage by note-taking for gist, and then assemble these gists to compose your own definition of moral panic. Elaborate this definition by (1) finding, from your experience, other examples of moral panic; (2) explaining why moral panic is an important focus for inquiry; and/or (3) reflecting on the role of the media in producing moral panic.

MORAL PANIC

I am going to suggest that the grammar furore [controversy over school curriculum in Britain in the 1980s and early 1990s, accompanied by many claims in the press and from political figures that young people didn't know grammar, and were illiterate] bears more than a passing resemblance to the sort of periodic hysteria cultural historians have labelled "moral panic" (Cohen 1987). Although there are differences as well as similarities, I believe the parallel is an illuminating one if we wish to understand why, in Simon Jenkins's words, "the nation's grammar stir[red] the political juices." Before we consider the grammar debate itself, it is therefore worth looking more generally at the phenomenon of moral panic.

A moral panic can be said to occur when some social phenomenon or problem is suddenly foregrounded in public discourse and discussed in an obsessive, moralistic and alarmist manner, as if it betokened some imminent catastrophe. In the past hundred years in Europe and America we have had out-breaks of this kind centring on prostitution and "white slavery," drugs, the "Jewish problem," juvenile delinquency, venereal disease, immigration, communism, overpopulation, pornography, rock music and pit bull terriers.

These are not claimed as cases of moral panic simply because they inspired public anxiety: some degree of concern about many of them would be perfectly reasonable. But there are times when concern goes far beyond what is reasonable. In the words of the criminologist Jock Young, "moral panic" describes "cases where public reaction [is] completely disproportionate to the actual problem faced" (*Guardian*, Letters, 9 July 1994). In a moral panic the scale of the problem is exaggerated, its causes are analysed in simplistic terms, anxiety about it climbs to intolerable levels, and the measures proposed to alleviate it are usually extreme and punitive. Analysts have suggested there are underlying sociological reasons why public concern gets "out of hand" in this way; and that vested interests are often at work encouraging it to do so.

Moral panic works by channelling, at least temporarily, the diffuse anxieties and hostilities that exist in any society towards a single, simple problem, such as "drugs," "Jews" or "communism." The discovery of the "problem" entails the creation of a scapegoat—the junkie, the fifth columnist, the Zionist conspirator. This generic "folk devil" is usually identified with a real social group, whose members then bear the brunt of hostility and blame. Moral panic thus has the potential to lead to such extreme forms of repression as witch-hunts and pogroms, and in some cases may even be orchestrated for that purpose.

Scholars have suggested that moral panic in the form we know it is a product of the modern mass media [....] The most commonplace incident or pedestrian report can be turned into an issue by media attention, whereas without that attention the same incident would go unnoticed and the report would gather dust. Having thus established something as an issue, the media can return to it under the guise of "responding to public concern"—even though that concern is of their own making.

Deborah Cameron 1995 *Verbal hygiene*. London: Routledge, 82–83.

7D The Social Profile of Abstractions and Their Different Roles in Different Disciplines

As we have seen, summarizing often entails using abstractions to marshal low-level details. Moreover, these abstractions—revolution, transnational communities—seem particularly likely to attract definitions. When we found abstractions in Chapter 4 to interpret the details of "Little Thumb," the sky was the limit: Do you notice that the father's attitude is odd? Let's call that *ambivalence*! Do you notice Little Thumb hiding under the stool? Let's call that circumstance *concealment*!

But it is not quite right to say that the sky is the limit, for as we move from one academic discipline to another we notice that some abstractions are more likely than others to participate in the scholarly conversation, and that different abstractions—what might be called **prestige abstractions**—prevail in different disciplines. To put it another way, in each scholarly community—among sociologists, historians, chemists—some abstractions are more likely to engage current scholarly concerns and issues, and more likely to enter into exchange with other abstractions which are currently highly valued. For example, amongst the excerpts we have read so far, we have encountered the abstraction *community* at work in a number of research sites. Similarly, reflecting on the positions and representations of ethnic minorities discussed by subjects of Verkuyten et al.'s research in Chapter 3, we might interpret these conditions as related to *marginality*, an abstraction current in many disciplines in the humanities and social sciences. If in reading the passages from Mary Englund's memoirs in Chapter 4 you came up with an abstraction like *colonial domination*, you would have begun to participate in discussion which circulates amongst those engaged in **post-colonial reasoning**. In every discipline, some abstractions enjoy more prestige than others: they attract scholarly interest.

This phenomenon should come as no surprise. Genre theory predicts that language will reflect the shared attitudes and interests of the community that produces it. The circumstances of prestige and interest are described by a scholar cited earlier in this chapter. Hyland observes that knowledge in research communities is a "social accomplishment"—the outcome of people listening to one another, addressing one another, being in the same neighbourhood, sharing topics and questions, developing some issues and neglecting others, negotiating common understandings and priorities.

Yet, while this kind of exchange is common to all disciplines, the **sociality of knowledge**—the ways in which knowledge is the product of social activities—differs somewhat in different disciplines, and the roles of communal abstractions differ accordingly. Roughly speaking, the differences arrange themselves along the continuum from the 'hard' sciences at one end to the humanities at the other, with the social sciences in between. In her detailed and valuable study of writing in the humanities and social sciences, focusing on literary studies, social history, and psychology, Susan Peck MacDonald (1994) observes that abstraction in literary study is much less constrained than it is in psychology. In literary study, interpretations of particulars can compete, and rival one another. Somebody might say, for example, that "Little Thumb" is *not* about *ambivalence* at all; rather, it is about *rivalry*—and there wouldn't be any way of settling this contest, except perhaps to wait and see whose interpretations got cited and used elsewhere, whose abstractions entered the conversation and got voiced by others. In psychology and the other social sciences, however, terms are used in ways that are methodical enough to "adjudicate" claims for the research community. MacDonald focuses especially on the abstraction *attachment*, which is in use in research in developmental psychology. *Attachment* is the relationship infants or small children form with their caregivers. It has many complexities and many (measurable) aspects and dimensions, and researchers ask many questions about it. But they (more or less) agree on which behaviours and attitudes to call "attachment" and which ones not to call "attachment." So, for example, if a literary scholar interpreted Little Thumb's father's conflicted attitude or his mother's tearful protests as *attachment*, these researchers would not likely regard the statement as contributing to *their* conversation about children and families. On the contrary, as MacDonald contends, the consensus among researchers in developmental psychology on what constitutes *attachment* emerges from a "conceptual frame," a means of "dismiss[ing] some kinds of interpretations and ask[ing] questions about others" (73).

Not surprisingly, researchers in the sciences handle abstraction differently from their colleagues in the humanities. In *Writing Science: Literacy and Discursive Power* (1993), M.A.K. Halliday and J.R. Martin offer means of discriminating amongst the roles of abstraction in different disciplines. They distinguish between abstraction in the sciences—which, they say, is "technical," and dedicated to the project of "classifying" the world—and abstraction in the humanities—which, they say, is not technical. To borrow an example from Martin, a physical geographer uses the abstract term *abrasion* as an element of a system that classifies forms of erosion (which is itself a technical abstraction). This system distinguishes *abrasion* from other types of erosion. If an historian, on the other hand, uses a term like *solemnity* to develop an interpretation of a memorial parade, *solemnity* does not classify the parade as technically distinct from, say, other forms of public gathering.

Similarly, the historian writing on the unsolved murder of a Scottish nanny used "contemporary knowledge," "scientific knowledge of the day," "common sense," "dominant understandings," and, especially, "discourses" to summarize and interpret a series of events in Western Canada in the 1920s. While his interpretation could invite correction and refinement or revision, or a suggestion of a better way to look at this case, it is unlikely that someone would say, "No, that cannot be classified as a discourse because a discourse is always and in every case *x*. What you refer to is not in fact *x*." But a geographer identifying a formation in the landscape as the result of abrasion might be contradicted: it is not abrasion, it is another (possibly as yet unnamed) type of erosion. What the geographer has pointed to is properly situated at some other place in the system of classification.

We can observe some of the classificatory work that abstractions do in the passage below, which is from an article that seeks to improve means of recognizing personality types. Among the terms that are in bold, which ones might you hear or utter in everyday, non-specialist talk? Of these, which would you estimate has a *technical* dimension in this context? Which terms seem to belong to the discipline of personality psychology and seem unlikely to make an everyday appearance? If we referred to Little Thumb's father as prone to "hypervigilance and ruminative rationalization," would personality researchers recognize our statement?

> Although members of each of the three high-distress groups are prone to **anxiety** and **depression**, they manifest very different personality structures. Although sensitized individuals (i.e., those with high distress and moderate restraint) report experiencing **excessive negative affect**, they do not seem to be especially predisposed to particular **personality disorders** (Weinberger and Schwartz, 1990). They are hypothesized to have moderate levels of **ego development** (conformist/conscientious) in which "neurotic" concerns about the inherent conflicts between the id (i.e., wishes, desires) and the **superego** (i.e., internalized prohibitions) are salient (cf. Fenichel, 1945). Consistent with traditional repression-sensitization literature (Byrne, 1961), the sensitized group is likely to cope with stress by employing **hypervigilance and ruminative rationalization**. Paradoxically, sensitizers tend to stew about nonessential aspects of their **affects**, often camouflaging the defensive nature of behavior that may often involve **displacement**. Their attachment model is hypothesized to vary within the preoccupied or fearful spectrum, where what is salient is a concern about their own **worthiness** in **relationships** (Griffin and Bartholomew, 1994; Mikulincer and Orbach, 1995).

> Daniel A. Weinberger 1998 "Defenses, personality structure and development: Integrating psychodynamic theory into a typological approach to personality." *Journal of Personality* 66 (6): 1061–77, 1074 (emphasis added).

Terms are working hard in this passage to classify behaviour, and being called on to improve and refine their technicality. But even in this highly classificatory atmosphere, we still see the signs that these terms are, as Ken Hyland says, a "social accomplishment," the result of a negotiated agreement between members of a scholarly community. For one thing, we see the reporting expressions that trace these claims and terms to their origins in the research community:

- … (Weinberger and Schwartz, 1990) …
- They are hypothesized to have …
- Consistent with traditional repression-sensitization literature (Byrne, 1961) …
- … is hypothesized to vary …

We also see appositives:

- moderate levels of ego development (conformist/conscientious)
- the superego (i.e., internalized prohibitions)

These appositive structures show the writer/researcher estimating the extent and stability of the terms (their social distribution), confirming their application for this purpose, and activating their components for this occasion. Even technical abstractions call for the cooperation and participation of readers.

The social dimension of abstractions can also be seen in the role definition plays as a research instrument, as in the following two passages. In the first example, economists gather abstractions that have been used to analyze the economic behaviour *charity* or *philanthropy*: specifically, in this case, the action of making donations to colleges or universities.

A THEORY OF GIVING

In the charitable giving literature, social scientists have distinguished several possible motivations for donations: 1) altruism, 2) reciprocity, and 3) direct benefits. Each of these will now be discussed in a college giving context.

Thomas H. Brugginck and Kamran Siddiqui 1995 "An econometric model of alumni giving: A case study for a liberal arts college." *The American Economist* 39 (2): 53–60, 53.

In the second example, physical anthropologists concentrate on the technical definition of *blade* to question longstanding assumptions of a connection between human evolution and the development of techniques for producing these blades.

WHAT ARE BLADES AND WHAT HAVE PEOPLE SAID ABOUT THEM?

The standard morphological definition of a blade is any flake more than twice as long as it is wide, although some investigators prefer ratios of 2.5 or even 4 to 1. The technical definition is somewhat narrower, limiting use of the term to elongated blanks with parallel or slightly curving edges.

Ofer Bar-Yosef and Steven L. Kuhn 1999 "The big deal about blades: Laminar technologies and human evolution." *American Anthropologist* 101 (2): 322–38, 323.

These two instances of technical definition reveal different motivations for using the definitions as research instruments. In the first case, efforts to technicalize abstract names for giving money away could have practical applications in planning fund-raising drives. In the second case, the record of the discipline's work on identifying blades will organize the researchers' critical review of traditional classifications of eras of human development and progress (are these people Stone Age?). In order to do this, there has to be some social consensus amongst researchers on what counts as a *blade*.

Researchers get so accustomed to the particular operations of abstractions in their field that these operations can seem "natural" to them—natural, that is, rather than social, and the outcome of exchange, cooperation, and negotiation. The way they use abstractions will seem to them "logical," "accurate," "clear," "precise," whereas other uses of abstraction will seem "illogical," "inaccurate," "vague," or "fuzzy."

Students, however, can have a different view. Taking courses in a variety of disciplines, they are not so likely to see the different uses of abstractions as "natural." In fact, in experiencing a range of sometimes contradictory reactions to their work, they would be justified in thinking that the acceptability or unacceptability of uses of abstraction is arbitrary, rather than natural. Sometimes what they write is logical, sometimes it's called illogical; sometimes what they write is clear, sometimes it is considered vague. Better than "natural" *or* "arbitrary," let's say "social." Different groups engaged in different kinds of research-and-writing activities (or different discourse communities) develop, through their association and communal purposes, different techniques for making and representing knowledge.

These differences can also affect the material conditions of learning in different courses. In disciplines that depend on technical abstractions, students spend a lot of time acquiring command of these terms and preparing to have their command of these terms tested. This can be hard work. But it might be even harder work, for some, to acquire facility with the prestige abstractions of the humanities, where the operation of terms is more covert and tacit, and less openly recognized as a matter of consensus and collaboration.

Exercise 4

In the following passage, Sandlin and Milam introduce and relate several abstractions. Identify the main abstractions and the instances of definition; analyze how they are related. How is one abstraction used to define other abstractions?

In this article we explore how two groups—Adbusters and Reverend Billy and the Church of Stop Shopping—use culture jamming as a means of resisting consumerism; we chose these groups because they are among the more widely known and enduring culture jamming groups. To frame our research, we draw from cultural studies and the critical curriculum literature focusing on public pedagogy. Specifically, we ground our work in a "Gramscian" cultural studies framework. This perspective conceptualizes popular culture as an active process, where cultural commodities and experiences are not simply passively consumed, but are the raw materials people use to create popular culture, within various contexts of power relations (Storey, 1999, 2006). From this view, popular culture is a prominent sphere in which inequalities of class, gender, race, and sexuality are made meaningful or brought to consciousness; it is also an arena for power struggles between dominant and subordinate social groups—a terrain on which hegemony, or consent, is fought for and resisted (Hartley, 2002; Storey, 2006).

Jennifer A. Sandlin and Jennifer L. Milam 2008 "'Mixing pop (culture) and politics': Cultural resistance, culture jamming, and anti-consumption activism as critical public pedagogy." *Curriculum Inquiry* 38.3: 323–50, 325.

Exercise 5

Compare the presentation of definitions in two or three of your textbooks from different courses (if possible, choose textbooks from at least two different disciplinary areas, that is, from areas named as sciences, social sciences, and humanities). Try to generalize about the approaches to definition preferred in each discipline. Consider some of the following questions:

- Where do the definitions tend to occur? In a glossary? In the body of the textbook?
- In general, do the definitions strike you as *technical* (i.e., stable and designed for classifying phenomena) or *non-technical* (provisional and open to reformulation by other writers)?
- What kinds of definitions tend to be presented as brief appositions?
- What kinds are presented as sustained definitions?
- Are definitions ever attributed to specific researchers?
- Do any terms receive more than one definition (proposed, perhaps, by different researchers in the field)?

Exercise 6

Analyze the use of definition in a scholarly article, perhaps one that you are using for a research essay in one of your courses. Consider some of the following questions:

- Where do the definitions tend to occur? What sorts of words or terms tend to be defined?
- How does the writer present definitions (i.e., apposition versus sustained)?
- Are definitions attributed to other researchers?
- What role does definition serve in the article? Does the writer seem to assume that the reader doesn't know the meaning? Does definition establish common ground? Does definition establish a precise, technical meaning?
- Are the meanings of words or terms contested or seen as having different possible meanings?

Compare your findings with those of your classmates.

8

Introductions

In the schoolroom essay, introductions are often determined by models relating to a number of elements of the social situation, including the need for students to do well on standardized, system-wide essay-writing exams that can be quickly graded. For example, think of the advice high school students are routinely given for writing introductions for five-paragraph essays: begin with a generalization, narrow the topic, and end the paragraph with a thesis statement identifying the three main points of the essay. But genre theory tells us that introductions are likely to serve quite different purposes in research writing, and so it is particularly important to consider how the scholarly situation shapes the beginnings of research essays. Obviously, in both schoolroom and research writing, introductions share the need to begin—to present a topic and establish grounds for discussion—and this need will bring some similarities. However, there are crucial differences that arise because of the knowledge-making demands of the research genres. This chapter will focus on **generalization**, **citation**, and **documentation** practices in order to identify some of these differences. In particular, it applies our knowledge of summary and the orchestration of voices, discussed in the first half of this book, to introductions in research writing. We'll consider how citation leads to estimates of the **state of knowledge** and **knowledge deficits**, features of academic writing that we have already encountered in research proposals and that make an appearance in introductions as well. We'll also take a close look at reporting style and the accompanying conventions of documentation. But first, let's consider the role of generalization and citation in establishing how a topic has been discussed before.

8A Generalization and Citation

Most people would probably agree that introductions typically begin at and sustain a relatively high level of generality. For the schoolroom essay, generality itself is often enough to get the essay under way.

> Throughout history, humans have sought to understand who they are.

Or:

> Imagination is a powerful force in our daily lives.

But if we transfer this habit of generality directly to the academic essay, we might find that academic readers are uncomfortable with—and may even be quite skeptical about—generalities like these. Academic readers are used to beginnings like the following passage, taken from an article:

> In the last 20 years, business organizations have been increasingly held accountable for their corporate social performance in a variety of areas (Wood, 1991). Firms have been confronted by an organized, activist, and concerned set of stakeholders (Ansoff, 1975; Freeman, 1984) clamoring for improved corporate performance on a wide range of social and political issues, from clean air and nutritional labeling to equal employment opportunities.
>
> Daniel W. Greening and Barbara Gray 1994 "Testing a model of organizational response to social and political issues." *Academy of Management Journal* 37: 467–98, 467.

It seems likely that most people—including the writers—already knew, at the time of the article's publication, that public consciousness of business and industry had changed. After all, at that time and still today, corporate spokespersons regularly appear on TV, and are often quoted in the print media to answer complaints about their products and practices. But, even though these circumstances seem to be part of common knowledge, the academic writer attributes their mention to particular sources. Why are statements that could easily be justified as belonging to the present writer attributed to other writers?

Recent research into academic discourse has shown that one of the moves writers typically make is to confirm that they are carrying on a

tradition of inquiry. Parenthetical citations show that a particular topic has been discussed in published research, which attests to its relevance and importance. In the academic community to which an article is addressed, people recognize this topic as something to be studied. So we could say that in the passage above Greening and Gray include these citations in order to show that other scholars have discussed the issue. The citation shows that the claim attached to it is verifiable by measures valued in research communities rather than simply coming from "common knowledge," which, as we will see in Chapter 10, can turn out to be in some way mistaken. We can call this practice **secured generalization**. It validates the topic as eligible for scholarly examination.

As well as putting a check on common sense—on unexamined though widely held views—attributing generalizations to others can also put a check on personal perceptions. We may notice, in our daily life, that the servers at fast-food outlets are elderly people. So we construct a generalization: "The fast-food franchise industries hire elderly people." But what if it is only the one or two outlets that serve the fried chicken we like that actually do hire elderly people? What if, in the next district or province, most servers are adolescents? Our limited experience—our particular position in the world—has distorted our knowledge of the situation. And what if our experience is limited in some other way, for example, by our attitudes and interests? Maybe we have a grudge against elderly people, and feel the world is overrun with them. We see them everywhere. Our unchecked personal perception would produce an unwarranted generalization, a stereotype, one which reflected our point of view but might not stand up to rigorous scrutiny. So, in academic writing, we find generalizations that typify sections of the population secured with citation to demonstrate that these categories are products of research and not stereotypes or untested personal perception:

> Some investigators have attributed ... low rates of delinquency and other behavior disorders [among "people of Asian descent in North America, particularly those of Chinese heritage"] to culture-related factors. That is, Asian culture emphasizes conformity, family solidarity, harmonious relationships, and respect for authority, especially the unconditional respect for parents, or filial piety (Fong, 1973; Hsu, 1981). The North American culture, on the other hand, emphasizes freedom and individualism. Consistent with this notion of cultural differences, Kelley and Tsang (1992) reported that Chinese parents

in North America used more physical control over their children and more restrictive child-rearing practices than did their non-Chinese counter-parts.

Siu Kwong Wong 1999 "Acculturation, peer relations, and delinquent behavior of Chinese-Canadian youth." *Adolescence* 34 (133): 107–19, 107–08.

As suggested by the terms of this example—"people of Asian descent in North America, particularly those of Chinese heritage"—the generalization has been produced in a context of scholarly research and exchange and is therefore less susceptible to the criticisms that can be levelled against untested "common knowledge," particularly when it relates to such sensitive issues as race or gender.

Exercise 1

Here are two examples of generalization occurring in opening sections of research articles. What would be the "common-sense" versions of these generalizations? What kinds of criticisms would the researchers be open to if they were to present these common-sense versions without citing any prior research?

PASSAGE 1

To combat racism effectively it is necessary to understand its complex features and underlying themes. In Britain it has recently been argued that such understanding is lacking in many anti-racism strategies (see Gilroy 1990; Rattansi 1992). Anti-racist understanding of racist thinking and arguing is not very sophisticated. Cohen (1992), for instance, typifies anti-racism as the disavowal of complexity for the sake of pursuing moral certainties. Anti-racism appears to be lacking in effectiveness because of its doctrinaire form and its lack of powerful arguments.

Maykel Verkuyten, Wiebe de Jong, and Kees Masson 1994 "Similarities in anti-racist and racist discourse: Dutch local residents talking about ethnic minorities." *New Community* 20 (2): 253–67, 253.

PASSAGE 2

Gender is one of the most important categories—if not the most important category—in human social life. The dichotomy between female and male is of crucial relevance to virtually every

---

domain of human experience (Bem, 1981; Huston, 1983; Ruble and Ruble, 1982). All known cultures specify that female-male is a fundamental distinction. They provide terms to distinguish boys from girls and men from women. More importantly, they associate men and women with different sets of characteristic features and with different sets of behavioral expectations (see Williams and Best, 1990).

Thomas Eckes 1994 "Features of men, features of women: Assessing stereotypic beliefs about gender subtypes." *British Journal of Social Psychology* 33: 107–23, 107.

8B Reported Speech

As we have observed, introductions in the schoolroom-essay genre and in the research genres share a tendency for high-level—i.e., general—beginnings. Both genres, it seems, strive thereby to establish a common ground of understanding with readers. The difference between them is that "common understanding" extends in different directions. In the schoolroom essay, introductory generalities seem to cast such a wide net as to grab any reader in sight. The research genres, on the other hand, compose introductory generalities to cast a narrower net in order to initiate a scholarly conversation—to resume the collaborative consideration of topics that research communities are working on. Accordingly, **reported speech** is an important (and very common) way to start a scholarly conversation.

As we saw in Chapter 2, reported speech is so crucial a feature in scholarly discourse that the research genres have developed their own distinctive ways of incorporating the speech of others. Intricate systems direct writers to quote a lot, or not much, to quote directly, or to paraphrase, or to put other writers' names in the reporting sentence, or to put them in parentheses, or even to leave some speakers unidentified. As we proceed to examine the roles played by reported speech, we may find some *guides* to this system, but we will not find the kind of *rules* that govern, for example, the preparation of a Works Cited or References page or the punctuation of a parenthetical citation in a certain discipline. Instead, we will find patterns that indicate the preferences and habits of different academic disciplines and communities.

First, let's think about how we incorporate the speech of others in everyday conversation. We can use **direct speech**, the exact words the other person used:

JANE to FRED: I'm so sorry. I forgot your birthday.

FRED to CATHERINE: And then Jane said, "I'm so sorry. I forgot your birthday."

Or, instead of direct speech, we often substitute our own words—**indirect speech**—which can be more or less close to the original:

JANE to FRED: I'm so sorry. I forgot your birthday.

FRED to CATHERINE: And then Jane said she regretted it. She was sorry she had forgotten my birthday.

When we are reporting the speech of others, our choice of whether to use direct or indirect speech depends on various factors, including whether we need to be completely precise, or condense the utterance into a smaller space, or accommodate it to a different context.

Like everyday speakers, academic writers make decisions about what they will quote directly and what they will incorporate indirectly. It appears that there are tendencies in how much direct versus indirect speech is used, and these tendencies reflect the writer's academic discipline: biologists, for example, quote much less frequently than do historians. Both direct and indirect speech, however, follow the function of the summary: they report what has been said, and in doing so may confirm it, dispute it, or go further. Moreover, there is a good chance that, particularly in indirect speech, the reporting terms will appear not as verbs, but as nouns. To continue with the example above, the writer might change "regretted" into the noun "regrets" (Jane said she had regrets). For other examples of verbs turning into nouns,

	suggests	
she	assumes	that ...
	argues	

—can become:

	suggestion	
her	assumption	that ...
	argument	

So, "Jane expressed regret ..." could become "Jane's expression of regret...." We will call this action of replacing verbs with nouns **nominalization**, and in Chapter 10 will look more closely at some of the reasons this phenomenon is so common in scholarly writing.

For the moment, however, let's consider some of the most common patterns of reported speech in academic writing. The simplest, baseline case of reported speech—both direct and indirect—is "*x* said *y*." Or "*x* said" can be replaced by a characterization of the original speech, followed by the gist, sometimes with a bit of direct speech retained.

> FRED to CATHERINE: Jane expressed regret about forgetting my birthday, saying she was "sorry."

But research writing often departs from these baseline cases. Commonly, the reported speaker leaves the sentence itself and relocates in parentheses.

> It has been reported that the expression of regret is a key factor in ongoing relationships (Short 1996; Gross 2000).

This form can even eliminate the speech verb (*say* and its many substitutes, such as *report, suggest*, etc.) while retaining the speaker:

> Heartfelt regret is an important element in ongoing relationships (Short 1996).

Alternately, sometimes the speaker or speakers can disappear entirely, and only the presence of a **reporting verb** alerts the reader to the existence of a speaker. In this case, the act of speech is represented with an **agentless expression**:

> It has been reported that the expression of regret is essential, and should be done regularly.

This last way of speaking seems to defy the research community's practice tying current scholarship to a tradition of inquiry by attributing statements. On non-scholarly occasions, agentless reports of statements may tend to make the statement seem more valid—coming from not just one person (who may or may not be reliable) but from more widely distributed sources, as in the famous first sentence of Jane Austen's novel, *Pride and Prejudice*:

> It is a truth universally acknowledged, that a single man in possession of a good fortune must be in want of a wife.

So the agentless report of speech can suggest some consensus. Inspecting the samples of reported speech below, you will have a chance to see whether this is the case in scholarly publications.

In a variation on the agentless report of speech, statements can some-times be attributed to a **typified group**—"informants," "researchers," "eugenicists," for example, in the scholarly genres; "experts," "officials," or "business leaders" in other genres. So our example, in a "group-speaker" form, could be rewritten:

> Interviewees report that the expression of regret is a key factor in friendships.

When statements are presented as reported speech in any of these forms, their quality as knowledge is indicated: the statement has been produced—somewhere. At first it may appear that, in the scholarly gen-res, to present a statement as coming from a position other than that of the present speaker may implicitly affirm that the statement is true: "this is not just my idea." But, as we saw in Chapter 6 ("Orchestrating Voices"), things are more complicated than this. Statements are reported not simply to ensure that only true things get down on paper. Writers also report statements to establish common ground, to identify an ongo-ing debate, or to sketch a community of speakers producing knowledge in a particular area. Reported statements produce a map of that knowl-edge domain. And a main concern of scholarly writers, as we will see, is to locate themselves on that map—maybe close to some speakers, or far away from others, maybe starting in densely populated locales where a lot has been said, but heading out into sparsely settled regions from which few statements have been transmitted so far.

We have called the baseline case of reported speech "*x* says *y*," but we have not said much about the many verbs that scholars use in place of "says." In variations on our example, we used a variety of verbs, includ-ing *suggest, assume,* and *argue* (all of which we also turned into nouns). Although we might use any of these in reporting the speech of our friends, they by no means exhaust the range of reporting verbs that aca-demic writers use, and many of the reporting verbs we use in everyday life (*express,* for instance, or *feel* or *portray*) almost never appear among the terms scholars use to report previous research. In Chapter 3, we noted the importance of choosing verbs that characterize the action of the original, such as *state, propose, suggest, maintain, claim.* Associated with verbs of speech is a set of verbs we could call "knowledge-making." Among the knowledge-making verbs, we find words like *analyze, investigate, exam-ine, discover, find, identify, observe.*

Analyzing shopping opportunities, Smith (2000) **found** that bargains were available.

Like the verbs of speech, these verbs can be turned into nouns, as in

Analysis of shopping opportunities has led to the **identification** of bargains (Smith 2000).

Where a range of wordings presents choices, the different choices tend to be associated with different functions. So, in everyday speech, to use *claim* as a reporting verb may in some situations have the effect of discrediting the statement, or at least suggesting that it needs review.

THOMAS to MARK: Well, Matthew claims to have found bargains.

It is not clear whether *claim*—as just one example—works the same way to express doubt in scholarly writing. But research has found some correlation between the choice of reporting verb and the position of the writer vis-à-vis the sources reported, with terms like *demonstrate* expressing greater confidence than, say, *speculate* or *suggest*.

Choice of reporting verb can also be influenced by the discipline in which the writer is working. In his study of citation practices in eight disciplines (molecular biology, magnetic physics, marketing, applied linguistics, philosophy, sociology, mechanical engineering, and electronic engineering), Ken Hyland (1999) found diversity in reporting expressions used. For example, marketing is distinctive for its "particularly high degree of author tentative verbs, with *suggest* accounting for over half of all instances" (350); philosophy and marketing are more likely than the other disciplines in the sample to name the cited author outside parenthetical references (358–59); physics favours the reporting verbs *develop, report, study*, while sociology prefers *argue, suggest, describe, note, analyze, discuss*. In the sample, none of the science papers used direct quotation (348). Hyland suggests that part of what people learn when they become part of a research community is a discipline-specific understanding of how scholarly work is organized, and how knowledge is made. Techniques for reporting the speech of others display this understanding.

Exercise 2

Examine the following samples of scholarly writing, which report the statements of others. Identify the extent to which the samples illustrate the range of expression and function described above: the summoning of the voices of others to gesture to an important issue or established line of research; the variation between direct and indirect speech; the naming, obscuring, or typifying of other speakers; the characterization of the production of statements with various words for speaking and/or making knowledge.

From these limited data, can you generalize your results? What do you notice about the reporting of statements in scholarly prose? Can you see any correlation between the features you identify and the disciplines in which the writers are working?

PASSAGE 1

In the second paradigm, gender is construed as a global personality construct. The concepts of masculinity, femininity and androgyny exemplify this approach (see, e.g., Archer, 1989; Cook, 1985; Morawski, 1987). In reviewing the literature concerning the sex-differences and the gender-as-a-personality-construct approaches, Deaux and Kite (1987) come to the following conclusion: "The scientific record on questions of sex differences, based on either biological or psychological distinctions, is shaky at best [...]. Yet despite evidence of considerable overlap and situational specificity of gender-related behaviors, beliefs in sex differences are held tenaciously" (p. 97).

Researchers adopting the third and most recent approach conceive of gender as a social category, that is, as a category on which perceivers base judgements, inferences and social actions. The central research issue here is not "how men and women actually differ, but how people think that they differ" (Deaux, 1984, p. 110).

Eckes 1994: 107–08.

PASSAGE 2

Many commentators on post-war Britain have suggested that the workforce and its unions must accept a large part of the responsibility for the country's continuing economic ills. British workers may or may not have been unusually strike prone, but they have certainly long colluded, it is believed, in a range of restrictive practices on the shopfloor, thus increasing costs, curtailing output and drastically limiting the scope for necessary industrial modernisation. As the distinguished Anglo-German academic Ralf Dahrendorf has recently put it, working people in Britain have tended to "stretch their work so that it begins to look like leisure."[1] In this situation, the inevitable consequence has been economic stagnation.

Over the following pages we aim to challenge this view and demonstrate that restrictive practices of this type have been nowhere near as common or serious as some have argued.

Note

1   R. Dahrendorf, *On Britain* (1982) p. 46.

Nick Tiratsoo and Jim Tomlinson 1994 "Restrictive practices on the shopfloor in Britain, 1946–60: Myth and reality." *Business History* 36 (2): 65–84, 65.

PASSAGE 3

Results are less conclusive for species richness than for abundance, with fewer studies reporting statistically meaningful comparisons of clear-cuts to older stands for multiple species. Petranka et al. (1993, 1994) found significantly fewer amphibian species on clear-cut plots in the southern Appalachians (approximately one half and one third of the richness of mature stands at high and moderate elevations, respectively). Similarly, for a community of stream amphibians in western Oregon, Corn and Bury (1989) reported that only 1 of 20 (5%) streams in logged stands contained all four of the species studied versus 11 of 23 (47.8%) streams in uncut forests. However, Raphael (1991) found no significant differences in patterns of richness between clear-cut and older seral stages, while several others found differences in species composition after cutting and a trend toward greater species richness on control plots (Bury 1983; Enge and Marion 1986; Corn and Bury 1991; but see Pais et al. 1988); these differences were not statistically significant. Finally, a review of the raw data presented by authors that did not explicitly test for differences reveals nearly identical richness values for clear-cut versus control stands (Bury and Corn 1988a; Foley 1994; Phelps and Lancia 1995).

Phillip G. deMaynadier and Malcolm L. Hunter, Jr. 1995 "The relationship between forest management and amphibian ecology: A review of the North American literature." *Environmental Review* 3: 230–261, 235.

Exercise 3

The distinctive appearance of the following is characteristic of publications in history. Describe the ways in which it departs from what we have come to regard as typical of scholarly introductions. Describe the distinct ways this writer establishes the generalities that frame research contributions.

In October 1888 the Colonial Office expressed deep disquiet at news that an officer of the Gold Coast Constabulary, Inspector Akers, while involved on an expedition to subdue Krepi, had inflicted harsh sentences of flogging upon men under his command who were accused of attempting to strike an NCO, drunkenness and cowardice. The nine accused Hausa constables were flogged publicly before the whole force, the worst offender receiving 72 lashes. Both the method of flogging and the number of lashes given were extremely severe and contrary to the standing orders of the Constabulary. In an enquiry that consumed a considerable amount of Colonial Office time and paper, the matter was thoroughly investigated and Akers, an officer with "many good qualities" but "having a violent and hasty temper," was invalided home.[1]

European use of physical violence, even excessive violence, against African subordinates was not particularly unusual in the late nineteenth and early twentieth centuries. However, the Akers case, coming less than ten years after flogging had been abolished in the British Army, marks an approximate point at which the Colonial Office began to exercise concern, and seek to regulate, the extent and severity of officially sanctioned corporal punishment inflicted on African soldiers and also labour. A discussion of official and colonial attitudes to the use of corporal punishment in British Africa is a large subject and beyond the compass of a brief article. What is attempted here is much more manageable: a discussion of the attempts by the Colonial Office, over a period of more than sixty years, first to regulate more closely and then to bring to an end corporal punishment in the African Colonial Forces. Colonial Office officials were agreed on the need to regulate corporal punishment; those advocating abolition steadily increased with the progress of the century. Both regulators and reformers in London had to contend with military officers and colonial administrators who argued that corporal punishment was necessary for the control and discipline of African troops, especially when on active service, and the steady pressure from various humanitarian lobbies in Britain denouncing severe practices in the colonies.

Note

1 Public Record Office, Kew [PRO], CO96/197/3064, 31 Dec. 1888; and CO96/197/3080, Griffith to Knutsford, conf., 30 Nov. 1888.

David Killingray 1994 "The 'rod of empire': The debate over corporal punishment in the British African colonial forces, 1888–1946." *Journal of African History* 35: 201–16, 201.

8C Documentation

Reporting expressions—direct and indirectly reported speech of other speakers, and the echoes of reporting in the nominalized style we have been considering—summon a community of voices and position the present writer amongst them. But as we know, these expressions are only part of the system that situates research amidst other research. These reporting expressions are linked to systems of documentation—footnotes, endnotes, References and Works Cited.

It is also well known that styles of documentation vary from discipline to discipline. Genre theory tells us that differing documentation practices relate to differences in the particular communities that produce them—divergent beliefs about what kinds of reported speech are most useful and what kinds of information need to be emphasized. Most disciplines in the humanities and social sciences use some variation on a system of parenthetical expressions in the body of the text which are keyed to an alphabetical list at the end. For example, the name of each writer (each source) listed at the end of this sentence—

> The idea of using assessment as a lever for school change is not a new one: many accountability tools in the 1970s and 1980s tried to link policy decisions to test scores (Linn, 1987; Madaus, 1985; Wise, 1979).

—signals an entry in a list called References at the end of the text:

> Linn, R.L. (1987). Accountability: The comparison of education systems and the quality of test results. *Educational policy* 1 (2), 181–198.
>
> Madaus, G., West, M.M., Harmon, M.C., Lomax, R.G., and Viator, K.A. (1992). *The influence of testing on teaching math and science in grades 4–12.* Chestnut Hill, MA: Boston College Center for the Study of Testing, Evaluation, and Educational Policy.
>
> Madaus, G.F. (1985). "Can we help dropouts? Thinking about the undoable." In G. Natriello (Ed.), *School dropouts: Patterns and policies* (pp. 3–19). New York: Teachers College Press.

The parenthetical "(Linn, 1987)" sends the reader to the first entry above, while "(Madaus, 1985)" sends the reader to the third rather than the second entry under "Madaus." (If Madaus had two entries, both by himself only and both from 1985, the writer could have distinguished them as "1985a" and "1985b.")

While documentation systems vary in detail, they all operate to achieve one principal effect: the reader's easy movement from the body of the text to the full documentation in the References or Works Cited pages. Let's compare the above example from a journal in education to the following passage, the first sentence of a study of how meerkats learn, published in a scientific journal:

> It is widely agreed that scientific endeavours to understand the evolutionary roots of human culture require knowledge of the extent to which the social transmission of information in human and non-human societies relies on homologous mechanisms [1], [2], [3].

Here, instead of clusters of names and dates, we find numbers that that direct the reader to entries in a reference list that includes (as is increasingly the case with online publications) links to electronically published studies:

1. Galef BGJ (1992) The question of animal culture. Human Nature 3: 157–178. doi: 10.1007/bf02692251
•View Article •PubMed/NCBI •Google Scholar

2. Tomasello M (1994) The Question of Chimpanzee Cultures. Chimpanzee Cultures. Cambridge: Harvard University Press. 301–317.
•View Article •PubMed/NCBI •Google Scholar

3. Laland KN, Galef BGJ (2009) editors (2009) The Question of Animal Culture. Cambridge: Harvard University Press.

Will Hoppitt, Jamie Samson, Kevin N. Laland, Alex Thornton (2012) "Identification of learning mechanisms in a wild meerkat population." *PLoS ONE* 7 (8): 1–11.

As later references in the study make clear, this documentation system relies on numbering studies in the order they are cited rather than alphabetizing by author: "This is consistent with recent empirical findings suggesting that, contrary to common assumption [31], social learning need not lead to within-group homogeneity [5], [12],[36]" (6).

Variation in systems of documentation can be found both in styles of reporting, in the body of texts, and in styles of listing, at the end of texts. Yet, despite differences in the ordering of information, documentation provides three important items of information: the name of writer, the title of the work, and publishing information necessary to distinguish the publication from all other publications. Making arrangements for the readers' easy movement from the body of the text to the full documentation is part of the writer's larger orchestration of the scholarly conversation. Most obviously, it enables readers—if they choose—to find the source in a library or elsewhere, read it, and join the conversation themselves.

Less obviously but equally important, the full documentation provides more information about the circumstances under which the cited statement was produced. A reader who may not in fact get the original and read it can still find relevant information about the conditions of the statement's production: Did the cited statement appear in a book or an article? If it was in a book, was it a chapter in a collected edition? Who edited the book? If it was an article, in what journal did it appear? What was the title of the book or chapter or article (i.e., how did it announce what it was about)? And, most important, when was the statement produced?

Exercise 4

The following passages are taken from introductions of research articles in various disciplines. In each case, examine the format of the in-text references to see what they suggest about how the discipline constructs knowledge. For instance, are different forms of in-text reference associated with different patterns of reported speech? Why do you think one passage uses page numbers, while two of the others use dates? Why does one passage use numbered references only, eliminating all other bibliographic detail?

From a medical study of Alzheimer's by Ute Dreses-Werringloer et al., published in *Cell*:

> Alzheimer's disease (AD) is a progressive neurodegenerative disorder characterized by a massive loss of neurons in several brain regions and by the presence of cerebral senile plaques comprised of aggregated amyloid-β (Aβ) peptides (Mattson, 2004, Selkoe, 2001). The first atrophy observed in the AD brain occurs in the medial temporal lobe, which includes the hippocampus, and is the result of a massive synaptic degeneration and neuronal death (Braak et al., 1991, de Leon et al., 2007).

From a study of language instruction by Margaret Early and Sondra Marshall, in *The Canadian Modern Language Review*:

> As is commonly known, for two decades now there have been rapidly growing numbers of students from ethnically, culturally, and linguistically diverse backgrounds flowing into classrooms in English-speaking countries around the world (Mohan, Leung, & Davison, 2001). Their presence creates both educational opportunities and challenges for students and educators alike. However, tracking studies conducted in Canada (Eddy, 1999; Derwing, DeCorby, Ichikawa, & Jamieson, 1999; Gunderson, 2004, 2007; Watt & Roessingh, 1994, 2001) all conclude that educational institutions need to do more to seize the opportunities and

overcome the challenges created by the presence of these students, since currently, high school graduation remains an elusive goal for an unacceptably high percentage of students for whom English is a second language (ESL).

From a study of climate change by Michiel M. Helsen et al., published in *Science*:

The Antarctic Ice Sheet is constantly adjusting its mass in response to changes in the accumulation of snow on its surface, which occur on centennial to millennial time scales (*1*), with a concomitant effect on global sea level. Although most coupled general circulation models predict the mass of the interior of the Antarctic Ice Sheet to grow in a warmer climate (*2, 3*), no clear trend has been found there over the past half century (*3, 4*).

From an essay on historical fiction by Kim Wilson, in *Children's Literature Association Quarterly*:

While many authors of historical fiction will admit they have evoked the power of imagination to write their story, they will also claim the work's reliance on and fidelity to historical facts. Ann Rinaldi claims she writes about real life (McGlinn), Nadia Wheatley confidently asserts the history recounted in her books is real ("History Alive"), William Durbin is doing his "best to depict the past as authentically as [he] can" ("William Durbin" 25) and Goldie Alexander—like all of the preceding authors—identifies sources of information to establish the authenticity of her tale ("Fictionalising History" 20). While the diaries are certainly understood to be fictional accounts of historical events, they are also declared as legitimate and "truthful" because they are based on real events. By connecting events of the diaries to real events or people outside the story, the ideas and values expressed by the author will accordingly be imbued with that prized epithet—"truth." Perry Nodelman writes in "History as Fiction" that by "denying its fictionality" history is "particularly effective as propaganda: acceptance of its truthfulness allows readers to absorb the meanings and values it contains" (72).

Exercise 5

Below are four samples of entries from reference pages at the end of articles in scholarly journals. Inspect these samples to determine the points at which they are similar and at which they vary (e.g., punctuation, use of capitals, order of information, and so on). How do scholars document a source that is (a) an article in a journal? (b) a book? (c) a chapter in a book? (d) an article in a book? What correlations do you see between the features you identify and the disciplines in which the writers are working?

From a Works Cited list in *PMLA* (a literary-critical journal, Publications of the Modern Language Association of America):

Ganapathy-Doré, Geetha. "Fathoming Private Woes in a Public Story: A Study of Michael Ondaatje's Anil's Ghost." *Jouvert* 6.3 (2002): n. pag. Web. 10 Apr. 2013.

Goldman, Marlene. "Representations of Buddhism in Ondaatje's Anil's Ghost." *Comparative Literature and Culture* 6.3 (2004): n. pag. Web. 10 Apr. 2013.

Guha, Ranajit. "Chandra's Death." *Subaltern Studies* 5 (1987): 135–65. Print.

Hoole, Rajan. *Sri Lanka: Arrogance of Power: Myths, Decadence and Murder.* Jaffna: University Teachers for Human Rights, 2001. Print.

Horowitz, Donald L. *Deadly Ethnic Riot.* Berkeley: U of California P, 2003. Print.

Mrinalini Chakravorty 2013 "The dead that haunt *Anil's Ghost*: Subaltern difference and postcolonial melancholia." *PMLA* 128 (3): 542–58, 557.

From a References list in *Language and Communication*:

Lo, A., Kim, J.C., 2012. Linguistic competency and citizenship: contrasting portraits of multilingualism in the South Korean popular media. Journal of Sociolinguistics 16 (2), 255–276.

Maira, S., 2004. Youth culture, citizenship and globalization: South Asian Muslim youth in the United States after September 11th. Comparative Studies of South Asia and the Middle East 24 (1), 219–231.

Mangual Figueroa, A., 2013. ¡Hay que hablar!: Testimonio in the everyday lives of migrant mothers. Language & Communication 33, 559–572.

Marshall, T.H., 1950. Citizenship and Social Class. Cambridge University Press, Cambridge.

Milani, T.M., 2008. Language testing and citizenship: a language ideological debate in Sweden. Language in Society 37 (1), 27–59.

Jennifer F. Reynolds and Elaine W. Chun 2013 "Figuring youth citizenship: Communicative practices mediating the cultural politics of citizenship and age." *Language and Communication* 33 (4): 473–80, 480.

From a References list in the *American Journal of Economics and Sociology*:

Krantz-Kent, R. (2009). "Measuring Time Spent in Unpaid Household Work: Results from the American Time Use Survey." *Monthly Labor Review* July: 46–59.

Lempert, P. (2007). "The 5-Minute Shopping List." Online. http://supermarketguru.com/page.cfm/355. (Accessed 26 February 2007).

Mayo, J. (1993). *The American Grocery Store*. Westport, CT: Greenwood Press.

McTaggart, J. (2005). "Diversified Investment." *Progressive Grocer* 84(9): 44–51.

Merchant, C. (1980). *The Death of Nature: Women, Ecology, and the Scientific Revolution*. San Francisco: Harper and Row Publishers.

Milkman, R., and E. Townsley. (1994). "Gender and the Economy." In *The Handbook of Economic Sociology*. Eds. Neil J. Smelser and Richard Swedberg, pp. 600–619. Princeton, NJ: Princeton University Press.

Shelley L. Koch and Joey Sprague 2014 "Economic sociology vs. real life: The case of grocery shopping." *American Journal of Economics and Sociology* 73 (1): 237–63, 261.

From a References list in *Genetic, Social, and General Psychology Monographs*:

Chassel, L. M. (1916). Test for originality. *Journal of Educational Psychology, 7,* 317–329.

Clapham, M. M. (2004). The convergent validity of the Torrance tests of creative thinking and creativity interest inventories. *Educational and Psychological Measurement, 64,* 828–841.

Claridge, G. (1997). *Schizotypy: Implications for illness and health.* Oxford, England: Oxford University Press.

Cohen, J. (1988). *Statistical power analysis for the behavioral sciences* (2nd ed.). Hillsdale, NJ: Erlbaum.

Colvin, S. S. (1902). Invention versus form in English composition. *Pedagogical Seminar, 9,* 393–421.

Mark Batey and Adrian Furnham 2006 "Creativity, intelligence, and personality: A critical review of the scattered literature." *Genetic, Social, and General Psychology Monographs* 132 (4): 355–429, 415.

From a References list in *Neurology*:

1. Wood-Kaczmar A, Gandhi S, Wood NW: **Understanding the molecular causes of Parkinson's disease.** *Trends Mol Med* 2006, **12:**521–528.

2. Kamel F, Tanner C, Umbach D, Hoppin J, Alavanja M, Blair A, Comyns K, Goldman S, Korell M, Langston J, Ross G, Sandler D: **Pesticide exposure and self-reported Parkinson's disease in the agricultural health study.** *Am J Epidemiol* 2007, **165:**364–374.

3. Frigerio R, Sanft KR, Grossardt BR, Peterson BJ, Elbaz A, Bower JH, Ahlskog JE, De Andrade M, Maraganore DM, Rocca WA: **Chemical exposures and Parkinson's disease: a population-based case-control study.** *Mov Disord* 2006, **21:**1688–1692.

4. Ascherio A, Chen H, Weisskopf MG, O'Reilly E, McCullough ML, Calle EE, Schwarzchild MA, Thun MJ: **Pesticide exposure and risk for Parkinson's disease.** *Ann Neurol* 2006, **60:**197–203.

5. Baldi I, Lebailly P, Mohammed-Brahim B, Letenneur L, Dartigues JF, Brochard P: **Neurodegenerative disease and exposure to pesticides in the elderly.** *Am J Epidemiol* 2003, **157:**409–414.

Dana B. Hancock, Eden R. Martin, Gregory M. Mayhew, Jeffrey H. Stajich, Rita Jewett, Mark A. Stacy, Burton L. Scott, Jeffrey M. Vance, and William K. Scott 2008 "Pesticide exposure and risk of Parkinson's disease: A family-based case-control study." *BMC Neurology* 8: 6.

8D State of Knowledge and the Knowledge Deficit

Investigating the role of reported speech in getting the scholarly discussion under way, we observed that, when statements are presented as issuing not from the present writer but from other writers, they include an implicit comment on their status as knowledge. They were produced by someone; they came from a site in the research community. If we take this perspective on scholarly statements, we can see reported speech as mapping a set of positions in the territory of knowledge producers. We have used the term *state of knowledge* to name this mapping activity: the ways a writer indicates what is known by researchers, the limits of knowledge, the conditions under which knowledge was produced, and the positions from which statements issue. And we used the term *knowledge deficit* to talk about how writers can identify what hasn't been said, what needs to be said. These indicators occur throughout a given piece of scholarly writing, but they often appear in a compressed form in introductions.

The state of knowledge in compressed form should be familiar because we have examined several examples already. Here is another example:

> There have been several well-conducted efforts to understand childhood disorders of emotion in terms of distinct and meaningful components (e.g., Fox and Houston, 1983; Ollendick and Yule, 1990; Papy, Costello, Hedl, and Spielberger, 1975). In particular, several investigators have found considerable overlap between the constructs of anxiety and depression (e.g., Lonigan, Carey, and Finch, 1994; Norvell, Brophy, and Finch, 1985; Tannenbaum, Forehand, and McCombs-Thomas, 1992; Wolfe et al., 1987) and have suggested a higher order construct of negative affect (Watson and Clark, 1984). Although the evidence for this relation is compelling, the latent structure of childhood negative emotions is only beginning to be conceptualized in detail (e.g., Joiner, Catanzaro, and Laurent, 1996).

Bruce F. Chorpita, Anne Marie Albano, and David H. Barlow 1998 "The structure of negative emotions in a clinical sample of children and adolescents." *Journal of Abnormal Psychology* 107 (1): 74–85, 74.

In this passage, Chorpita et al. provide a summary of certain research activities. You will notice that the overall pattern begins by identifying the area of study ("childhood disorders" in terms of "components"). It then focuses on a type of finding (the "overlap" of "anxiety and depression") and how it has been interpreted (a "higher order construct of negative affect"). Following this, some caution is expressed ("childhood negative emotions" are "only beginning to be conceptualized"). At each step, these research activities are located by way of parenthetical citation that usually names more than one research publication. Without advancing an explicit position or comment of their own, Chorpita et al. have told the story of the research that precedes their own. They have created a map on which we might expect they will locate their own work.

One way researchers can locate themselves on the map is by claiming to add to existing knowledge: a space that has been recognized as unoccupied or only tentatively claimed gets filled up with a claim based on new data or further reasoning. Sometimes the space has not yet been recognized: it has gone unnoticed by others. Another way scholars get title to a position on the map is to evict the current occupant: they show that previously established knowledge cannot hold that ground because it is faulty or incomplete in some way.

In making moves on the knowledge map, the writer identifies a knowledge deficit. There is something we don't know, some space on the map where there is a gap, a spot where no one has so far settled to take careful account of the place. Or there can be some error in what is held to be true. The only way such a deficit can be identified is through a review of what is known, or taken to be known. Reported speech—the whole practice of citation and summary—*is used to establish the deficit in relation to published research.* On the one hand, reported speech provides a positive rationale for the current writer to speak, because it shows that the research community is already talking about an issue. On the other hand, by allowing the current writer to respond to a deficit, reported speech provides a negative rationale by indicating why the discussion so far is not complete.

When the current writer first responds to a knowledge deficit, we can expect to find a distinct change in style of expression. The writer might make an appearance, using expressions like "I think" or "I suspect" to indicate limitations to the current state of knowledge. We will call this use of the first-person pronoun, which signals the presence of the writer in the capacity of researcher, the **discursive *I***. We will look more closely at this phenomenon in Chapter 11. **Modalized** expressions—words like "seems" or "could" that express reservations or uncertainty—may also emerge, overtaking reporting expressions and sometimes appearing alongside the discursive *I*. These features typically point to the current study's **research question**—a question, sometimes implied but sometimes explicit, that the writer addresses in order to expand or correct the state of knowledge.

One such indication of the research question can be found in writers' formal statements of their **hypothesis**: the statement which is deemed plausible, but which is, so far, untested and will be shown to be tested in the course of the article. Modalized expressions show up in statements such as this one:

> Two main hypotheses are addressed in this study: (1) that unidentified and untreated learning difficulties **may** be related to teenage girls becoming pregnant, deciding to raise their children, and dropping out of school, and (2) that teenage pregnancies **may** *not* be characteristically "unintended."
>
> Rauch-Elnekave 1994: 92 (italic emphasis in original, bold emphasis added).

But many research publications do not specify the hypothesis in this way, and still make use of **modal expressions** and the discursive *I*. So rather than attach these features simply to the hypothesis, it may be better to locate them in the larger process of constructing a knowledge deficit. Here we spot them showing up as a writer poses his research question about "low ability" classes where "high quality instruction fosters significant learning among students":

> What characterizes such phrases? To address this question, **I draw** on evidence from earlier studies by other authors, and **I provide** two new illustrations taken from a larger study of eighth- and ninth-grade English classes in 25 midwestern schools. Although these examples are far from conclusive, common elements emerge that, taken together, **may** help to characterize effective instruction in low ability classes in secondary schools.
>
> Adam Gamoran 1993 "Alternative uses of ability grouping in secondary schools: Can we bring high-quality instruction to low-ability classes?" *American Journal of Education* 102: 1–22, 2 (emphasis added).

The question identifies an as-yet unoccupied location on the knowledge map: we don't know what goes on in these classes. Plotting his approach to this space, the writer moves speculatively. Conceding the limits of the evidence available to him, he says his work "may help" to make this unknown area known. Compare the unmodalized, unqualified version of the same statement:

> Common elements emerge that characterize effective instruction in low ability classes in secondary schools.

The unmodalized version may actually be more in keeping with the traditions of the schoolroom essay. Students are often advised to take a stand, state their opinion, be decisive in their writing. And as readers of print or digital news, we expect editorial writers and columnists to take a decisive stand. Yet in scholarly writing, where knowledge is laboriously constructed, the modalized version is more typical. Scholarly statements leave traces of their sources and their status. To identify the knowledge deficit, the writer of the above example must show that the current state of knowledge (called "this view" below) is inadequate.

> According to this view, observed differences among studies in the effects of grouping are due to chance; taken together, the studies indicate that no real effects on achievement exist. Another interpretation **seems** equally **plausible**. The inconsistent findings may have resulted from uncontrolled differences in the way ability grouping was implemented in the various school systems under investigation.
>
> Gamoran 1993: 3–4 (emphasis added).

In moving to show that a published view from a respected source comes up short, and leaves the state of knowledge in this area unfinished, the writer does not simply deny the view ("This interpretation is wrong"). He doesn't even say that another interpretation "is equally plausible," or "more plausible." It only "*seems* equally plausible." And the reinterpretation is itself modalized: "inconsistent findings *may* have resulted from uncontrolled differences" rather than "inconsistent findings resulted from uncontrolled differences."

Exercise 6

The samples in the exercise below show two distinct ways that writers identify knowledge deficits. Inspect these passages and identify the ways in which each one establishes the writer's (or writers') right to speak positively (i.e., by connecting the present work with established concerns) and negatively (i.e., by identifying a knowledge deficit).

PASSAGE 1

In this article, we examine the cultural categories and the conceptual logic that underlie the orthography debates about kreyòl that have taken place over the last 50 years. In Haiti, as in many countries concerned with nation building, the development of an orthography for vernacular literacy has been neither a neutral activity nor simply about how to mechanically reduce a spoken language to written form. The processes of transforming a spoken language to written form have often been viewed as scientific, arbitrary, or unproblematic. However, the creation of supposedly arbitrary sound/sign (signified/signifier) relationships that constitute an orthography always involves choices based on someone's idea of what is important. This process of representing the sounds of language in written form is thus an activity deeply grounded in frameworks of value.

Shieffelin and Doucet 1994: 176.

PASSAGE 2

In many ways, the influenza pandemic of 1918–19 is the "forgotten" epidemic; forgotten, at least, by scholars studying British Columbia's First Nations. Much attention has been paid to the timing and severity of late eighteenth- and early nineteenth-century epidemics for what they tell us about the proto-historic and early contact culture and population change. Scholars have argued the significance of these epidemics in softening up indigenous societies for the onslaught of colonization. Few, however, have examined later disease patterns for what they tell us about the nature of cross-cultural relations in the early twentieth century.

Mary-Ellen Kelm 1999 "British Columbia First Nations and the influenza pandemic of 1918–19." *BC Studies* 122 (Summer): 23–47, 23–24.

PASSAGE 3

My conclusions on morphology have led to a reconstruction which differs in many important respects from all earlier ones. There was not one pair of eyes, but two pairs on short stalks and a median eye. The frontal process was not an eversible proboscis, the anterior part of the alimentary canal was U-shaped, and the mouth backward facing. The gill appendage was not trilobite-like, and was situated dorsally to the lateral lobe of the trunk. Therefore I reject the view, maintained since Walcott's work, that *o. regalis* was an arthropod, either an anostracan brachiopod or a trilobitoid. It was a segmented animal perhaps descended from a group ancestral to some arthropod phyla and/or annelids, a reminder of how little we know of the evolution of such creatures.

H.B. Whittington 1971 "The enigmatic animal *Opabinia regalis*, middle Cambrian, Burgess Shale, British Columbia." *Philosophical Transactions of the Royal Society, London*, 3.

8E Student Versions of the Knowledge Deficit

As a student writer, you may be reluctant to say that nobody has ever studied this before, or that everybody has got it wrong so far. But, with some adjustments, you can still replicate the move which identifies a knowledge deficit. Consider the following example from a scholarly article:

> There are several studies which have analyzed the discourse functions of quotation. Some researchers have analyzed languages other than English (e.g., Larson 1978; Besnier 1986; Glock 1986). Others have analyzed English, but most did not examine discourse samples to determine if their analyses are actually supported by data (e.g., Wierzbicka 1974; Halliday 1985; Li 1986; Haiman 1989). Additionally, these studies have not addressed the question of whether direct quotations are really quotations. In other words, how authentic are direct quotes? Do they represent actual previous utterances, or are they inventions of the speaker? This paper focuses on these questions as well as on the functions of quotation in informal spoken English. Unlike these other studies, my analysis is based on discourse samples.
>
> Patricia Mayes 1990 "Quotation in Spoken English." *Studies in Language* 14 (2): 325–63, 326.

A student writer could recast this knowledge deficit to show that there is something interesting to be found out:

Although speakers often resort to sayings they attribute to other speakers, and listeners accept these sayings as appropriate elements of conversation and other speech genres, we might still ask what role such quotations play in these speech acts. What conditions motivate speakers to repeat others' claims? Is the repetition exact or approximate? authentic or fictionalized? In short, how and why do we represent our own speech as originating with someone else?

Or it could be recast to mark the writer's position in relation to one other speaker (instead of seven):

Halliday (1985) provides a useful account of the functional grammar of reported speech, but his analyses do not explain the role of quotation in conversation and other speech acts. What conditions motivate speakers to repeat others' claims?

That is, where a professional version of the statement of the knowledge deficit would summarize many (if not all) published claims about a research entity, the student version can summarize one or two.

In some situations, student projects may cite no other speaker. In those cases, the introduction can instead propose plausible ideas about the object of inquiry and then show that these ideas, reasonable as they seem, are problematic: they leave some questions unanswered. The example below in effect invokes possible statements about the object of inquiry, bringing these statements into a kind of conversation with one another, and allowing a question to emerge from this conversation.

As For Me and My House can be read as a system of concealment: Mrs. Bentley skips days at a time, shifts her focus suddenly to the weather, offers little information about her own background while she relentlessly exposes her husband's personal history. Yet the idea of concealment suggests an audience—and *As For Me and My House* is represented as a diary, a genre which assumes no audience but the writer herself. If the narrative is indeed a pattern of withholdings, how can we reconcile this condition with the book's generic presuppositions about audience? From whom is the missing information being concealed? Perhaps by revising the idea of concealment, and recasting it as a system of attention to painful matters, we can understand Mrs. Bentley's diary on its own terms, as a diligent, deliberate—and sometimes desperate—personal inquiry into the circumstances of her life.

You will see from these examples that a question tends to follow the problematizing activity, or the identification of a knowledge deficit.

For student writers and professional scholars alike, arrangements for speakers—those schemes of scholarly conversation we investigated in Chapter 6 using the term **orchestration**—can take the writer to the verge of a knowledge deficit, and incite questions. Engaging *speaker x* to *speaker y*, and summarizing the statements of each one, the writer arranges for a new exchange between these positions, and introduces the reader to a new scholarly contribution.

Exercise 7

Draft an introductory paragraph to an essay that you are working on for one of your classes. Briefly introduce two or three scholarly studies you have read by characterizing their approach to your topic. Position your own approach in relation to these sources by introducing the deficit that you will address or a question you will try to answer.

9

Readers Reading II

Chapter 5 put us in touch with our readers. The **think-aloud proto-col**, an alternative method of giving reader feedback, put us in hearing range of the reading process, and revealed that readers employ a variety of strategies for understanding while reading. We've seen that attitudes about language affect speakers' judgements about usage. And the particular context or circumstance for reading affects readers' expectations and reception of a written document. This chapter extends our study of readers by looking at various theories about reading and interpretation. Understanding readers' **social** and **cognitive responses** will help us draw a more accurate portrait of our readers; in turn, we'll become better predictors of their particular needs. To this end, we'll continue practising think-aloud protocols, and, in this chapter, learn to analyze and convert reader feedback into strategies for revision.

9A Think-Aloud and Genre Theory

Writers know—or get to know—how to write in ways that will satisfy a situation, and readers read in ways that include their recognition of a situation. Genre theory begins with this tendency: the mutual recognition of and responses to recurring types of **situations**. It's not rules and enforcements that make writing acceptable but *contact and familiarity* with recognizable instances. Genre theory finds the *regularities* (not rules) of writing in readers' and writers' *social experience*.

Think-aloud techniques coax out this readerly know-how. By focusing on readers' experience of reading—readers' efforts to understand—think-aloud articulates what would otherwise remain unspoken. The focus is on what works for readers, what they expect, rather than on what satisfies rules. If you, as a writer, receive think-aloud protocols from different readers, over time you will be able to identify occasions where readers typically have trouble, as well as those occasions where the trouble may be more or less idiosyncratic. Think-alouds also reveal both social and cognitive occasions for trouble. The following two examples of think-aloud illustrate the difference between a social response and a cognitive response.

The example below shows a scholarly reader stopping at an unqualified and unattributed generalization.

TEXT	READER THINKING ALOUD
For centuries, women had no alternative but to marry or go into religious orders.	*Well that might have been true in some cases but there were alternatives, a woman could become the housekeeper of a widowed father or brother for example, and different areas of Europe...*

The think-aloud response reveals a particular reader's position, which is conditioned by a particular experience in the world. This reader expects to find complexity, limitation, and openness to exceptions when she reads scholarly writing, expectations that typify writing in the research genres. Other readers—ones experienced in journalistic genres, for example—might not stop at all at this statement. Other social expectations would condition them to accept the generalization without hesitation.

How could the writer assist a reader who exhibits this sort of response? Perhaps simply acknowledging exceptions would help: e.g., "For centuries, women had *few* alternatives but to marry or go into religious orders." Or, perhaps, introducing reporting expressions and identifying the **generalization** as coming from a given researcher would help the reader see that the claim is part of a conversation. These changes would address social needs that arise out of the scholarly situation.

Sometimes, however, a reader might stop for reasons we could see as more *cognitive* than social—that is, a problem with understanding that would likely cause almost anybody to stop. The following example refers to an anthropological study of RVers that we looked at briefly in Chapter 3. As we noted then, RVers spend much of their year in recreational vehicles: motorhomes, truck-campers, trailers. In the original study, "boondockers," who park their recreational vehicles—usually for free and unofficially—on (US) federal lands, are distinguished from "private-park RVers," who stay in organized, commercial facilities. In the example below, a reader looks for connections between statements: a reason for the second sentence to appear in the context of the first.

TEXT	READER THINKING ALOUD
RVers have pot-luck dinners, and they exchange addresses before they hit the road again. "Private-park" RVers object to the way "boondockers" live.	*oh ... what's the connection between these statements? pot-luck and addresses, that sounds like friendliness, but then there are objections. Maybe the boondockers don't have pot-luck dinners? Is that why the private-park people object? Or maybe both types of RVers have rituals but they don't get together? Is that the contradiction here? I don't know. I need some help.*

Having no guide from the writer, the reader struggles on her own. This could be seen as a cognitive response—an unsuccessful attempt to understand why the writer is linking potlucks and addresses.

How could the writer of the example on RVers assist a reader with this sort of cognitive response? Research done in the early 1980s suggests that readers take cues from higher-level content in interpreting details, and in storing the meaning of those details (see Section 3B on levels of generality). The think-aloud response above indicates that a difficulty arises when the reader tries to understand the relation between details: address-exchange and pot-luck dinners seem positive, but objecting to how boondockers live seems negative. This cognitive need can be addressed by introducing abstractions that instruct the reader in how to use or relate the details.

> RVers have pot-luck dinners, and they exchange addresses before they hit the road again. **Yet this reciprocity occurs alongside stigmatization. For example**, "private-park" RVers object to the way "boondockers" live.

Now pot-luck dinners and address-exchange mean "reciprocity," and reciprocity is posed as at least partly conflicting with "stigmatization." The scholarly practices of abstraction we explored in earlier chapters are not just formalities: they have important cognitive functions as guides for readers, helping them relate details.

Understanding and anticipating readers' cognitive needs will be further explored in Section 9B below. But first, the social needs of readers warrant further study. In the example above of a social response involving the historical roles of women, the reader expresses concern based on the social expectation that academic writing will be careful about exceptions and qualifications. As we noted, this is not a response that all readers would have. Readers with different expectations may accept this sort of generalization. In this sense, the response is social and not exactly cognitive. But in the example involving the RVers, while the response is clearly cognitive—an attempt to understand how details relate to one another—the suggestion to use abstractions to help a reader seems to rely on social expectations. For example, a reader accustomed to journalistic rather than academic genres might pause over the abstractions "reciprocity" and "stigmatization."

As we have seen in Chapter 7 (Section 7D), abstractions have a social as well as a cognitive aspect. For instance, in the humanities and some social sciences, some abstractions enjoy more prestige than others; these abstractions seem to have an important role in the life of the discipline, as meanings are challenged and changed over time. By contrast, in the sciences and (again) in some social sciences, technical abstractions are often the product of collaborative effort amongst researchers; the circumstances in which they are used are widely agreed upon, and their meanings remain stable over time.

As useful as abstractions can be, not all genres call for them. We have seen that narrative may touch abstractions only intermittently, and in some cases not at all. Telephone books have high-level, generalizing titles—"Calgary," "San Diego"—and then plunge into details of names and addresses and phone numbers. How do people manage with genres like telephone books, when they seem to have trouble with mention of pot-luck dinners?

People using telephone books don't read, stop, and say "I'm having trouble with this. What's the connection here? What is this about?" They don't need high-level abstractions to guide their understanding of the details of names and addresses because they bring a question of their own to the page ("What's John Karamazov's phone number?"). The question provides a context for interpretation. Conversely, unless they are preparing for some RVing of their own and wondering whether to take lasagne ingredients, readers of "RVers have pot-luck dinners" may not have a ready-made context of interpretation for this statement.

One way of understanding the contexts of interpretation and understanding is to apply **relevance theory**. The conditions which make a statement understandable are described by linguists Sperber and Wilson (1986) as having to do with **relevance**. The term "relevance," in its everyday sense, is easy to grasp: someone might say, regarding mention of pot-luck dinners, "How is this relevant?" But for Sperber and Wilson, the term also measures *degrees* of relevance: a statement is relevant in inverse relation to the effort it takes to find the context in which it is meaningful. In other words, the more processing effort it takes a reader to find a context for interpretation, the less relevant the statement is for that reader. For example, in the following—

> JANE: John, what's your phone number?
> JOHN: 888-9999

—"888-9999" is highly relevant to Jane because the context—Jane's question—is immediately accessible. It takes very little effort for Jane to find this context. On the other hand, the reader who encountered mention of private-parkers' criticisms of boondockers in the context of mention of pot-luck dinners and address-exchange has to make a much bigger effort to discover a larger context in which the criticism is meaningful.

We can apply relevance theory to what we know about genre. Genres serve contexts which both reader and writer recognize, but this familiarity doesn't prevent apparent difficulties from arising as they did in the pot-luck dinner passage. Often the connection between adjacent statements—the relevance of one to the other—is not clear on the surface. In reference genres, like encyclopaedias or computer manuals, sentences next to each other can seem to bear only a general relation to one another. Here is an entry from *The Encyclopaedia of Aquarium Fish* for Brachygobius or "bumblebeefish":

> A native of Indian and south-east Asia. Has a yellow body with broad, vertical, dark brown or black bands. It is most at home and spends most of its time close to the bottom of the aquarium.

> David J. Coffey 1977 *The encyclopaedia of aquarium fishes in color.* New York: Arco, 70.

This is generally about the bumblebeefish, but what is the connection between the fish's origin, its appearance, and its favourite spot? Does the author mean to say that, *because* of its dark-striped yellow body, the fish lurks at the bottom? What does the fish's colour have to do with the bottom of the aquarium? However, most readers would not ask such questions. The social use of encyclopaedia genres is such that readers bring information requirements with them ("What's a bumblebeefish? I have to do a report for school"), and these requirements contribute to the context for interpretation of details.

I wonder why my bumblebee-fish stays at the bottom. Is it sick?

Oh. I see. It prefers the bottom. It's not sick.

So the reader's *context of understanding* makes the sentence, "It is most at home ... close to the bottom of the aquarium," relevant and meaningful. It has immediate contextual implications.

Abstractions can also be analyzed for their relevance. Some abstractions are poised at the thresholds of many easily accessible contexts in certain disciplines. They can operate powerfully to make details meaningful, although all abstractions, in academic contexts at any rate, probably contribute to relevance. In this sense, the writer responding to the reader's cognitive need to understand the connection between pot-luck dinners and boondockers uses the abstractions "reciprocity" and "stigmatization" and builds a transition between two apparently contradictory details. At the same time, the abstractions also signal relevance by providing a context in which the details are potentially meaningful.

Exercise 1
Working with a partner, read the following three passages aloud. As you read, stop and offer comments about what works for you as a reader, and what gives you difficulty. Offer also your expectations of the particular passage by drawing on your background experience,

or lack thereof, with the genre. Now analyze the think-aloud commentary. Are particular difficulties or successes in reading and understanding connected to

- prevailing rules for "correctness"?
- relative experience with the genre?
- cognitive needs?
- social expectations?

How might the writers of the respective passages revise in order to address your responses?

PASSAGE 1: AN ENCYCLOPAEDIA ENTRY
KOSOVO, small south central republic in what was YUGO-SLAVIA between MACEDONIA, SERBIA, and ALBANIA. Its 10,000 ha/24,700 acres of vineyards in spectacular inland mountain and valley settings are largely devoted to the production of Amselfelder branded wine for sale in Germany. Train-loads of light red are sent in bulk to Belgrade for STABILIZATION, sweetening, and shipment. The light aromatic fruit of the PINOT NOIR was certainly the inspiration behind this brand. CABERNET FRANC, MERLOT, PROKUPAC, and GAMAY are also part of the region's production.

Kosovo is a poor region and throughout the 1980s was heavily dependent on its exports of the Amselfelder range. This dependence became a serious liability when Yugoslav turmoil made the German importers realize how easily other eastern European vineyard areas could copy the style.

A.H.M.

Angela Muir 1994 "Kosovo." In *The Oxford Companion to Wine*, ed. Jancis Robinson. Oxford: Oxford UP, 542.

PASSAGE 2: THE BEGINNING OF A STUDENT ESSAY
With the rising popularity of social networking sites, selfie photography has become a defining form of self-expression among today's youth. This style of photography's popularity has exploded in recent years in correlation with the accessibility of the internet and availability of front facing camera smart phones, making it

possible to easily upload photos straight to social networking sites such as Myspace, Facebook, or Instagram. Their popularity is not only due to recent technological advancements, however. I have applied Jean Baudrillard's theories of hyperreality and simulacrum to my own understanding of selfies as a member of the generation that popularized this style of photography. In addition, I have found research examining the habits of college students on social networking sites, the most common environment to find selfies. As I will demonstrate, I have concluded that selfies are a cultural product of a generation of North American youth raised to value individualism in an environment that has experienced a contemporary societal shift to become a "culture of the simulacrum" (Storey, 193). Selfies simultaneously represent both subject and object: a declaration of identity and an endlessly reproduced image.

Greta Negrave 2013 "Selfie generation: Simulacrum of individuality." Research essay completed for Interdisciplinary Studies 100: Popular Culture and University Writing, Vancouver Island University.

PASSAGE 3: THE BEGINNING OF A STUDENT ESSAY
In Cameron's article (1995) she observes that improper grammar can cause people to make unfair or discriminatory judgements about the speakers or writers who make these errors. Attitudes towards language are often based on social prejudice: low-class people are condemned by members of the elite for being lazy and undisciplined. As Milroy and Milroy point out (1991), prejudices that would be unacceptable to express in any other context are acceptable in talking about grammar. (Milroy and Milroy 1991) Nevertheless, I believe that it is important for people to have the skills necessary to express themselves in ways that earn them the social respect they deserve.

9B The Mental Desktop

We will explore one more technique for composing our portrait of the reader. Derived from cognitive studies, this technique pictures the reader organizing a **mental desktop**: a space on which statements arrive, one after the other, as the reader advances through a text.

If your actual desktop is like many people's, it gets covered with piles of paper, and you end up paying attention only to what's on top—the most recently arrived material—until these pages themselves get covered by new arrivals. Reading can be like this, too, if what we are reading is very difficult for us: we concentrate on one sentence or a few sentences at a time. In the meantime, previous sentences are sometimes forgotten.

The reader's mental desktop is a finite area. It can't get bigger. In other words, the reader's attention span—or short-term memory—is inelastic. No matter how hard readers try (or how much you wish they would try), they can concentrate on only a relatively small number of things at a time. This is the way the human brain works. Writers have to learn to live with this inescapable condition of reading comprehension.

This small, inelastic space for paying attention may make the reader seem like a limited being, hardly worth addressing with an interesting paper. Moreover, the limitation does not match other qualities of our own reading experience: we read articles, chapters, books, and we have a sense of remembering a lot more than the handful of items that happened to be the last ones to pass across our mental desktop.

According to the theories behind the mental desktop image, readers manage their desktops—successfully under good circumstances, less successfully under other circumstances. Up to a certain point, it's the *writer rather than the reader* who is responsible for these circumstances.

To the picture of the reader and desktop we will add a **management device**. The management device arranges and uses mental space. The mental space is furnished with, in addition to the desktop, a sort of side-table for temporary storage, and filing cabinets for long-term storage. To manage the flow of information and make the most of it, the reader operates the management device to assign statements to these different mental spaces. The reader operates the device to detect the following:

1) items that can be combined; 2) items that can be put aside for the moment; 3) items that can be neglected; and 4) items that can be sent into long-term memory.

To illustrate how readers can manage their mental desktops, let's consider the following passage.

ASIAN CORPORATIONS

Corporate growth—the development of multiunit firms—can be explained in terms of business response to the conditions of industrialized markets. According to Chandler (1977), when markets grow, businesses need to develop efficient systems of management to handle increased volume and coordinate multiple activities. Another theory also explains corporate development in industrial economies in terms of the market: as the number of transactions increases in the process of transforming raw materials into market goods, uncertainty increases (Williamson 1977, 1981, 1983, 1985). To reduce uncertainty, businesses grow, internalizing transactions and thereby governing them more reliably. These explanations of corporate development, however, do not fully account for corporate growth in Japan and South Korea, where prevailing organizational structures predate industrialization.

The Japanese economy is dominated by large, powerful, and relatively stable enterprise groups. One type of enterprise group consists of horizontal linkages among a range of large firms; these are intermarket groups spread through different industrial sectors. A second type of enterprise group connects small- and medium-sized firms to a large firm. These networks are normally groups of firms in unrelated businesses that are joined together by central banks or by trading companies. In pre-war Japan, these groups were linked by powerful holding companies that were each under the control of a family. The zaibatsu families exerted strict control over the individual firms in their group through a variety of fiscal and managerial methods. During the US occupation, the largest of these holding companies were dissolved, with the member firms of each group becoming independent. After the occupation, however, firms (e.g., Mitsui, Mitsubishi, and Sumitomo) regrouped themselves.

In Japan in the Tokugawa era, from 1603 to 1867, a rising merchant class developed a place for itself in the feudal shogunate.

Merchant houses did not challenge the traditional authority structure but subordinated themselves to whatever powers existed. Indeed, a few houses survived the Meiji Restoration smoothly, and one in particular (Mitsui) became a prototype for the zaibatsu. Other zaibatsu arose early in the Meiji era from enterprises that had been previously run for the benefit of the feudal overlords, the daimyo. In the Meiji era, the control of such han enterprises moved to the private sphere where, in the case of Mitsubishi, former samurai became the owners and managers. In all cases of the zaibatsu that began early in the Meiji era, the overall structure was an intermarket group. The member firms were legal corporations, were large multiunit enterprises, and could accumulate capital through corporate means.

In South Korea, the chaebol—large, hierarchically arranged sets of firms—are the dominant business networks. In 1980–81, the government recognized 26 chaebol, which controlled 456 firms. In 1985, there were 50 chaebol that controlled 552 firms. Their rate of growth has been extraordinary. In 1973, the top five chaebol controlled 8.8% of the GNP, but by 1985 the top four chaebol controlled 45% of the GNP. In 1984, the top 50 chaebol controlled about 80% of the GNP. The chaebol are similar to the pre-war zaibatsu in size and organizational structure. Their structure can be traced to premodern political practices and to pre-World War II Japanese industrial policy which directed Korean development after Japan's colonization of Korea in 1910.

Adapted from Gary G. Hamilton and Nicole Woolsey Biggart 1988 "Market, culture, and authority: A comparative analysis of management and organization in the Far-East." *American Journal of Sociology* 94, 552–94.

With its array of historical references, unfamiliar Japanese and Korean terms, and precise numbers, the passage may seem dauntingly complex, and no reader could be expected to retain everything. But readers can manage details so that intelligible patterns emerge. As mentioned above, items *can be combined* to form a single item, often at a higher level of abstraction, thus leaving room on the mental desktop for new items to be concentrated on:

> "Mitsui ... Mitsubishi ... Sumitomo ..." *OK, these three examples all show family networks associated with corporate growth ... I'll combine them as such. Now there's room for more.*

Items that are not centrally relevant at this point *can be put aside* on a nearby mental side-table so that they can be retrieved when they are necessary:

> *Hmm ... Most of this isn't about* family, *but* family *is bound to come up again. I'll just put the idea of* family *and* corporate growth *here, within easy reach when it's needed.*

Some items *can be neglected*, left to fall off the desktop as other material arrives—

> *I see. The American market is just an example, not part of the main focus.*

Connections can be captured by important gists:

> *The zaibatsu arose when merchant houses allowed themselves to be subordinate instead of challenging dominant powers. This subordination is feudal rather than industrial. So, commercial growth in Japan developed out of a feudal culture. Mitsubishi is an example of how this feudal culture endures in modern Japan.*

These gists can be placed in the centre of the desk and returned to with subsequent gists.

There are, of course, limits to what a management device can achieve. When there is no immediate, accessible context for interpreting details, the reader can't *use* them for their contextual implications. Here we see a cognitive outcome of a *structural* feature: a passage that stays low, and doesn't make higher, interpretive levels accessible, can confound a reader.

> *Here are a number of dates associated with numbers of firms regarding the South Korean chaebol: 1980–81, 1985, 1973, 1984. I see these demonstrate growth, but do I need to remember these precise figures? They seem important, so I'll just keep them in mind and figure out their importance later.*

Moreover, when the management device is not properly directed to a clear context for interpretation, it may make some very inefficient decisions about long-term storage. Encountering a big claim early in an essay, and finding it neither developed nor repeated in subsequent passages, the device may judge that it is not important enough to keep handy. So the claim gets sent to the long-term memory files—that big, elastic capacity that houses the person's experience and knowledge of the world.

American markets haven't come up again. I predict they won't. I'll send this to long-term storage and make room for other things.

In this case, the material is not exactly forgotten, but it is no longer in mind. And, stored in long-term files, it is relatively inaccessible compared to items on the desktop and on temporary side-tables. If the device has made a mistake, and it turns out that this material *is* needed, the reader has to go and retrieve the item from the long-term files.

Now, what's this about? It seems to presuppose ideas about American markets. Do I have something on that? Maybe in my files ... where did I put that?

The retrieval takes up attention capacity. During the time the reader spends retrieving something from long-term storage (assuming he *can* retrieve it, and hasn't simply forgotten it), the desktop gets untidy. When he returns, he finds that things have fallen off, and have to be recalled by rereading.

Our earlier discussion of levels of generality (see Chapter 3B) can also help us analyze a reader's experience of a passage like "Asian Corporations." Stranded in a valley of detail, the reader has to find his own way out.

Exercise 2

Read the following revised version of the "Asian Corporations" passage. The passages in bold have been added in an attempt to manage a reader's mental desktop. How do these revisions address the challenges you faced in reading the original passage? How do they assist a reader's management device to help keep the mental desktop organized (see the four examples of uses above)?

ASIAN CORPORATIONS

Corporate growth—the development of multiunit firms—can be explained in terms of business response to the conditions of industrialized markets. According to Chandler (1977), when markets grow, businesses need to develop efficient systems of management to handle increased volume and coordinate multiple activities. Another theory also explains corporate development in industrial economies in terms of the market: as the number of transactions increases in the process of transforming raw materials into market goods, uncertainty increases (Williamson 1977, 1981, 1983, 1985). To reduce uncertainty, businesses grow, internalizing transactions and thereby governing them more reliably. These explanations of corporate development, however, do not fully account for corporate growth in Japan and South Korea, where prevailing organizational structures predate industrialization. **While the historical conditions of industrialization may explain why North American and European corporations operate the way they do, Japanese and South Korean corporate structure can be better explained as the result of other conditions: cultural factors which favour family links and which have all along adapted corporate management to older, pre-industrial forms of authority.**

The Japanese economy is dominated by large, powerful, and relatively stable enterprise groups **of business units—groups whose structure can be traced to traditional patterns of authority and family connection. Contemporary corporate structures in Japan are distinguished by characteristic systems of family connection that have persisted throughout this century, re-emerging powerfully in the post-war period. Today in Japan,** one type of enterprise group consists of horizontal linkages among a range of large firms; there are intermarket groups spread through different industrial sectors. A second type of enterprise group connects small- and medium-sized firms to a large firm. **The networks of large firms are the modern descendants of the pre-World War II zaibatsu—powerful, family-controlled holding companies.** These networks are normally groups of firms in unrelated businesses that are joined together by central banks or by trading companies. In pre-war Japan, these groups were linked by powerful holding companies that were each under the control of a family. The zaibatsu families exerted strict control over the individual firms in their group through a variety of fiscal and managerial methods. During the US occupation, the largest of these holding companies were dissolved, with the member firms of each group becoming independent. After the occupation, however, firms (e.g., Mitsui, Mitsubishi, and Sumitomo) regrouped themselves. **While market conditions can account for some features of the Japanese corporate structure, these persistent network linkages are better explained by cultural frames that influenced the organization of commerce long before industrialization reached Japan.**

Commercial growth in Japan arose amidst, and adapted to, traditional authority in a feudal rather than an industrial culture. In Japan in the Tokugawa era, from 1603 to 1867, a rising merchant class developed a place for itself in the feudal shogunate. Merchant houses did not challenge the traditional authority structure but subordinated themselves to whatever powers existed. Indeed, a few houses survived the Meiji Restoration smoothly, and one in particular (Mitsui) became a prototype for the zaibatsu. Other zaibatsu arose early in the Meiji era from enterprises that had been previously run for the benefit of the feudal overlords, the daimyo. In the Meiji era, the control of such han enterprises moved to the private sphere where, in the case of Mitsubishi, former samurai became the owners and managers. In all cases of the zaibatsu that began early in the Meiji era, the overall structure was an intermarket group. The member firms were legal corporations, were large multiunit enterprises, and could accumulate capital through corporate means. **In Japan, the corporate framework of industrial society preceded the appearance of expanded industrial markets, and that framework—indigenous and culturally specific—persists today.**

Like the Japanese economy, the South Korean economy depends on large groups of firms which are the descendants of traditional forms of authority and commercial cooperation. Today in South Korea, the chaebol—large, hierarchically arranged sets of firms—are the dominant business networks. In 1980–81, the government recognized 26 chaebol, which controlled 456 firms. In 1985, there were 50 chaebol that controlled 552 firms. Their rate of growth has been extraordinary. In 1973, the top five chaebol controlled 8.8% of the GNP, but by 1985 the top four chaebol controlled 45% of the GNP. In 1984, the top 50 chaebol controlled about 80% of the GNP. **But this surge of growth— recent and unmistakable—is nevertheless a phenomenon related to older patterns of commercial affiliation.** The chaebol are similar to the pre-war zaibatsu in size and organizational structure. Their structure can be traced to premodern political practices and to pre-World War II Japanese industrial policy which directed Korean development after Japan's colonization of Korea in 1910. **Intermarket linkages among business units coordinated by family affiliation rather than managerial principles are expressions of preindustrial culture as much as they are responses to expanding markets.**

Exercise 3

This exercise resembles the activity discussed in section 4B, where low-level stories were interpreted by finding abstractions that expressed their significance. The passage below is flat: it does not ascend to higher levels of generality and abstraction to claim the relevance of the data presented. Revise the passage by adding sentences with higher-level abstractions or phrasings to guide the reader's management device. You might want to break the passage into several paragraphs.

Here are a few suggestions for building higher-level abstractions to guide the reader's management device:

- find general names for what the passage is about and for what the noted changes and practices belong to;
- identify the main characteristics of the practices and situations described;
- express the significance of the data: what do we learn by finding out about these ancient occurrences?

At ancient buffalo-jumps, like the one at Head-Smashed-In, Alberta, prehistoric hunters drove buffalo over cliffs to their death. From the beginnings of this practice, about 5,700 years ago, until about 2,000 years ago, the hunters consumed only the choice cuts of the slaughtered animals and left the rest to rot. Then practices changed. The hunters began dragging much of their kill at Head-Smashed-In to flat land close by. After drying or roasting the bison flesh on hearths, they crushed the animals' long bones into splinters, boiling the fragments to render bone grease. To boil bones, prehistoric families first had to heat stones in a fire and then drop them into a hide-lined pit filled with water. Good boiling stones were rare at Head-Smashed-In, for the local sandstone crumbled during heating. So band members brought their own stones with them—tons of quartzite and other rocks from more than a mile away. The bone-boiling process was necessary to the production of pemmican. During prehistoric times, the Peigan and other members of the Blackfoot Nation rendered bone grease to stir into mixtures of smashed dried meat and Saskatoon berries, making massive 40-kilogram bags of the long-lasting food. The grease not only added to the usable protein in the meat but made the mixture extremely stable. According to one account from the Canadian fur trade, a bag of pemmican was slit open and safely consumed 20 years after it had been prepared. After techniques for producing pemmican developed, later bands began to pitch semipermanent camps in the nearby Oldman River Valley. Having extensive stores of pemmican for the winter, they no longer had to range so far afield for food.

Adapted from Heather Pringle 1988 "Boneyard enigma." *Equinox* May–June: 87–104.

Exercise 4

Exchange your own writing—perhaps a draft of an essay or even an old essay—with a classmate and practise think-aloud protocol. Using what you discovered about your classmate's experience of reading your work, revise your writing to better assist your reader's management device.

Exercise 5

The following passages are taken from articles in biology, sociology, literary studies, forestry, geography, Canadian studies, and business management. Working with a partner, take turns reading each passage aloud using the think-aloud protocol. Together, note features that you encounter in more than one passage—i.e., what similarities do you observe?—and those that seem to distinguish a discipline. Pay special attention to how each writer (or set of writers) establishes relevance.

PASSAGE 4: ABSTRACT FROM AN ARTICLE ON STEM CELL RESEARCH

Trophoblast stem cells (TSC) are the precursors of the differentiated cells of the placenta. In the mouse, TSC can be derived from outgrowths of either blastocyst polar trophectoderm (TE) or extraembryonic ectoderm (ExE), which originates from polar TE after implantation. The mouse TSC niche appears to be located within the ExE adjacent to the epiblast, on which it depends for essential growth factors, but whether this cellular architecture is the same in other species remains to be determined. Mouse TSC self-renewal can be sustained by culture on mitotically inactivated feeder cells, which provide one or more factors related to the NODAL pathway, and a medium supplemented with $FGF4$, heparin, and fetal bovine serum. Repression of the gene network that maintains pluripotency and emergence of the transcription factor pathways that specify a trophoblast (TR) fate enables TSC derivation in vitro and placental formation in vivo. Disrupting the pluripotent network of embryonic stem cells (ESC) causes them to default to a

TR ground state. Pluripotent cells that have acquired sublethal chromosomal alterations may be sequestered into TR for similar reasons. The transition from ESC to TSC, which appears to be unidirectional, reveals important aspects of initial fate decisions in mice. TSC have yet to be derived from domestic species in which remarkable TR growth precedes embryogenesis. Recent derivation of TSC from blastocysts of the rhesus monkey suggests that isolation of the human equivalents may be possible and will reveal the extent to which mechanisms uncovered by using animal models are true in our own species.

Michael R. Roberts and Susan J. Fisher 2011 "Trophoblast stem cells." *Biology of Reproduction* 84 (3): 412–21.

PASSAGE 5: SOCIOLOGICAL STUDY OF POPULAR CULTURE

How might we approach a general understanding of popular culture and stigma? We can begin by recognizing that stigma occurs in a broader social context in which social class and other social group distinctions play a role in the articulation of stigma theories in popular culture. The general position of popular culture in the United States already articulates social class distinctions (Gans, 1974); for example, the debate over mass culture during the 20th century articulated social class distinctions in the framing of high art and popular art (Swingewood, 1977; Storey, 2001). Beisel (1993) also shows how debates concerning obscenity in the early 20th century articulated class distinctions in the stigmatization of popular pornography, while the nudes enjoyed by an elite audience were defended as high art. And Sternheimer (2003) points to the special role that children as a social group play as victims amid adult fears engendered by broad social change that make popular media a convenient scapegoat. Social class and social group distinctions play out in a variety of ways in how and when stigma occurs in popular culture.

Paul Lopes 2006 "Culture and stigma: Popular culture and the case of comic books." *Sociological Forum* 21 (3): 387–414, 391.

PASSAGE 6: LITERARY ANALYSIS OF BRAM STOKER'S NOVEL *DRACULA*

Bram Stoker's *Dracula* (1897) participates in that modernizing of Gothic which occurs at the close of the nineteenth century. Like Stevenson's *Dr. Jekyll and Mr. Hyde* (1886) and Wilde's *Picture of Dorian Gray* (1891), Stoker's novel achieves its effects by bringing the terror of the Gothic home. While Gothic novelists had traditionally displaced their stories in time or locale, these later writers root their action firmly in the modern world. Yet critics have until recently ignored the historical context in which these works were written and originally read. Most notably, criticism has persistently undervalued *Dracula*'s extensive and highly visible contacts with a series of cultural issues, particularly those involving race, specific to the 1890s. This neglect has in part resulted from the various psychoanalytic approaches taken by most critics of Gothic. While such approaches have greatly enriched our understanding of *Dracula*, and while nothing in psychoanalytic critical theory precludes a "historicist" reading of literary texts, that theory has in practice been used almost exclusively to demonstrate, as Stoker's most recent critic puts it, that *Dracula* is a "representation of fears that are more universal than a specific focus on the Victorian background would allow." Yet the novel's very attachment to the "Victorian background"—what *The Spectator* in 1897 called its "up-to-dateness"—is a primary source of Stoker's continuing power. Late-Victorian Gothic in general, and *Dracula* in particular, continually calls our attention to the cultural context surrounding and informing the text, and insists that we take that context into account.

Stephen Arata 1990 "The Occidental tourist: 'Dracula' and the anxiety of reverse colonization." *Victorian Studies* 33 (4): 621–45, 621–22.

PASSAGE 7: FORESTRY ARTICLE ON MOUNTAIN PINE BEETLES IN BRITISH COLUMBIA

Since 1999, the population of mountain pine beetle (*Dendroctonus ponderosae* Hopk. [Coleoptera: Scolytidae]) has grown to an epidemic level in western Canada, expanding into areas previously thought to be outside the mountain pine beetle's geographical range (Westfall and Ebata, 2008). Endemic to British Columbia, the preferred host of the beetle is lodgepole pine (*Pinus contorta* Dougl. Ex. Loud var. *latifolia* Engelm.); however, any species of pine is at risk of attack (Furniss and Schenk, 1969). Factors contributing to the current epidemic include alterations to established climatic limitations to mountain pine beetle survival (Réginière and Bentz, 2007; Aukema et al., 2008; Raffa et al., 2008) and an abundance of suitable hosts resulting from almost one hundred years of successful fire suppression (Taylor and Carroll, 2004).

By 2008, mountain pine beetle had impacted more than 13 million hectares of pine forest in western Canada (Raffa et al., 2008). The total cumulative volume losses associated with the current epidemic in British Columbia are estimated at 620 million m³, representing 46% of the total merchantable pine volume on British Columbia's timber harvesting land base (Walton et al., 2008). The magnitude of the current mountain pine beetle epidemic has converted the forest in the impacted area from a small net carbon sink to a large net carbon source (Kurz et al., 2008). Concern is now focussed on the possibility of further range expansion by the beetle into the pine forests of Canada's boreal region (Westfall, 2006; Raffa et al., 2008).

Michael A. Wulder, Stephanie M. Ortlepp, Joanne C. White, Nicholas C. Coops, Sam B. Coggins 2009 "Monitoring the impacts of mountain pine beetle mitigation." *Forest Ecology and Management* 258 (7): 1181–87, 1181.

PASSAGE 8: GEOGRAPHICAL STUDY OF URBAN DESIGN

Eco-city projects are increasingly popular globally: they are often marketed as 'new' urban environments focused on achieving sustainable urban living while promoting a low-carbon technological and industrial base. Many such projects are being built from scratch in a variety of locales, from the Gulf to East Asia. These eco-cities stem from different planning traditions, economic development strategies, and political and ideological contexts. What is common to several of these projects, however, is the aim of constructing eco-cities as energy-independent communities which produce little to no waste while being economically sustainable: they can be conceived as experiments in entrepreneurial zero- or low-carbon urban economies (Jonas et al., 2011a; 2011b; Bulkeley and Castán Broto, 2012). Indeed, eco-city projects often seem rooted in a specific view of the city's urban metabolism as a closed system of flows, inputs and outputs. Although much research in the tradition of urban political ecology has focused on the metabolic relations around specific metabolic components of the city, such as water, little critical work has focused on cities' thermal aspects. A focus on thermal relations is key to analyzing new 'eco' urban developments in an era concerned with adaptation to climatic warming. This article argues for the need to consider the thermal aspects of urban metabolism while focusing on the link between individual buildings and eco-city master plans and wider economic development strategies at a state level. In so doing, it encourages critical analysis of eco-city design and planning while focusing on the role of specific building structures within eco-cities as examples of the intermeshing of what can be termed a "political ecology of scale." This stretches from specific buildings' climatic characteristics, to the metabolic master plan for eco-cities, to provincial, regional and state-level plans for the integration of eco-cities within wider economic and political development trajectories.

Federico Caprotti and Joanna Romanowicz 2013 "Thermal eco-cities: Green building and urban thermal metabolism." *International Journal of Urban and Regional Research* 37 (6): 1949–67, 1949–50.

PASSAGE 9: CANADIAN STUDIES ARTICLE ON THE FRANKLIN EXPEDITION

The end of the twentieth century witnessed the publication of a plethora of novels and other literary treatments that re-imagined the career of Sir John Franklin (1786–1847) and the tragic circumstances of the expedition under his leadership which sought to traverse the Northwest Passage through the Arctic in 1845. The disappearance of this expedition, one of the most prominent episodes in the history of exploration, incited frenzied speculations about its fate throughout the Victorian era and beyond in which spiritualists and clairvoyants, as well as writers and investigators, endeavoured to imagine what really happened (Ross

2003). Through the mystery of its disappearance, the Franklin expedition came to occupy a spectral place in contemporary culture: as Margaret Atwood put it, "Because Franklin was never really 'found', he continues to live on as a haunting presence" (1995: 10).

The impact of the loss of HMS *Terror*, *Erebus* and 129 men, and subsequent revelations of cannibalism, on Victorian society has been compared to that of the *Challenger* space shuttle disaster in late-twentieth century society (Stein 2007), and sporadic attempts were made, starting in the 1850s, to piece together a coherent narrative through the mapping of skeletons (see Figure 1). Contiguous with the emergence of 'Franklin fiction'—speculative, postmodern, postcolonial and historical re-imaginings of the Franklin expedition—the searches for relics, bodies and the Franklin shipwrecks in what is now Nunavut, Canada, which commenced on a large scale in the 1980s, disclosed a ghostly inheritance haunting modern Canada. If the North has functioned in Canada as a grand national myth for the past century—the "True North, Strong and Free"—an idea more than a location (Francis 1997: 152–71; Grace 2007), then the particular details of this disaster can be seen to occupy a central role in how the nation deals with its Arctic possessions.[1]

Note

1 Certainly, Canada and Britain were not alone in their fascination with the Arctic archipelago: private and government-sponsored expeditions from the United States of America entered the Arctic sphere in response to the loss of Franklin in the 1850s with a mixed bag of geographical, commercial and nationalist aims. See Robinson 2006.

Shane McCorristine 2013 "Searching for Franklin: A contemporary Canadian ghost story." *British Journal of Canadian Studies* 26 (1): 39–57, 39–40.

PASSAGE 10: BUSINESS MANAGEMENT STUDY OF BUZZWORDS

Identifying the benefits of management buzzwords is not a straightforward task. Studies looking at the use of buzzwords in organized settings point out the difficulty of categorizing certain terms as buzzwords as, more often than not, we can find instances where the same terms represent a more precise use of language (Atkins, 1997; Cornwall, 2007; Godin, 2006; Hunter & Barker, 1993; Lee, 2000; Nicklin, 1995; Simberloff, 1983; Thomas, 1996). Without accepted examples, management buzzwords have been looked at as an issue of fashion rather than as a particular type of language use (Collins, 2000). Austin's (1975) work is instructive here. Austin constructs ideal types to show how we do different things with words. He tells us that this approach is not designed to identify robust distinctions between particular terms but to help us to recognize general differences in the ways language is used.

So, after providing a definition of buzzwords and exploring the history of the term, this paper adopts Austin's perspective to set out three ways managers use buzzwords. As we will see, managers use buzzwords to claim authority in their organizations, to facilitate action within their organizations and to deal with the anxieties of making decisions that may damage their societies, economies and environments. The paper concludes that management buzzwords are not just meaningless clichés, mumbo-jumbo or business school bullshit. They also solve specific organizational problems for managers—problems that would not disappear if we eradicated buzzwords from organizational life.

Robert Cluley 2013 "What makes a management buzzword buzz." *Organization Studies* 34 (1): 33–43, 33–34.

10

Scholarly Styles I: Nominal Style

Scholarly writing is often ridiculed in the popular media. Like the speech of people who have not internalized schoolroom rules of usage, it is deplored by those who believe in "good" writing. Most scholarly expression goes on out of earshot of the rest of the world—in scholarly journals and at scholarly conferences. But when the sounds of scholarship do leak into more public settings, they can come in for some criticism. In this chapter, we will examine some of the stylistic features that give rise to that criticism.

10A Common and Uncommon Sense

Criticism of scholarly expression is sometimes most vociferous where academic research meets public policy. For instance, when a curriculum document reaches the attention of the popular press, any wordings which are traceable to otherwise secluded research domains can leave people indignant or amused. The following example of such "edubabble" comes from a curriculum report that was presented to Ontario's Minister of Education:

> A certain minimum fluency is required before students are able to reflect critically on their own language use. Attention to language forms and conventions should therefore increase gradually as

language skill develops and should arise specifically out of the reading and writing being done. Students are more likely to achieve good punctuation and spelling and surface correctness through extensive practice in reading and writing rather than conscious attempts to apply rules out of context.

The newspaper article that cites this passage describes it as "bureaucratic babble" and lines up readers who characterize it as "meaningless and offensive," "pretentious," and "arrogant." The article then goes on to report that the passage (along with the 100-page report it came from) was rewritten in **plain language**:

> Students are more likely to learn correct language uses, punctuation, and spelling by reading and writing than by learning rules in isolation.

Ottawa Citizen, reprinted in *The Vancouver Province*, 5 July 1994, A14.

Whatever the defects of the original or the virtues of the rewrite, the rewrite gets rid of material like "a certain minimum fluency is required," "attention to language forms and conventions," and "through extensive practice in reading and writing rather than conscious attempts to apply rules out of context." Such expressions bear the marks of scholarly activity. For example, we can detect instances of the kind of nominalization we encountered when we looked at reported speech in introductions (Chapter 8B). Events are turned into things ("x pays attention to" y = "attention to" y; "x attempts to apply" y to z = "attempts to apply" y to z), and so are attributes ("x is fluent" = "fluency"). As verbs and adjectives are turned into nouns, agents of actions and possessors of attributes disappear (*Who* pays attention or attempts to apply? *Who* is fluent? *Who* requires fluency?). In getting rid of these features and emphasizing the agents (in this case the students), the rewrite might be said to restore "common sense" to the original. But at the same time, it seems to reduce the conceptual complexity of the original: for example, the emphasis on "language forms and conventions" is reduced to a set of "rules."

With genre theory in mind, we could argue that it's not that the original is in itself bad, or that the reaction is mistaken. Rather, there has been a series of **genre violations**: the writers of the curriculum report transferred the sounds and styles of scholarly research too directly to a non-research document, in this case one meant to be read by government officials. And the ministry officials who objected and the rewriters who responded to these objections failed to acknowledge the fact that the documents on which this report was based were addressed to professionals: researchers, teachers, and educational administrators who are familiar with these uses of language. In other words, the curriculum report retained elements that served research situations that were not shared by most readers of the *Ottawa Citizen* or the indignant politicians whose consternation was reported.

This example illuminates the conflict between what Halliday and Martin (1993) have called the **common sense** of, roughly speaking, our everyday experience of the world and the **uncommon sense** of the learnèd domains of research.

From a distance, it seems tempting to vouch for common sense and to deny uncommon sense as unnatural, pretentious, or even deliberately deceiving. Yet common sense has also been the source of some questionable ideas—that whales are fish (to use one of Halliday and Martin's examples)—or less innocent ideas, such as that women are inferior to men, or that children benefit from stern discipline, or that rivers are a good place to get rid of industrial waste. That is to say, sometimes common sense is simply unexamined assumptions which perpetuate conditions that benefit some people and disadvantage others—or benefit no one in the long run. Although these assumptions are so widely held—that is, so common—that they appear self-evident, they may in fact be wrong.

Research activities seek to subject common-sense assumptions to examination, and this process of examination is represented in the distinctive language of the scholarly genres. For example, in a common-sense world, we all understand the word *think* and use it in various situations:

[Fred and Jane are taking a car trip.]

FRED: When did we get gas?	JANE: Hmm. Let me *think*.
FRED: We're going an average of 85 kph. When will we get to Mariposa?	JANE (looking at a map): Wait. I'm *thinking*.
FRED: What are you doing?	JANE (looking at a map): I'm *thinking* about where we should go next.

But cognitive scientists who want to find out how people think would distinguish amongst these situations, seeing that one is a matter of remembering, another is a matter of calculating an answer to a particular question, and the third is a more complex procedure that involves assessing alternatives. For the third case, they might (and have) come up with a specialized term: *nonspecific goal strategy in problem solving*. Rarely would we hear this term outside scholarly circles—or, indeed, outside the even smaller circle of the discipline of cognitive science.

Some advocates of plain language and common sense complain about this kind of wording. They suggest that it is an unnecessarily complicated way of speaking. Why not just say "thinking"? They suggest that, by choosing the specialist term, research writers exclude readers who rely on common sense and isolate scholars in a false distinction made of elaborate language. And some suggest that this kind of wording is not only pretentious and exclusionary, but also hard to read. Let's examine the grounds for these complaints.

10B Is Scholarly Writing Unnecessarily Complicated, Exclusionary, or Elitist?

Later sections of this chapter will offer broader perspectives on this question, looking at how the structure of an expression like *nonspecific goal strategy in problem solving* cooperates with other features of scholarly genres to produce the discourse which typifies and maintains research activities. In the meantime, we could grant that, sometimes, scholars might be advised to say "thinking" instead of "nonspecific goal strategy in problem solving."

But we can make this concession to critics of scholarly style only in light of other considerations. In efforts to reorganize common-sense knowledge of the world into uncommon sense, researchers analyze issues and entities into smaller parts, differentiating those parts into segments which may be scarcely visible to the untrained observer. Those segments—produced by research activity—then become objects of study, and to report results precisely it becomes necessary to apply a different name to each of these objects.

Be that as it may, our opinion of the wording *nonspecific goal strategy in problem solving* may come down to our opinion of research activity itself. If we believe the results of the research are useful or important, we're likely to identify the inherent complexities of expression as *necessary*; if we don't, we're more likely to dismiss those complexities as *unnecessary*.

This is a big issue, and it is further inflated by our culture's ambivalence toward higher learning, expertise, and what counts as legitimate research. On the one hand, we invest heavily—materially and socially—in professional research. Tax and corporate dollars support scholars' activities; experts are called in as authorities on many matters, from family life to outer space. But, on the other hand, we not only ridicule expert language but also question our investment in "pure" research that doesn't have any immediately foreseeable use. If we are concerned about famines on earth, we may be skeptical of funding for research into particle physics. Moreover, we may be troubled about the applications of research in new technologies: we complain that they have spoiled cherished aspects of our customary ways of life or we worry about the ethical implications of, for example, new medical technologies.

Our judgement about the complications of scholarly language would eventually have to take into account this ambivalence. For now, we might say that, if the activities that appear to depend on wordings like *nonspecific goal strategy in problem solving* have useful, real-world implications, then the wording is not *unnecessarily* complicated—though it may still be complicated. And one of these results might be a clearer picture of how people reason: how certain kinds of schoolroom problem-questions (*If A is travelling at 50 kph and B is going 56 kph in the opposite direction ...*) may trigger in children reasoning different from that which the teacher anticipates, or how a doctor's diagnostic questioning may trigger replies that obscure rather than illuminate a patient's condition.

Often accompanying the criticism that scholarly writing is unnecessarily complicated is the accusation that it's elitist. In fact, there can be little doubt that scholarly style excludes many readers. Even within the larger academic community, readers who are members of one discipline can be excluded from the ongoing discourses of other disciplines—palaeontologists and cognitive scientists do not tend to understand one another's research very well. While researchers seem to be generally respectful of those working in other fields, smirks and raised eyebrows are not unknown when a researcher comes within earshot of the wordings of another discipline. The "postmodernism" of the humanities and some of the social sciences can inspire ridicule amongst those who do not work with those terms. And, equally, the classifying vocabularies of the sciences and some other social sciences can arouse suspicion amongst those who work with less technical terminologies.

Genre theory predicts that this will be so: the more highly defined and particular the situations which language serves, the more distinctive will that language be, and the more inscrutable to people unfamiliar with those situations. So we might also predict that any social group—skateboarders or pilots or childcare workers—will develop and maintain speech styles which serve and represent the routines which organize their activities. And these styles will, to a greater or lesser degree, exclude people who don't belong to the group and incur the risk of social reactions to that exclusion.

Exercise 1

The following passage appeared in an online discussion forum. What features strike you as likely to exclude the non-specialist reader? Are these elements "unnecessarily complicated" or do they reflect complexities that are inherent in the subject matter? In your estimation, what would be the effect on the intended reader—someone who frequents this forum and who knows a lot about Macs—of expanding the abbreviations and defining difficult terms?

I'm suspecting that this must be a software/driver issue, but I'm stumped ... MacBook Air Mid2012 with 10.8 and latest updates.

The symptom is the following: SanDisk 64GB UHS card in the SD Card slot. Formats fine both FAT and ExFAT. Attempting for format HFS (any combination of encrypted, case sensitive, etc.), the card formats but can't mount. Repair fails too.

Now here's the kicker, put the same card in an external SD Card Reader (via USB), it formats HFS and mounts fine. Still can't mount via the internal reader though. Tried other SD cards, down to 4GB, same deal....

Hope someone has seen this before!

Thanks

Exercise 2

The following two passages discuss eco-city (i.e., sustainable city) projects. One passage is taken from a newspaper article published in the *Edmonton Journal*, while the other is from the conclusion of a research article published in the *International Journal of Urban and Regional Research*. Compare the two passages' treatment of their subject. Identify specific features of each passage that relate to their intended audience. What elements of the second passage are likely to cause difficulties for the general reader for whom the first passage appears to have been written?

PASSAGE 1

It is blatantly untrue that Canada can do nothing about global warming and carbon emissions. Canada has a wonderful opportunity to innovate if it can tear itself away from fossilized patterns of thinking. If it cannot, it actually runs the risk of falling technologically behind the rest of the world.

China has commissioned the design of an eco-city which should be ready to be lived in in 2010. It will house 80,000 people at first but will eventually be home to 500,000.

None of the buildings will be more than eight stories high. Turf and vegetation will cover the roof to insulate and recycle waste water.

Pollution-free buses powered by fuel cells will be used. An intranet service will give travel times and connect people who want to use cars. Electric scooters and bicycles will be used. Roads will be laid out so walking and cycling to work is quicker than driving.

Sara-Anne Peterson May 22 2006 "China's eco-city sets example." *Edmonton Journal*: A17.

PASSAGE 2

Studies of eco-city projects often take into account sustainability indicators or other measures of a proposed new urban area's ecological footprint. At the same time, as argued above, critical analyses of urban projects rooted in political ecology highlighted how nature and the city are intermeshed and mutually produced in a system of dynamic metabolic relations. This article argues for the need to include urban thermal metabolism within studies of eco-cities, and to do so at the scale of individual buildings, seen as enzymatic components of a wider urban metabolic system. Furthermore, the Masdar eco-city example shows that current flagship eco-city projects can be categorized as belonging to a broad political and ideological category which sees eco-cities as rooted in central planning, but which are dependent upon the investment and input of industrial actors (from developers to engineering corporations, to architectural and design firms) to bring projects to fruition. Furthermore, industrial and commercial firms are utilized to ensure that eco-cities "fit" within wider, strategic economic visions elaborated by central planners at the state or provincial scale.

Caprotti and Romanowicz 2013: 1962.

10C Nominal Style: Syntactic Density

Criticism of scholarly expression—in particular, the claim that it's hard to read—has sometimes focused on what has been called its heavily **nominal style**. This characterization refers to its preference for nouns over verbs, and the way that preference results in long **noun phrases** (i.e., a phrase formed by a noun and all its modifiers) like the one that we have been using as our example: *nonspecific goal strategy in problem solving* is longer than *thinking*. This difference is visible to the naked eye and needs very little grammatical analysis to reveal it. Once nouns are preferred over verbs, noun phrases bear a particularly heavy load, carrying content that would otherwise have been distributed throughout the sentence. These concentrated loads appear likely to challenge readers on two fronts: (1) the **syntactic density** of noun "strings," and (2) the potential **ambiguity** of these strings. Let's begin by examining syntactic density, the first of these conditions.

In English, the noun phrase is capable of expanding by picking up other sentence elements. In the following series, you will see noun phrases growing by absorbing material from other parts of the sentence.

(a) *the noun phrase absorbs an adjective*
This behaviour is **criminal**.
This **criminal** behaviour ...

(b) *the noun phrase absorbs another noun*
The reports record **offences**.
The **offence** reports ...

(c) *the noun phrase absorbs a predicate—verb and adverb*
Some strategies **work forward**.
Some **forward-working** strategies ...

(d) *the noun phrase absorbs a predicate—verb and (object) noun*
Strategies **solve problems**.
Problem-solving strategies ...

There are limits to what the noun phrase can absorb, but these examples don't even approach those limits. They exemplify only some of the simplest noun-phrase expansions.

You can see that the capacity of the noun phrase to incorporate other sentence elements provides one of the normal economies of English. For example, by installing "work forward" in the noun phrase (c), the writer leaves the rest of the sentence free to carry other information:

> **Forward-working strategies** enable the problem solver to explore the problem space to see what moves are possible.

Speakers of English use the capacity of the noun phrase all the time to achieve economies of expression. Instead of saying—

> My car has broken down. It is brand new.

—the speaker can economize, presenting the same information in fewer words:

> **My brand-new car** has broken down.

Yet, while this *appears* to be the same information, the choice between the two versions is not entirely free or arbitrary: it has to do with **topic development**. For instance, if the speaker were to continue reporting his predicament, the second version would *tend* to lead to development of the "break-down" topic—

> My brand-new car has broken down. I was going along and heard this BUMP-BUMP.

—whereas the first version would *tend* to pave the way for development of the "brand-new" topic:

> My car has broken down. It's brand new. I just got it last month.

In reflecting on the noun phrase's capacity to absorb material from other parts of the sentence in ways that are patterned rather than arbitrary, let us first take a cognitive approach. Consider the effect of the heavy noun phrase on readers' working conditions. How does the decoding of a long noun phrase impose on readers' limited resources for paying attention?

Most theory and research in this area suggests that as readers make their way through sentences, they predict, on the basis of the word they are currently reading, the syntactic category of the following word or phrase. So, if readers encounter a *determiner* like—

> **the** ...

—they predict, as most likely but not inevitable, that a *noun* will come next:

> the **goal** ...

If their expectations are disappointed, and they find not a *noun* but an *adjective*—

> the **nonspecific** ...

—they recover easily, and now predict a noun, since adjectives following determiners have a high probability of being followed by a *noun*:

the	nonspecific	**goal**
determiner	*modifier (adj)*	*nominal head (noun)*

This seems to complete the noun phrase, and readers are ready for a *verb*—the goal *is* something, or *does* something. They predict a verb. But what if they encounter another *noun*?

> the nonspecific goal **strategy** ...

the	nonspecific	goal	**strategy**
determiner	*modifier*	*modifier*	*nominal head*
	(adj)	*(noun)*	*(noun)*

Now they revise their hypothesis about the sentence and its structure: *goal* is not the head of the noun phrase, but only another modifier. Notice that we have not yet approached the structural limits of the noun phrase. Somebody could conceivably write "the nonspecific goal strategy research innovation project."

Analysis of the above procedure first isolates noun strings—nouns modified by other nouns—as a site of such **failed-then-revised hypotheses** sequences. Then it proposes that these recursive predictions burden readers' attention capacity. (We could see this burden as a micro version of the larger efforts after meaning that we explored in Chapter 9, when we inspected the state of readers' mental desktops as they worked to construct the relevance of lower-level information to higher-level concepts.) So far, our evaluation of the syntactic density of noun phrases has been cognitive only: we have been estimating readers' reasoning as they meet long noun strings. But readers also respond in ways that stem from their social experience. And research shows that, while noun strings may cause trouble for some readers, they are no problem for other readers. Are some readers dull and others brilliant?

In fact, as we saw in Chapter 9, the difference lies in readers' different experience of the world. Readers' social milieu and the background knowledge they have acquired play a big part in their understanding of what they read. It all depends on readers' previous contact with the subject treated by the text. For example, when the primary author of this book was investigating stylistic features in management studies, she came across the term *relationship marketing*. Being unaccustomed to the topic, she didn't know what that was—a dating service? professional matchmaking? Reading on, she was able to infer—from appositives, synonyms, and other elements of the context—that *relationship marketing* is a sales strategy which emphasizes techniques for building an enduring relationship with customers: keeping in touch after one sale had been made, building a context for future sales. Presumably, readers more familiar with these aspects of the discourse on management would not have had to experiment with the noun phrase *relationship marketing* in this way.

Conditions people have in mind when they talk about "clarity" and "conciseness" in the scholarly genres may have as much to do with the *identity* and *position* of the reader as they do with the style of the writing. Exploring this possibility, a student in an undergraduate class in writing in the research genres carried out a small study of readers' level of difficulty in encountering scholarly forms of expression. She selected introductions from three articles, one each from scholarly publications in biomedical science, geography, and literary studies. She asked two readers to evaluate the passages for "clarity." The first subject, a physician, rated the biomedical passage as "most clear," and the literary studies passage as "most unclear." The second subject, a first-year student in a university-transfer program at a college, rated the literary studies passage as "most clear," and the biomedical article as "most unclear."

Let's put the reader back together as a **socio-cognitive** being, and ask the question again: is scholarly style hard to read? Yes, it is—for some people. Students new to a discipline, for example, may find the nominal style of scholarly writing difficult to read. Perhaps, then, these students can benefit from first seeing the scholarly noun phrase as a structure which absorbs other sentence parts, and then methodically unpacking that noun phrase, understanding why it is causing them trouble but not letting it get the upper hand. As *readers*, students can overcome these obstacles once they understand the structure of the obstacle, and where the footholds and handholds are.

As *writers*, students can be wary of all-purpose rules for plain writing—or computer style checkers—that call for verbs instead of nouns, and deplore noun "strings." Their readers will not necessarily have trouble with a heavily nominal style. But writers can also keep in mind the cognitive load imposed by noun strings. There may be times when unpacking a big noun phrase for readers will offer them cognitive relief. For example, the second passage below may sometimes be preferable to the first (where the target noun phrase is shown in bold):

> **A recent comparative study of multi-family housing development and maintenance costs based on 1986 construction experience** showed that three-storey buildings ultimately provided cheaper housing than high-rises.

> A study recently compared costs of developing and maintaining multiple-family housing. It was based on 1986 construction experience, and it showed that three-storey buildings ultimately provided cheaper housing than high-rises.

Exercise 3

The following noun phrases are taken from published articles in a variety of scholarly disciplines. Analyze them, following the example ("the nonspecific goal strategy") above: what predictive hypotheses would readers first make and then revise as they navigate their way through these noun phrases?

delayed sleep phase syndrome
labour supply decision-making
voluntary employee turnover
issues management structures
other-race face recognition
eating pathology scores
risk management science
droplet size distribution measurements
sea-level maximal oxygen uptake
supramolecular structures formation

Exercise 4

The following passage examines "community," a concept whose scholarly sense you have become familiar with from readings in previous chapters. Using the think-aloud techniques discussed in Chapters 5 and 9, ask two or more classmates to read and comment on the passage. Do the results differ according to readers' backgrounds—their area of study, for example? Ask someone from outside the class to read the passage: how does their experience of the passage compare with those of readers in the class?

I am less concerned with the conceptual aporia of community-capital contradiction, than with the genealogy of the idea of community as itself a "minority" discourse; as the making, or becoming "minor," of the idea of Society, in the practice of politics of culture. Community is the antagonist supplement of modernity: in the metropolitan space it is the territory of the minority, threatening the claims of civility; in the transnational world it becomes the border-problem of the diasporic, the migrant, the refugee. Binary divisions of social space neglect the profound temporal disjunction—the transnational time and

> space—through which minority communities negotiate their collective identifications.
>
> Homi K. Bhabha 1994 "How newness enters the world." In *The Location of Culture.* London: Routledge, 231.

10D Nominal Style: Ambiguity

We have seen that noun phrases are hospitable to other sentence elements: they will take in just about anything. As these bits and pieces are accommodated in the noun phrase, other elements are left behind. However, when parts get left behind, **ambiguity** can result. Sometimes the effort required from the reader to resolve the ambiguity is so negligible it is scarcely measurable. The bold-faced noun phrases in the following passage, which appeared in a daily newspaper, make demands on readers that they meet almost automatically.

> The body, discovered in the basement of **a concrete building**, was identified as the remains of **a newspaper boy** who had lived in the neighbourhood in the late 1960s.

A concrete building means that the building was made of concrete. But *a newspaper boy* doesn't mean that the boy was made of newspaper: it means that the boy delivered newspapers. The noun phrases don't make these distinctions: they are lost when the noun phrase absorbs other elements. So, it's *readers* who make these distinctions, by consulting their knowledge of the world (no people are made of newspaper). And readers make the distinctions easily, without significant processing demands.

Other noun phrases can be slightly more distracting. The next passage comes from a news report about social conditions in the United States.

> Homeless experts say that the problem will only get worse as the summer goes on.

What is a "homeless expert"?

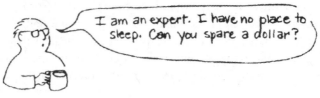

A more likely interpretation soon supersedes the less likely one.

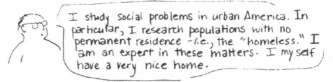

I study social problems in urban America. In particular, I research populations with no permanent residence – i.e., the "homeless." I am an expert in these matters. I myself have a very nice home.

Readers resolve the ambiguity in the noun phrase by consulting their knowledge of the world.

Other noun phrases can be more stubbornly ambiguous. Like the example *relationship marketing*, the following noun string cannot be resolved by simply consulting our knowledge of the world:

> police arrest information

Does this refer to information that police use when they arrest people? Or information police compile when they arrest people? Or does it refer to information about police arresting people? Without surrounding context (or maybe even with it), this noun phrase remains ambiguous.

Finally, when style is heavily nominal—that is, when information is concentrated in expanding noun phrases—an accompanying feature appears which can also contribute to ambiguity. This feature, which we encountered at the beginning of this chapter in the document on Ontario's school curriculum, we will call **agentlessness**. The doers of actions slip away when the actions are turned from verbs to nouns. So, while the verb *attend* requires (in active voice) that the doers of the action be identified—

> **Forty-five property owners and six tenants** attended the meeting.

—the noun *attendance* allows these agents of the action to withdraw from the sentence:

> **Attendance** was high.

Agentless writing has been condemned as both ambiguous and deceptive, an instrument of concealment. Leaving charges of deception aside for the moment, we must concede that long noun phrases which eliminate agents are liable to be ambiguous. For example, in *labour supply decision-making*, who is making the decision? (and about what?) Someone who has not read the article from which this phrase was taken might be surprised to learn that the decision makers were Bangladeshi women in London who chose to do piecework at home rather than look for jobs in garment factories.

The ambiguity and syntactic density of a heavily nominal style are both potential troublemakers for readers and writers. Yet scholarly style risks these troubles. This way of writing must therefore provide some benefits, some important service to scholarly situations. In the next section we will observe these benefits and services.

Exercise 5

Look in the passage below for dense noun phrases. Rewrite by unpacking them, spreading their elements out into other parts of the sentence and other sentences. For example, "Incarceration-based measures are the most common in national prison-use assessment" could be rewritten as "Some measures are based on the frequency with which criminals are incarcerated. These rates are the measure most commonly used to assess the way nations use prisons." (Note that the rewrite will not necessarily be an improvement—merely another version, less nominal, possibly more friendly to readers in certain situations.)

> The Australian basic-wage Royal Commission of 1920, seeking working-class standard-of-living criteria, was chaired by a widely read and respected living-wage champion, husband of a controversial family-planning advocate. Despite the liberal-reform inclinations of the Commission's chair and its nearly 40% recommended basic-wage increase, one of the main legacies of the Commission was the unquestioned equation of the "family" wage with the male-provider wage.
>
> Adapted from Kerreen M. Reiger 1989 "'Clean and comfortable and respectable': Working-class aspirations and the Australian 1920 Royal Commission on the Basic Wage." *History Workshop* 27: 86–105.

Exercise 6

The advertisement below appeared in the Career Opportunities section of a national newspaper. Other advertisements in this section included descriptions of positions available in engineering, private- and public-sector administration, personnel and sales management.

> Examine the advertisement for features we have identified as belonging to scholarly expression: that is, nouns that represent actions or events, and that in doing so lose agents (doers) and the objects acted upon. What questions might someone ask about who does what to whom? Evaluate this passage for its potential ambiguity and syntactic density. Speculate on why these ways of speaking, which seem characteristic of research genres, turn up here in a business genre.
>
> ### SENIOR CONSULTANT
> #### Automotive marketing
>
> Blackburn/Polk Vehicle Information Services (BPVIS) is Canada's leading supplier of motor vehicle and marketing information services to the automotive industry and its allied businesses. We are looking for a Senior Consultant to work with our clients to market our full range of products and services. We require an individual with the following skill set:
> - knowledge of the automotive market and its information requirements
> - general understanding of geo-demographics and market research
> - general knowledge of direct marketing.
>
> Our services for the automotive industry include market performance evaluation and benchmarking, network planning and location analysis, customer profiling studies, and support services for direct communication and customer retention programs.
>
> The successful candidate will have strong presentation and interpersonal skills and be self-motivated.
>
> Compensation is performance related and is commensurate with experience. Please apply in confidence to _____.

10E Sentence Style and Textual Coherence

Here are three scholarly passages which raise questions:

> The insertion of a Fourth World of indigenous populations who have a distinct vision of their place in a world that until recently has ignored them (Graburn 1976) cultivates an awareness of the political potential of submerged nationalities that are emerging once again

in the postmodern world. This belated recognition of submerged ethnicities comes in the wake of the demise of the Second World, which no longer provides the paradigmatic base for analyses, as the structures of capitalism, socialism, and imperialism are undermined.

June Nash 1994 "Global integration and subsistence insecurity." *American Anthropologist* 96 (1): 7–30, 8.

Who inserts a Fourth World? Who is aware? Who belatedly recognizes? Who analyzes? What nationalities and ethnicities are these? Who or what submerged them?

Our study advances and tests a model incorporating both institutional and resource explanations for why firms adopt certain structural modifications, namely, issues management structures. The study ... provides a model to account for variation in the development of issues management structures across firms.

Daniel W. Greening and Barbara Gray 1994 "Testing a model of organizational response to social and political issues." *Academy of Management Journal* 37 (3): 467–98, 469.

Who explains? Who modifies what? Who manages? What are the issues and what does it mean to manage them? Who develops structures?

This article analyses labour supply decision-making for a particular group of women workers in a particular segment of the London clothing industry. It takes as its starting point the concentration of Bangladeshi women in the homeworking sector of the East London rag trade (Mitter, 1986a).

Naila Kabeer 1994 "The structure of 'revealed preference': Race, community and female labour supply in the London clothing industry." *Development and Change* 25: 307–31.

Who makes decisions? What is supplied? Who labours? Who or what concentrates? What is concentrated?

These samples—all heavily nominal—seem to confirm the view that scholarly writing is difficult. Yet they appeared in respected journals. This style must in some way benefit scholarly writers and readers, and serve scholarly situations.

Halliday and Martin (1993) argue that this "language of the expert" gives priority to **taxonomy**: that is, to schemes for classifying and ordering phenomena. Such schemes depend on *names* for things. So, in the second passage, the action *modify* becomes the noun *modification*, which can then take an attribute ("structural"), which distinguishes it from other "modifications." The action or event stabilized as a noun can then be worked into an arrangement with other named phenomena, "institutions" and "resources." These arrangements, Halliday and Martin argue, are designed to reveal relations of *cause*. This is evident where the authors explicitly ask "*why* firms adopt ... structural modifications." In this ordering search for causes, the grammar of research genres ends up with heavy **nominalizations**.

We might also note tendencies in current scholarship in many disciplines to *integrate*—to bring together theories, conditions, analyses, dimensions. So, for example, in the third passage, "labour supply decision-making" names an effort to combine—or integrate—analyses of labour supply (availability of workers) with analyses of how people and households make decisions about what jobs they will seek, or keep, or quit. The grammatical outcome of this research initiative is a big noun phrase.

To this social analysis of nominal expressions we can add a cognitive, or socio-cognitive, dimension. In Chapter 9 we imagined readers working with passages of sentences, seeking higher-level terms in which to understand stretches of detail, or to understand the relevance of statements in context. Not all genres instruct the reader's efforts after meaning in the same way, and not all genres produce relevance in the same way. The scholarly genres typically maintain coherence and relevance by repeated references to high-level abstract topic entities.

Other genres—like websites, newspaper reports, or computer manuals—don't do this, although they may use nominalization for the purposes of economy or to identify highly specific technical terms. Nominalized headlines like "Proposed film tax law a step backwards, Cronenberg" or "Low vitamin D heightens breast-cancer mortality rate" are common; some can be genuinely difficult, as in the case of a CNN headline— "Freed mafia acid bath killer storm"—which was used to introduce a story about a public outcry that occurred when a killer who had used acid to dispose of the body of his victim was released from prison. Technical writing—in this case a manual for a scanner—routinely refers to things like "the Digital ICE photo retouch function" or "a built-in IEEE 1394 interface port." In none of these cases, however, does nominalization serve the research functions of maintaining textual coherence through repeated reference to important high-level abstractions.

With these conditions in mind, we can begin to see the role of heavily nominalized expressions in supporting these repeated movements between abstract and concrete, generalities and detail. If, over several paragraphs, one were to write about a number of cases where employers preferred to train young employees on the job and tended not to hire people with secondary-school diplomas, one could compress these many cases into *skill requirements in the workplace* and *educational attainment* and specify the relation between them as *not* synonymous. These expressions eliminate the employers who hired and taught and the workers and students who learned or failed to learn. But they also provide an ascent to the high level of abstraction that will hold this section of the discussion together. Then, as they are repeated, they serve as tokens for—or efficient reminders of—this section as the discussion develops over 10 or 20 pages: it is almost as if these expressions assume the status of single words. These abstract terms—the nominal versions of actions and events—can be reinstated at each of those points when the academic reader's mental desktop needs instructions on managing information. While the details on particular firms and industries and school curriculum can be filed away, the high-level terms should be kept handy.

Scholarly writers seem to need a concentrated expression they can reinstate to bind together parts of their discussion and to manage extensive stretches of lower-level information. These expressions are like elevated platforms from which the extent of the argument can be captured in a glance. There is not much standing room on these platforms, so, when the arguments are complex, the expression can be dense. In the article on Bangladeshi garment workers, "labour supply decision-making" has to capture at once the article's distinctions as a contribution to the analysis of labour markets. The author examines labour as offered by workers rather than required by firms—hence "labour supply." And she examines the conditions which determine the decisions people make about work in an immigrant community where husbands' wishes about the wives' work may not coincide with the women's wishes, and where both sets of choices are hemmed in by racial attitudes in the surrounding community. *Labour supply decision-making* is the platform from which expanses of statistical and interview data can be viewed.

These viewing platforms are situated throughout the scholarly article, often working to incorporate summary of other writers' statements. Below, in an article on *voluntary employee turnover* (people quitting their jobs), *employee turnover* is ground shared by the other writers and the current authors, while the expressions *job alternatives* (If I quit will I be able to get another job? Will it be a good one?) and *job satisfaction* (Am I happy in my work? Do I get along with my boss? Will I be promoted?) themselves compress information. And these abstractions not only point back to accumulated reasoning but also can be extracted from the publication and indexed as *key words*—to signal to researchers the site of scholarly conversation on a topic shared in a research community. Abstractions sum up previous research attention and the current episode—and they point forward, too, as reference or orientation for other researchers' future work:

> In a major conceptual advance from previous research directions, Hulin and colleagues (1985) recognized that job alternatives and satisfaction could have substantially different effects on employee turnover across various populations. For example, job alternatives but not job satisfaction might have a substantial and direct effect on turnover among marginal and temporary employees (often described as the secondary labor market). In contrast, both alternatives and job satisfaction might have significant effects on turnover among permanent and full-time employees.
>
> Thomas W. Lee and Terence R. Mitchell 1994 "An alternative approach: The unfolding model of voluntary employee turnover." *Academy of Management Journal* 19 (1): 51–89, 54.

Nominal expressions also tend to appear as writers end one section of argument and move on to the next stage. Here, the writer concerned with subsistence economies concludes a three-part account of the "world crises" affecting the "submerged ethnicities." She uses three expressions which nominalize verbs (and remove their agents) to compress the preceding discussion and make it portable, able to be carried forward compactly to the next section:

> These world trends of **integration of economies, dependence on finance capital**, and **erosion of subsistence security** have profound consequences for the societies we study, whether they are located in core industrial countries or in developing areas. I shall illustrate their implications in three case studies of integration into the global economy where I have carried out fieldwork.
>
> Nash 1994: 13 (emphasis added).

Unlike many other genres, scholarly genres must live up to demanding coherence requirements, hinged on abstraction and spread through deep descents to specifics and sharp ascents to generality. We could say that these large patterns of abstraction and specificity at text level determine smaller patterns at sentence level.

Earlier in this chapter, we asked what benefits come from long expressions which many measures would estimate as cognitively costly (hard to read). Now we have the answer: cognitive cost at the level of sentence and phrase brings benefits at the level of textual coherence.

Yet the model of the reader's mental desktop warns us that those sentence-level costs can be high—to readers who give up, and to writers who can't get through to exhausted readers. So you will find academic writers stopping to **unpack** a passage and relieve some of the congestion on the desktop.

> Pleck suggests that Afro-American women worked more as a reaction to their greater long-term potential for income inadequacy than to immediate economic deprivation. It was as if they were taking out insurance against future problems.
>
> James A. Geschwender 1992 "Ethgender, women's waged labor, and economic mobility." *Social Problems* 39 (1): 1–16, 7.

Sensing perhaps that "immediate economic deprivation" (being poor? not having enough money?) and "long-term potential for income inadequacy" (worry about not having enough money later?) are complicated ways of speaking, the author rephrases these expressions in everyday language.

In other words, while the research genres privilege the heavily nominal phrase—for reasons we have just examined—they also compensate for the difficult socio-cognitive conditions produced by their own styles. They do this by giving the reader easier access to the viewing platform offered by the noun phrase. This access is achieved by a feature we encountered in Chapter 7: the appositive expression. The appositive says it again, in other words, giving the reader a second chance at an important but difficult concept. For instance, after the writer in the passage immediately above says "long-term potential for income inadequacy," he repeats the idea in simpler, if less technically precise terms: "future problems."

Seeded throughout research writing we find two tiny expressions which signal writers' efforts to aid the reader's understanding of difficult nominal phrases by saying it again: *i.e.* and *e.g.* The expression *i.e.* (an abbreviation for *id est*, a Latin expression meaning "that is") signals that an element in the preceding statement (or statements) will be repeated; *i.e.* works *laterally*, putting an additional expression next to the one which the writer estimates as important but difficult, or important and complex, and deserving further attention. Synonymous with *i.e.* are *that is*, *namely*, *in other words*, *that is to say*. On the other hand, *e.g.* (*exempla gratia*, another Latin term, meaning "for example") signals that an element in the preceding statement will be exemplified at a lower level of generality; *e.g.* works *vertically*, descending from high levels to lower levels of specificity. Synonymous with *e.g.* are *for example*, *for instance*. Although they are not interchangeable, both *i.e.* and *e.g.* can work as appositives—enriching readers' understanding of a term, inviting their cooperation in its use in the particular context.

By these means, writers can reduce the cognitive costs of heavy nominal expressions to the reader. But what can readers do when they face imposing clumps of nouns? Rather than give up, they can unpack those clumps for themselves, finding the everyday wordings that would represent the ideas at stake, and trying to think of examples of what the writer is talking about.

Exercise 7
Take the three passages at the beginning of this section and unpack them for yourself. In each case try to construct concrete examples of what the writers are talking about. Using i.e. and e.g., rewrite the passages, incorporating answers to the set of questions immediately following each passage.

11

Scholarly Styles II:
Messages about the Argument

In Chapter 9, we considered the common complaint that scholarly style is difficult to read. We found that readers' previous contact with the subject and their different experiences of the world explain some of these reading difficulties. We also saw that the research genres are distinguished by nominalization and the superstructure of abstraction that it builds. Both nominalization and abstraction can appear in other genres, but they do not work in the same way they do in the research genres, where they consistently enforce the special coherence of scholarly writing and attach individual research contributions to an ongoing scholarly conversation. In this chapter, we will inspect **messages about the argument**, including four stylistic features that distinguish the academic genres: **self-reference**, the **discursive *I***, **forecasts**, and **emphasis**. These messages help readers understand the organization of academic writing.

11A Messages about the Argument

The following passage, which appeared in a geography journal, exhibits several features we will investigate. This passage refers to itself ("This paper"); it refers to the author ("We" and "Our"); and it forecasts the argument to follow ("After a brief discussion," "we consider," "We then turn," and "Our conclusion").

... the study of gender issues generally in rural areas remains relatively neglected (Little 1991).

This paper is an attempt to begin to redress the balance by concentrating on the gender divisions apparent in the material collected by the Rural Church Project, and aims also to highlight the need for further specific study of gender and the rural church. **After a brief discussion** of the history of staffing in the Church of England, **we consider** recent published studies on gender roles in the Church and our own material from the Rural Church Project survey on the staffing of parishes in five dioceses. **We then turn** to rural parishioners and consider the influence of gender on church attendance and religious belief, together with attitudes towards women priests. **Our conclusion** is an attempt to reconcile the very different pictures of the rural church which emerge from the information on staffing on the one hand and attendance, belief and attitudes to women priests on the other.

Susanne Seymour 1994 "Gender, church and people in rural areas." *Area* 26 (1): 45–56, 45.

To sharpen your sense of these features as distinctive, call to mind other genres, familiar from everyday life. Before we look at messages about the argument found in this passage, let's think back to Chapter 8 where we found that introductions often construct a state of knowledge and identify a knowledge deficit. Here, the passage begins, "the study of gender issues generally in rural areas remains relatively neglected (Little 1991)." Would a newspaper report or a thank-you note situate what is currently being said in relation to what others have said, or not said?

Little information about this event has been published, since it only happened yesterday.	No one has so far expressed gratitude for this gift in writing.

It's unlikely. In fact, newspaper stories often repeat what has already been reported as if it were news, while thank-you notes repeat earlier thanks, perhaps in-person, to create emphasis.

Would you find a newspaper report or a thank-you note referring to itself?

This report provides information on protest at the legislature.	This thank-you note expresses gratitude for two gifts received last week.

Probably not, although there are instances where other genres (very formal business letters, for example, or legal documents) refer to themselves. Would you find a newspaper report or thank-you note referring to the author in this (limited) sense?

| I/we present a series of quotations from participants at the protest. | I/we describe the gift in favourable terms. |

Probably not, although the thank-you-note writer may refer to himself in other senses ("I have been very busy at school and look forward to the holidays"). Would you find a newspaper report or thank-you note forecasting its discussion?

| These quotations will be followed by quotations from political figures responding to the protest. | Following the description of the gift, brief news about the recipient's family will be presented. |

Again, probably not.

In the next sections, we will examine these features, which distinguish the cited passage from—at least—newspaper reports and thank-you notes.

Exercise 1

The passage from Seymour above includes self-reference: "This paper" refers to the article that Seymour is writing, "Gender, church and people in rural areas." Identify instances of self-reference in the following passage from an article on the geologic history of Mars. For each instance, explain why the writer uses self-reference.

Since 1996 three spacecraft have successfully landed on the martian surface and four have been placed in orbit. These vehicles have returned enormous amounts of data that are transforming our understanding of what Mars is like and how it arrived at its present state. The purpose of this paper is to summarize what the new data might imply for the geologic evolution of the planet (Fig. 1). It focuses mainly on surficial processes such as erosion, sedimentation and weathering, rather than primary terrain-building processes such as impact, tectonism and volcanism since surficial processes arguably present the most puzzling aspects of Mars' geologic evolution. The role of liquid water is particularly puzzling. With a mean annual temperature close to 215 K at the equator and a mean surface pressure of 6.1 mbar, the surface pressure is below the critical pressure for liquid water over half the planet's surface and everywhere temperatures are such that any liquid water that forms will rapidly freeze. Yet geologic evidence for the widespread presence of liquid water is compelling, particularly for early Mars, and claims have also been made of present-day water activity. Thus while the emphasis of the paper is on geology, the discussion has implications for climate and atmospheric evolution.

Michael H. Carr and James W. Head 2010 "Geologic history of Mars." *Earth and Planetary Science Letters* 294 (3): 185–203, 186.

Exercise 2

Inspect essays you have written recently or are currently drafting: do you find expressions that refer to the essay itself? (Keep in mind that such wordings appear at points where writers make major claims or promises.) How do you feel about saying, "This study focuses on three explanations for ..."? Would you feel better saying, "This paper ..." or "This essay ..."?

11B The Discursive *I*

One feature in the above passage on gender roles in rural churches that sometimes surprises students is the author's tendency to refer to herself. Although the first-person singular *I*—and the plural *we*—occurs in the scholarly genres with nowhere near the frequency that it does in daily conversation (where it is a favoured sentence opener), it is by no means absent from published scholarship (though favoured in some disciplines more than others).

Sometimes students ask their teachers if they want them to use *I*, or to avoid it. This question is often accompanied by a question as to whether the teachers are interested in the students' own opinions. In the long history of the teaching of writing, *I* and "opinion" have become connected. However, in conventional, mainstream scholarship, where *I* occurs under limited conditions, it would be hard to connect *I* with the ordinary sense of "opinion."

Let's examine the limits or constraints on *I* in published scholarship. See if you can infer the conditions that control the use of *I*. (Analysis follows, but try to make this out for yourself before looking at the analysis.)

> **After reviewing** the original motivation for the formulation of string theory and what we learned from it, **I discuss** some of the implications of the holographic principle and of string dualities for the question of the building blocks of nature.
>
> Leonard Susskind 2013 "String theory." *Foundations of Physics* 43 (1): 174–81, 174.

> Lesbian theory and feminism, **I want to suggest**, are at risk of falling into a similar unhappy marriage in which "the one" is feminism.
>
> Calhoun 1994: 568.

> ... **I shall focus upon** expectations and evaluations regarding the participation of married women, with husband present, in the waged labor force. **I begin with** a discussion of the "cult of domesticity," explore ethnic variations in commitments to the cult, examine the causes and consequences of its decline in influence, and evaluate the consequences for ethnic groups of difference in rates at which married women work for wages. **I close with** a consideration of policy implications.
>
> Geschwender 1992: 1.

> This article has two purposes. The first is to show that ability grouping in secondary schools does not always have the same effect, and therefore it is worth seeking ways of using it more effectively than commonly occurs. A brief review of earlier studies, and a reinterpretation of the conclusions of an earlier synthesis, provide the support for this claim. The second goal is to explore instances of relatively successful uses of ability grouping, in the sense that high-quality instruction fosters significant learning among students assigned to low-ability classes. What characterizes such classes? **To address this question, I draw on evidence** from earlier studies by other authors, and **I provide** two new illustrations taken from a larger study of eighth- and ninth-grade English classes in 25 midwestern schools.
>
> Gamoran 1993: 1.

On the one hand, the *I* of the writer in these passages seems to hover on the vanishing point. In most cases, the *I*-construction could be eliminated without depleting content. It could simply disappear ("Lesbian theory and feminist theory are at risk of ...") or be replaced by one of the text-referring words like "study" ("this study focuses"), and the last passage mixes such words ("article," "review") with instances of *I*.

Given the frequency with which *I* makes its appearance in the scholarly genres, we might look at the typical habitat of the first-person pronoun: what does it occur with? Then we notice that all the verbs that have first-person subjects refer to some **discourse action**, something the writer is doing:

I want to suggest	I close
I begin with	I draw on evidence
I shall focus	I provide
I explore, examine, evaluate	

Analysts who specialize in the study of the research genres would distinguish among these verbs, finding different categories of discourse action. But, for our purposes, it is enough to note their general similarity: they all describe the speaker in his or her capacity as a writer/researcher. Let us call this use of *I* in the scholarly genres **the discursive *I***.

As a writer in the scholarly genres, you can refer to yourself, pointing yourself out to your reader. But, as the passages above suggest, your identity is limited to your activities as a researcher. Attitudes to these limitations run to extremes. So many students report that their teachers and professors have instructed them not to use *I* that there must still be some *I*-avoidance afoot. Perhaps this can be explained by the limitations on *I* when it occurs in scholarship. Those who would disallow *I* translate the limits into a blanket prohibition.

Taking a different view, some scholars criticize the research genres for the limits they put on *I*. Conventions that limit writers to the discursive *I* erase elements of identity that are, in fact, relevant to research and its results. Such criticisms propose that who we are, as social and political beings, influences what we choose to study, how we gather information, and how we interpret that information. The discursive *I* obscures those influences and limits not only the surface expression of scholarship but its deeper character as well. In the next chapter we will look at instances in which *I* preserves a greater degree of the researcher's personal identity, but for now we should recognize the frequency with which the discursive *I* appears in the research genres.

Exercise 3

What do you think of the reference to the "author" in the following passage? Does it help you to know that this paper was written by a psychologist? Can you devise any other way of writing this passage—without using the first person singular?

> The author decided to investigate the academic achievement levels of the teenage mothers with whom she was working after being told repeatedly that their favorite subject in school was math—an unexpected and perplexing finding because girls are generally reported to feel they are not good at, and thus dislike, math (Parsons, Adler, and Kaczala, 1982).
>
> Rauch-Elnekave 1994: 97.

Exercise 4

Inspect essays you have written recently or are currently composing: how do you represent yourself when you write an academic paper? Are you happy with this representation? Would your friends and family recognize you? What options do you feel you have? Do the options vary according to the discipline you are working in?

11C Forecasts

Like references to the text itself, the discursive *I* of scholarly writing often occurs along with forecasts: statements about how the argument will be organized, what readers can expect.

> **First**, I will summarize prior research indicating that instruction is typically inferior in low-ability classes. **Second**, I will briefly show that new data from a study of midwestern secondary schools mainly conform to this pattern. **Third**, I will give four examples—two drawn from past research, and two original cases taken from the study of midwestern secondary schools—that illustrate that high-quality

instruction can occur in low-ability classes. **Finally**, I will consider the limitations and implications of these illustrations.

Gamoran: 4–5.

We have attempted to overcome these limitations with reconstructions by first developing new concepts for reconstructions, incorporating them into a new software system, and then using the procedures to develop a new set of global plate reconstructions. **We use** GPlates,[3] a new software system for interactive plate tectonic reconstructions linked to geodynamic models and GIS databases (Boyden et al., in press). The program incorporates evolving closed plate polygons to represent tectonic plates and incorporates both a data representation of closed plate polygons as well as onscreen capabilities allowing the user to interactively create polygons with geological data. The program also incorporates utilities to read in files from geodynamic models and prepare data files that control geodynamic simulations.

In this paper, we describe the continuously closed plate algorithm, provide a brief overview of the GPlates system, describe the CCP algorithm as implemented within GPlates, and illustrate the construction of a global reconstruction with continuously closing plates with data from existing traditional reconstructions. **We conclude** with some preliminary examples of using the new reconstructions in geodynamic models as illustrations.

Michael Gurnis, Mark Turner, Sabin Zahirovic, Lydia DiCaprio, Sonja Spasojevic, R. Dietmar Müller, James Boyden, Maria Seton, Vlad Constantin Manea, and Dan J. Bower 2012 "Plate tectonic reconstructions with continuously closing plates." *Computers and Geosciences* 38 (1): 35–42, 36.

Forecasts can also show up in agentless forms—that is, without either the text itself or the discursive *I* promising a particular course of discussion.

Before proceeding to a more precise description of **the research methods** used and a detailed discussion of sample matched reader-writer protocols, **the relevance of this study** to current theoretical disputes over appropriate rhetorical techniques and planning processes for appellate advocates **should be put into sharper focus. Two basic issues will be addressed:**

1) What rhetorical techniques in briefs do current brief writing theories recommend appellates use, and what conflicts exist between these theories?

2) What problems has empirical research investigating these theories encountered?

James F. Stratman 1994 "Investigating persuasive processes in legal discourse in real time: Cognitive biases and rhetorical strategy in appeal court briefs." *Discourse Processes* 17: 1–57, 7.

This passage achieves its agentlessness by using the **passive voice**: "the research methods used" (*who* used the methods?); "the relevance ... should be put into sharper focus" (*who* should do this?); "two basic issues will be addressed" (*who* will address the issues?).

The passive voice has been condemned by many, and defended by few. Despite its bad reputation amongst people who compose rules for writing, however, it is very common in scholarly expression, as well as elsewhere. In the three **passive constructions** listed above, for example, the themes of the sentences ("the research methods," "the relevance," and "two basic issues") are more important than *who* is "using," "addressing," or "putting them into sharper focus." The passive voice enables this focus on sentence themes.

While we do not run across forecasts (either with or without passive constructions) so often in everyday life—

MATTHEW: What have you been up to?

MARK: In addressing your question, I will first express my philosophy of life. Next, I will show that philosophy operating in my recent activities. Finally, I will describe my plans for the future.

—they are extremely common in the scholarly genres. It seems that forecasts play an important role in helping readers manage the contents of their mental desktops (see Chapter 9B). Forecasts guide readers in determining when one section is finished and another is beginning— determining, that is, when to file lower-level information, compacting its gist into higher-level statements that can be kept handy as the discussion goes on to other areas.

Exercise 5

Analyze the use of forecasting in the following passage from an article on botanical gardens. How do the writers combine self-reference and the discursive I (or "we" in this case) to create a forecast? Compare their style of forecasting with that of Gamoran, Gurnis et al., and Stratman in the passages above.

In this study, we take data on spontaneous seed and vegetative reproduction in a botanical garden and examine their relationships with a number of soft traits that are available from species databases and have typically been used in the literature as proxies for specific demographic processes of plants. Further, we search for possible trade-offs between vegetative and seed reproduction in the garden and examine whether corresponding trade-offs can be found in the trait data. The traits we work with are plant height, leaf size and SLA, which are used as proxies for growth rate or competitive ability, and seed size as a proxy for seed dispersal and chance of seedling establishment. For clonally growing species, we also use a number of essentially morphological traits (Klimešová, Doležal & Sammul 2011a; Klimešová et al. 2011) to assess the potential for vegetative growth and also relate these traits to the garden's reproductive data.

We work with approximately one thousand central European species grown in the Botanical Garden of Charles University in Prague. The garden is rather environmentally heterogeneous, with each species maintained separately in conditions that can be reasonably assumed to be close to its natural habitat, but with competitive interactions (namely interspecific) largely reduced by weeding and thinning. Still the reproduction in the garden results from plants' responsive behaviour to their environment, which forms a key component of the species' demographic processes in nature. We hence view the data as information on vegetative and seed reproduction of individual species under favourable conditions.

Tomáš Herben, Zuzana Nováková, Jitka Klimešová, and Lubomír Hrouda 2012 "Species traits and plant performance: Functional trade-offs in a large set of species in a botanical garden." *Journal of Ecology* 100 (6): 1522–33, 1524.

11D Emphasis

Readers are also served by statements of emphasis. Here are some examples.

> The **crucial point** for this essay is that between 1939 and 1944 the organization attracted *popular support*.

> Our **main interest** here is the style of the printed language—how did it reconcile with the everyday language of the predominantly oral world?

Thiathu J. Nemutanzhela 1993 "Cultural forms and literacy as resources for political mobilisation: A.M. Malivha and the Zoutpansberg Balemi Association." *African Studies* 52 (1): 89–102, 92–93 (bold emphasis added, italic emphasis in original).

> The **general point here** is that there are instances—this [campaign for non-sexist language] is one—where we can locate the specific and concrete steps leading to an observable change in some people's linguistic behaviour and in the system itself.

Deborah Cameron 1990 "Demythologizing sociolinguistics: Why language does not reflect society." In *Ideologies of Language*, ed. John E. Joseph and Talbot J. Taylor. London: Routledge, 91.

> What I want to **highlight** in Wittig's explanation of what bars lesbians from the category "woman" is that it claims both too much and too little for lesbians as well as reads lesbianism from a peculiarly heterosexual viewpoint.

Calhoun 1994: 563.

A common means of achieving emphasis is to use the **cleft** form of a sentence (i.e., a sentence that begins "It was X that ..." rather than "X ...". Many guides to "good" style disallow sentences beginning with *it*. These sentences are said to be boring or "empty." Yet *it* in English serves as a built-in grammar of emphasis. Notice how *it* works in these ordinary, conversational sentences to stage the importance of a particular part of the sentence.

Julie brought the cookies.   It was Julie who brought the cookies. [not anybody else]

A speaker could use intonation—"*Julie* brought the cookies"—to achieve emphasis. Writers can't use intonation—but they can (and do) use the cleft form of the sentence. (Notice how, if you say the second sentence above, stress falls on "Julie.") If the speaker or writer wanted to emphasize the contribution rather than the contributor, they could say or write:

> It was the cookies that Julie brought [not the lasagne].

In research writing, cleft sentences beginning with *it* can accomplish emphasis, e.g.,

> It was Foucault's work that mobilized research of institutions under the "surveillance" theme.

And, while we are thinking about sentences beginning with *it*, we can also observe that on many occasions the tendencies of English will use the **end-weight principle** to shift heavy material to sentence-end, leaving the sentence beginning "empty." Of the following pair, the first is more likely to be produced by English speakers and writers.

> It may be argued that this neglect is due to a lack of scholarly interest in the rural church rather than in gender relations in the Anglican Church as a whole.

> That this neglect is due to a lack of scholarly interest in the rural church rather than in gender relations in the Anglican Church as a whole may be argued.

The reason that the first is usually preferred is that it obeys the "end-weight" principle in English: a tendency for sentences to tilt, letting heavy material slide to the end, and producing what's called **anticipatory-it** or it-extraposition. Like the passive voice, sentences beginning with *it* have been criticized by authorities on "good" style, but there seems to be little basis for these criticisms. As we can see in the following example from molecular biology, the *it*-clause prepares readers for "generally accepted" information—information that is shifted to the end of the sentence.

> Although not formally proven, it is generally accepted that the spike is a timer of gp120-gp41 heterodimers....

Michael B. Zwick et al. 2003 "Molecular features of the broadly neutralizing immunoglobulin G1 b12 required for recognition of human immunodeficiency virus type 1 gp120." *Journal of Virology* 77 (10): 5863–76, 5863.

These uses of emphasis are not, however, universal in academic writing. Some research articles provide neither forecasts nor emphasis pointers. Movements along the hierarchy of generalization—from high-level abstraction to specifics and back again—themselves convey implicit messages about the argument, messages that will alert experienced readers to important points in the text. Nevertheless, many research articles do use expressions of emphasis, and most seem to offer some kind of forecast.

Similarly, most instances of the discursive *I* could be removed, and the expression in which they occur adjusted to get across equivalent information. But *I* occurs nevertheless, with some frequency. Perhaps both techniques not only benefit readers' mental desktops but also provide writers with greater control over the use that readers make of their texts. Perhaps forecasts and emphasis pointers would have, on some occasions, controlled some of those unruly readers/instructors who missed your point. While we could speculate that both forecasts and emphasis (and the associated references to the text itself and its writer) are signs that scholarly genres can be domineering or overpowering in their measures for controlling readers' interpretive work, we can perhaps also sympathize with writers' desires to overrule the hazards of misunderstanding.

The scholarly genres can seem aloof productions, remote from the personal contact and proximities of more mundane genres or of everyday conversation. Yet the features we have looked at in this chapter all summon writer and reader to the same spot, putting the writer in close touch with the reader.

Exercise 6

Imagine a reader from outside the academic community encountering the passage below (which is taken from the last three paragraphs of an introduction). How could you prepare that reader for contact with this example of scholarly expression? How would you explain the features of the passage so the imagined reader would understand them as functional expressions of the academic community's routines and procedures? (It might help to imagine a particular reader—a friend, family member, neighbour, co-worker, or maybe yourself at an earlier stage of your education.)

This article considers the global exchange of human hair, a business implicated in structuring First and Third World femininities, consumer and producer relations between the West and the rest, as hair is culled and then spun into a "repulsive gift"[5]—hair extensions—bestowed upon the scalps of a First World clientele. [...]

In the discussion that follows, I draw significantly on Chandra Talpade Mohanty's vision of the exploitative relationship between Third World producers and First World consumers, as well as on her discussion of invisible labour. In the context of the West's penchant for women's hair and its lustrous lengths, hair has historically operated to fill in a perceived bodily lack for Western women. Tracing the origins and networks of the trade, in particular the multinational hair extensions company Great Lengths International, I examine what happens when hair becomes a commodity in the global capitalist arena, suggesting that bodily products "exist as much outside of and between bodies as within or on them,"[6] and that the ethics of the global hair trade need to be delineated alongside the unequal relationship between First World consumers and Third World producers.

While I consider here the ways in which the global hair trade makes "getting lucky" involve the interfacing of one's corporeality with the imaginative power of corporate globalization, I also explore hair's living-dead undecidability, which, in the context of its commodification, invokes both the politics and ontology of what I call the zombie commodity.

Notes

[5]   Although space does not permit me here to discuss hair as a manifestation of the abject, it is worthwhile noting that Julia Kristeva situates abjection in between self and other as something that is discardable, droppable, sheddable. The abject is a "repulsive gift that the Other [...] drops so that the 'I' does not disappear in it but finds, in that sublime alienation, a forfeited existence. Hence a jouissance in which the subject is swallowed up but in which the Other, in return, keeps the subject from foundering by making it repugnant." Julia Kristeva, *Powers of Horror: An Essay on Abjection*,

trans. Leon S. Roudiez, New York: Columbia University Press, 1982, p 9.

6   Eugene Thacker, cited in Catherine Waldby and Robert Mitchell, *Tissue Economies: Blood, Organs and Cell Lines in Late Capitalism*, Durham, NC: Duke University Press, 2006, back matter.

Esther Berry 2008 "The Zombie commodity: Hair and the politics of its globalization." *Postcolonial Studies* 11 (1): 63–84, 63–64.

12

Making and Maintaining
Knowledge I

When research findings are reported to the public, in broadcast or general-circulation print and digital media, they are normally "popularized." That is, specialist or technical terms are translated and replaced with everyday ones. We can expect that, thereby, careful distinctions produced by technicality itself will be lost: "hedonic balance" and "life satisfaction," which to psychologists are important components of "subjective well-being," vanish on the road to journalistic accounts of the much more recognizable term *happiness*; climatologists' careful distinctions between "albedo" and "radiative forcing," "insolation" and "irradiance" disappear to make way for generalizations about *climate change*. But this is only part of the story. Research publications typically pay a lot of attention to the ways in which knowledge is produced, and we might expect that some of these concerns will also be lost in popularizations, which tend to emphasize research results over research processes. Since most new readers of scholarly prose are familiar only with journalistic approaches to reporting research, they may find that they need to be especially attentive to researchers' accounts of the *processes* by which knowledge is produced.

In earlier chapters, we saw that summary and orchestration of voices are central features of scholarly writing and that through them academic writers make audible a **state of knowledge**: what is known by researchers working in the field, the conditions under which this knowledge was produced, the positions from which statements issue. Orchestration can also identify limits to the state of knowledge and lead to a **knowledge deficit**: what still needs to be said, or even what has been mistakenly said and needs to be corrected. In some circumstances, particularly research proposals and introductions to scholarly papers, the knowledge deficit may be followed by an account of the processes by which new knowledge will be produced. This chapter examines those processes, and how they differ from discipline to discipline.

12A Making Knowledge

Consider for a minute what it means to make knowledge. Say that one particularly hot Labour Day weekend Matthew concludes that that summer had been the hottest in living memory. His friend Mark disagrees and so the two make a bet. To support his position, Matthew points out how frequently he went swimming to cool off and slept in his basement at night to avoid the heat; he can't recall doing those things as often in previous years. But Matthew's claims don't convince Mark, who knows that memories can be unreliable, and that, in any case, some summers Matthew has been out of town and some other summers the swimming pool had been closed. Faced with such skepticism, Matthew discovers that he needs to find some more reliable, objective standard—something less dependent on his own memories and impressions—for comparing the current summer to previous ones. And so he begins to look for old news stories about heat waves, and then for Environment Canada's records of daily temperature highs and lows over the years. Such inquiries become quite complicated, involving the calculation of daily mean temperatures and, because Mark remains skeptical, some weighting of night vs. daytime averages. In the end, settling the bet demands not only numbers, but a considerable amount of math as well.

Whatever the outcome of the bet, let's also imagine that in the course of his inquiries Matthew notices that people like telling him stories about past summers. His elderly uncle Thomas remembers the 1950s as having the most pleasant summers of all, and he tells eloquent stories about warm evenings at the drive-in theatre and the darkness of the skies when there were fewer city lights. These stories prompt Matthew to write something about the relation between memory and nostalgia, using his uncle as a case study. Later, however, he wonders how his particular relationship to Thomas shapes the stories he's recorded. Matthew and Thomas are both men, after all, and members of the same family—maybe Thomas presents the past differently to strangers or to women, or maybe Matthew listens to his uncle in ways he wouldn't listen to strangers. This realization makes Matthew try to account for his own role, as observer, in shaping his findings.

In this sequence of knowledge-making actions, we have, very roughly, travelled through the range of **methods** in the research disciplines, from the "hard" sciences (in which interpretation is sustained by research instruments that measure phenomena) to some branches of the humanities (in which qualities are open to interpretation but resist quantitative measurement) to what we might call "reflexive" interpretations in which the interpreter's position is taken into account in the production of knowledge.

Even without delving into complex philosophical questions of how we know what we know, we can see that knowledge-making procedures differ from discipline to discipline. These differences are reflected in the styles of research writing: variations in the ways that language represents the processes of making knowledge. The most conspicuous stylistic differences distinguish publications with lots of numbers from those with no numbers. They reflect the differences between **quantitative** and **qualitative** study.

Quantitative method aims to approach knowledge making as objectively as possible: that is, it seeks to set aside biases caused by an individual's beliefs or immediate experience of the world by observing controlled studies or experiments and quantifying results using as broad a sample as possible. In the example above, when Matthew abandons his own impressions in favour of gathering and analysing objective data on temperature, he steps into the realm of quantitative study. A classic example of the success of quantitative study is the Copernican revolution, in which the earth-centred view of the solar system was replaced with the sun-centred model. The invention of the telescope and the observations of planetary motion by Galileo provided empirical evidence that the earth revolves around the sun, despite deeply ingrained beliefs to the contrary and the apparently obvious evidence of our senses when we observe the sun rising and setting on a daily basis. In another famous example of the quantitative method, James Watson and Francis Crick used data showing that in DNA adenine was always present in the same amount as thymine, with the same holding true for guanine and cytosine. These ratios helped invalidate previous three-strand models of DNA and confirm Watson and Crick's hypothesis that DNA is structured as a double helix. This sort of method, which you probably associate with the sciences, attempts to quantify empirically reproducible findings.

A significant part of undergraduate education in the sciences and social sciences is devoted to learning established methods for quantitative study. These methods vary according to discipline and the phenomena studied, but, as genre theory suggests, the central importance of quantitative knowledge making in these disciplines should lead us to expect stylistic expressions that reflect the researchers' situation, a subject we'll examine more closely in the next section. However, these methods are not without their limits, even within disciplines that favour quantitative research.

For disciplines that study purely physical phenomena—for example, astronomy or chemistry—quantitative method is a relatively reliable and unproblematic way of understanding reality (although, as historians of science have pointed out, even the decision about *what* to measure is the result of the researcher's position in a social world). But when quantitative method encounters the complexities of social interaction, its limitations become clear. Once phenomena—events and attitudes, and the people who are involved in those events or harbour those attitudes—are translated into countable units, and the numbers are subjected to routines of statistical interpretation, they get separated from the meaningful complexities of real-life contexts. So a study of, for example, "learning outcomes" in a hundred classrooms might identify three relevant conditions: the socioeconomic identity of the learners (as measured by a standard scale), their learning styles (as measured by a standard method of classifying learning styles), and their performance in a subject area (as measured by a standardized test). The results could lead to changes in curriculum or teaching strategies. Critics of this kind of research argue that such quantifications erase the classroom moment, the experience of students and teachers, the complex interactions amongst them. Research quantifications therefore produce a limited or possibly skewed version of the world, and their applications can be unrealistic. In place of—or in addition to—quantitative research, these critics propose qualitative research.

Qualitative research can take various forms. One way to look at it is to say that it distinguishes itself from quantitative research by replacing the *many* instances (which are open to statistical interpretation) with *one* or at most a few instances. The one instance is examined in detail, often with an emphasis on qualities that elude the kind of measurement that instruments provide (whether those instruments are standardized tests or mass spectrometers). The long-distance panoramas of quantitative research are replaced by close-up views. So, in the qualitative version of the learning-outcomes study, researchers would locate themselves in one classroom and watch—for days, months, even years. They would record what they saw, taking notes, using video or audio tapes; they would collect documents and artifacts (the teacher's lesson plans, tests, students' work, and so on); they would talk to the teacher and to the students. Unlike quantitative researchers, who arrange measurable situations (controlled instruction, perhaps; tests administered solely for the purpose of the study), qualitative researchers try to leave things as they are. The only change is the presence of the researchers themselves. Back at their desks, the qualitative researchers interpret the material they have gathered. Surveying their data, they look for patterns and regularities, and, consulting the theoretical tools available to them, they develop explanations for what they have observed.

Both quantitative and qualitative techniques seek generalizations, but they establish the *authority* of their generalizations by different means. Quantitative studies represent their validity by numerousness. They use standardized means of manipulating a large number of instances to coax out statistically significant results. Qualitative studies have only the one instance (as in a "case study") or the one group (such as a group of young women who read teen romance fiction). So, while the "objective" style of quantitative research and the rhetorical force of that style are very important (consider, for a moment, the implications of our discussions on limits of the discursive *I* in Chapter 11B), qualitative research may actually be even more dependent on *style of reporting* to persuade readers to accept generalizations developed from limited instances. Moreover, as qualitative study generates an abundance of detail, the means of controlling these data, and transforming them into text that readers can understand, are perhaps more demanding for writers than the customary techniques used for producing text to report quantitative research.

Qualitative techniques show up in various disciplines, and, while many scholarly journals are exclusively quantitative in the submissions they publish, and many others tend toward qualitative research, yet other journals publish both quantitative and qualitative work. You will also find articles that are themselves a mix of quantitative and qualitative techniques.

Given this variety in form and occurrence, it would be rash to list rules for reporting research. Nonetheless, the shared concern for the sources of knowledge and an interest in tracing the production of knowledge lead to some features common to both quantitative and qualitative research. The prominence of reported speech is an obvious sign of these interests and concerns (see Chapters 2 and 3), but it is not the only sign of them. Appearing with some regularity throughout reports of research are typical expressions which signify that knowledge is under construction and in the process of being made, and that it comes from a particular position in the research community. In Chapter 13 we will inspect some of these expressions and try to arrive at generalizations about their use; we will also consider the relation between tenses and knowledge making. First, though, we will glance at the research genres' most explicit demonstration that knowledge is being made. Along the lines that distinguish quantitative from qualitative study, research genres are also distinguished by whether they make provision for a "Methods" section—an explicit account of how the researchers produced the knowledge they are now reporting—or leave method implicit.

Exercise 1

Consider how knowledge is made in different disciplines. What do researchers *do* in different disciplines? Drawing on your experience of different courses you have taken, reading you have done, and the experiences of friends, compare knowledge-making practices or methods in the natural sciences (e.g., biology and physics), social sciences (e.g., psychology and sociology), and humanities (e.g., English, history, and philosophy). Which would you identify as primarily qualitative? Which are quantitative? Which seem to combine both methods? In what ways do features such as individual observation and interpretation, data gathering, quantification of data, statistical analysis, experiments using control groups, and so on define each discipline's knowledge-making practice as qualitative or quantitative?

12B Method Sections

Method sections expose the procedures by which knowledge has been produced, and they are especially common in disciplines that use quantitative methods. The rhetoric of method sections has been much studied, for these sections exhibit some interesting stylistic features. For one thing, they tend toward **agentless expressions** (see Chapter 10D and 11C). So you will find language like the following, from a study on the neurology of emotions: "Before the scanning session the purpose of the study was explained, and each subject was asked to name specific events in her life that, when recalled, would make her sad (two events) or happy (two events) (George et al. 1995, 342)." Here the person doing the explaining and the asking disappears from the sentence, and it is impossible to tell which of the study's six authors did the interviewing, or whether several or indeed all of them conducted interviews. This feature of style has excited a lot of commentary, and sometimes it is interpreted as a way of persuading readers that the researchers' methods display an **objectivity** that is not open to personal bias or interpretation. The importance of reproducing results in a quantitative study may also explain the emphasis on actions rather than on the agents of that action.

However, while method sections tend toward agentless expressions, it would not be true to say that the agent is always excluded. Sometimes agentless expressions appear alongside statements employing what we might call the **methodological *I***, as in the following passage:

> The electrical resistance was measured using the four terminals with an applied a.c. measuring current of 1 mA. For the sample chamber with a diameter of 50mm, **we drilled** a hole in an Al_2O_3 layer which was fitted into a rhenium gasket. The Al_2O_3 layer electrically insulates the metal gasket from both the sample and from the electrodes. **We checked** the insulation between the electrodes and the gasket during compression and all processes. **We attached** the diamond anvil cell **and loaded** the sample directly onto the mixing chamber of a 3He/4He dilution refrigerator.
>
> K. Shimizu, K. Suhara, M. Ikumo, M. Eremets, and K. Amaya 1998 "Superconductivity in oxygen." *Nature* 393: 767–69, 768.

We have come across research uses of the first-person pronoun before, in the discursive *I* (Chapter 11B), and we noted that in such cases the first-person pronoun is associated with a **discourse action**. In the case of the methodological *I*, the first-person pronoun is often associated with *physical* actions—the handling of equipment, the excavation of sites, the interviewing of subjects.

Another interesting feature of method sections is their unusual pattern of coherence: although sentences are all, roughly, about "method," sometimes the relation between sentences is obscure. So, in the second passage in the exercise below, you will find:

The participants in this study were educationally and socially advantaged, middle-class, urban children who were predominantly white. The children attended the day-care centre for full days, year round, and had known each other for 1–3 years.

If this were not a method section, a reader could very well ask, "What is the connection between, on the one hand, race and socioeconomic status and, on the other hand, full-time attendance at daycare? Why select these details? Is it a causal connection? And what does any of this have to do with the topic of the article?" Readers probably won't ask these questions because they assume the details are relevant to the method—they are accustomed to encountering these sorts of apparently unrelated details in a method section. But it is worth asking exactly why these details are included. How do they relate to past studies? How might they be used in the future?

Exercise 2

Two samples of method sections appear below. (Passage 1 is not complete.) Analyze these samples for agentlessness and connectedness. Then consider the overall function of these passages: If you were to generalize from these limited data, what would you identify as the main concerns of researchers composing an account of their methods? What kinds of questions are the researchers answering about their work? Can you detect differences in these questions in two disciplines?

PASSAGE 1

2.2 Subjects

The sample consisted of adult patients (over the age of 18 years) who met one of the selection criteria: (a) surgery in the past 24–72 h and pain in the last 24 h, or (b) diagnosis of cancer, care in oncology units or hospice units, and pain in the last 24 h as assessed by the research assistant. Two hundred thirty-four patients were recruited for this study, including 100 postoperative patients, 100 oncology patients, and 34 hospice patients. The response rate was 94% for the surgical group, 89% for the oncology group, and 68% for the hospice group. The sample size of the hospice group is small because some hospice patients were too fragile or even cognitively impaired at the time this study was conducted. Of these 234 patients, 49% (n = 115) were male and 51% (n = 119) were female. The age range was from 18 to 87 with a mean (SD) of 52.8 (15.9) years. Sixty-five percent of the participants (n = 152) were married. Their religious affiliations included Buddhist (51.7%), Taoist (12.4%), Catholic (1.0%), Jewish (7.7%), and none or other (27.2%). Twenty-seven of these patients had a high school-equivalent education and 44% had completed college education. Demographic characteristics of the patients in each of the study groups are presented in Table 1.

2.3 Instrument

The outcome questionnaire of this study was adopted from the study by Ward and Gordon (1994). This questionnaire was translated into Chinese by using a translation and back-translation method to ensure correct translation. The questionnaire was based on the American Pain Society Standards (Max et al., 1991). This questionnaire included (1) patients' assessment of pain severity and satisfaction with how pain was managed by physicians and nurses, (2) patients' perceptions of the time between a complaint of pain and receipt of medication, and (3) patients' perceptions of the time between a complaint of inadequate medication and the receipt of different or stronger medication. Patients were asked if their doctors or nurses discussed with them the importance of pain management. The specific items in the outcome questionnaire, based on the PAS standards, are listed in Table 2. Finally, a one-page demographic sheet covering basic information, such as age, gender, and education was included in the questionnaire.

2.4 Procedure

Patients who met the selection criteria were approached individually by the research assistant. Patients who met criterion (b) (diagnosis of cancer) were approached within 72 h of admission to the unit. The research assistant described the study and obtained oral consent. Special emphasis was made that the patients' confidentiality would be protected and that their care providers would not know any individual's answers. Patients were asked to complete the questionnaire without assistance from others. If a patient [...]

Chia-Chin Lin 2000 "Applying the American Pain Society's QA standards to evaluate the quality of pain management among surgical, oncology, and hospice inpatients in Taiwan." *Pain* 87: 43–49, 43–44.

PASSAGE 2
Subjects
The subjects were 64 girls, ranging in age from 12 to 17, who voluntarily enrolled in a comprehensive program for teenage mothers and their infants that was provided by the local public health department in a large city in North Carolina. Of the 64 girls, four were white and 60 were African-American. They had been sexually active from a young age, the average age at first intercourse having been 13.3 years (range 10 to 16, median 14). Average age at the time of first birth was 15.5 years (range 12.5 to 17; median 15). One girl who gave birth at the age of 12 1/2 years had been raped by her mother's boyfriend. Less than half of the girls' mothers had been teenage mothers themselves. Although 43% of the fathers frequently participated in the care of their infants, 19% maintained only minimal contact, and 38% had none. Half contributed to the support of their child. Although school attendance by parenting teenagers was encouraged in the school district, 12 of them (18%) were not attending school at the time of initial intake into the program.

Procedure
Girls were required to attend the clinic at regular intervals, depending upon the age of their infant (i.e., mothers of younger infants attended more frequently), although many appointments were not kept. Efforts were made to administer a structured interview and a measure of self-esteem (Piers-Harris Children's Self-Concept Scale). In addition, the records of some of the girls' performances on the California Achievement Tests (CAT) were obtained from local public schools ($N = 39$). The scores reported were those most recently completed by each girl. They include the results of testing done in the sixth ($N = 9$), seventh ($N = 8$), eighth

(N = 20), and ninth (N = 2) grades between 1984 and 1988.

The Mental Scale of the Bayley Scales of Infant Development was administered to infants at their 9th and 18th month clinic visits, where possible. Because of logistical difficulties (e.g., missed appointments, attrition) all data are not available for every girl.

Rauch-Elnekave 1994: 93.

Exercise 3

The following passage appears in a methods section of an archaeological study. Begin by analyzing the passage for agentlessness and the methodological *I*. Then consider this: as a discipline, archaeology often combines quantitative and qualitative methodology. Do you detect any moments where a qualitative method emerges?

2.1. Field procedures

We selected three of the previously excavated 2 × 2 m sectors (P6, N4 and I2). The aim was to continue the excavations in at least one of these to bedrock, and to date the entire cultural and faunal sequence. For each selected sector, backfill was removed to expose *in situ* deposits. We then used timber shoring of the baulks for safety as the excavations deepened. We also plotted and bagged artefacts, faunal remains, seeds and charcoal found by the excavators; dry sieved excavated deposits with a 2 mm mesh; and took bulk samples of stratigraphic units for sediment, pollen and phytolith analyses. Westaway (2006) also took samples for luminescence and uranium-series dating of excavated materials, and used speleothems from other caves in the vicinity to reconstruct a local palaeo-climatic history spanning much of the last 100 ka.

2.2. Dating procedures

Ages of the Song Gupuh deposits were determined with the thermoluminescence (TL), optically stimulated luminescence (OSL), thermal ionisation mass spectrometry (TIMS) uranium-series and radiocarbon dating methods. U-series dating was applied to *in situ* flowstone deposits that were precipitated onto collapse material lying on the floor of the cave. The results of these samples will provide maximum and minimum age constraints for the timing of sediment deposition above and below the collapse material using analytical procedures described elsewhere (Zhao et al., 2001).

M.J. Morwood, T. Sutikna, E.W. Saptomo, K.E. Westaway, Jatmiko, R. Awe Due, M.W. Moore, Dwi Yani Yuniawati, P. Hadi, J.-x. Zhao, C.S.M. Turney, K. Fifield, H. Allen, and R.P. Soejono 2008 "Climate, people and faunal succession on Java, Indonesia: Evidence from Song Gupuh." *Journal of Archaeological Science* 35: 1776–89, 1778–79.

12C Qualitative Method and Subject Position

Not all disciplines use method sections. Research in disciplines in which scholars do not share recognized instruments and procedures are less likely to state explicitly the means by which knowledge has been made. So, in literary criticism, you will not find:

> The novel was read and notes were taken. Annotation took place at each point where the annotator could detect mentions that might signify something.

But even in disciplines where methods are tacit—generally but silently understood, and not much talked about—there can still appear traces of method. In these disciplines, theories and concepts take the place of instruments and procedures, producing knowledge by operating on a particular set of data. Sometimes the implicit method can be seen most clearly in the **abstract**, the brief summary that sometimes precedes an article or accompanies bibliographical information found in an index. For example, consider the following abstract of Gregg Hurwitz's article "Freud, Jung, and Shakespeare's *Pericles*":

> This essay applies a Freudian psychoanalytic and Jungian archetypal narrative analysis to Shakespeare's first and oft-criticized romance. The author argues that key structural and thematic elements of *Pericles* are best illuminated when viewed through a psychological interpretative lens, and that the play is best comprehended when examined in the context of its associative, rather than linear, richness. Masculinity and femininity, central themes of the narrative, are explored both in relation to the Oedipal complex and psychological individuation. *Pericles* also provides an excellent basis to examine key differences between Freud's and Jung's approach, particularly

Jung's widening of the primarily sexual psychoanalytic approach to encompass broader archetypal meaning.

Gregg Hurwitz 2002 "A tempest, a birth and death: Freud, Jung, and Shakespeare's *Pericles*." *Sexuality & Culture* 6 (3): 3–73, 3.

In the case of this article, the method involves a way to read the play. Hurwitz applies a technique borrowed from psychology to look at Shakespeare's *Pericles* in terms of associations rather than plot or dramatic development in order to isolate certain themes. In turn, reading the play this way allows him to compare different psychoanalytic techniques. In the article proper, this method is explained, but it is not done so in such a compact manner. The introduction begins by introducing *Pericles* and comparing it to other works by Shakespeare, before gradually explaining how psychoanalytic issues can be seen in the drama. The abstract brings the method into focus.

In disciplines that use qualitative rather than quantitative methods, explanations of method can be more explicit, sometimes resembling the style of the quantitative methods section but without the clear demarcation of a section. Consider, for example, the following introduction from Sue Jackson's article "To be or not to be? The place of women's studies in the lives of its students."

> In considering the experiences of women students in higher education, it was important to me that I enabled the women to develop their thoughts, ideas, feelings and opinions over a period of time. This would also enable me to consider any changes that took place in their experiences and perceptions during this period. I eventually interviewed 14 women although, because of their changing circumstances, I was not in the end able to interview all of the women through all of the three years. I interviewed the women four times during the period of their degrees: in the first semester; in the second semester; halfway through their second year; and halfway through their third year. Each interview lasted between 45 minutes and an hour. From the start, I wanted to centralize the students' voices and experiences.

Sue Jackson 2000 "To be or not to be? The place of women's studies in the lives of its students." *Journal of Gender Studies* 9 (2): 189–97, 189.

You will notice that in explaining her method, Jackson places considerable emphasis on her own role in the knowledge-making process. Earlier, in our examination of quantitative method sections, we noted that the researchers were largely missing from the explanation (and when they were there, they tended to appear as physical doers—handlers or manipulators of equipment and objects). Why does Jackson think it is important to include her own position and role as a researcher? She answers this question later in the article:

> From the outset it was important to me to locate myself in my research. Indeed, how could I not? I did not want to pretend to be a disembodied researcher, nor that the research was somehow "outside" of me. I am not an unseen and unmarked voice, but a person situated in my own complexities and lived realities. [...] From the outset, then, I identified my research as feminist, taking a feminist standpoint which engages in political struggle and centralizes women's experiences....
>
> Jackson 2000: 190.

The example from Jackson provides a good illustration of how genre responds to changing social situations. It could be argued that it was **feminist reasoning**, at the end of the twentieth century, which most sincerely invited the *subject*—the thinking, feeling being, experienced in the complexities of daily life—back into scholarly writing. Feminist reasoning has criticized research practices for being carried out from a *masculinist* position or point of view, and then representing that position as *universal*. So feminist research would be inclined to dismantle the form of knowledge constructed by traditional research practices and expose that knowledge as not only not "objective" but also as serving the interests of those who work at it. But some types of feminist research would also do more than expose the **subjectivity** of established regimes of knowledge. They would acknowledge the impossibility of the independent "fact" (and possibly even deny its desirability), and require that the researcher identify himself or herself.

Fleshed out beyond the discursive *I* we met in Chapter 11B, the "subjective" researcher would expose the relevant social and political— *personal*—elements of his or her experience of the world. These elements would constitute the **subject position** from which the researcher speaks. The knowledge the researcher then offers would be contingent on that position: not absolute or universal, but relative to that position.

It is hard to say how far this project for remodelling scholarly writing has advanced. Publications in disciplines which deal with gender-related topics are still perhaps the most likely to invite the fleshed-out subject to the page (and even then, in the presence of gender issues—as we have seen from the excerpts from articles on gender-related topics in previous chapters—the traditional scholarly voice can still prevail). But, even among articles which are not about gender issues, we can find writers stepping out from traditional styles and saying who they are, and what happened to them, personally, to make them think the way they do now:

> In the forty years that I have been doing fieldwork in Latin America and the United States, my own awareness of how the events I recorded are related to the world around them has expanded along with (and sometimes belatedly to) that of my informants. This follows trends in the field as the unit of investigation has progressed from one of bounded cultures where the task was to recapture a traditional past to a multilayered, historically situated inquiry where the authoritative stance of a privileged observer was no longer condoned. In tracing my own ethnographic journey, I shall try to capture some of those experiences in which I was forced to encounter the world dimensions of everyday struggles for survival.

Nash 1994: 13–19.

This article is not about gender issues, yet perhaps its style has been influenced by the feminist reasoning which suggests that researchers identify themselves. It's interesting, too, that this researcher represents herself as changing—as a thinker and observer—over time. She knows things now that she didn't know before; she has been influenced by others, she has changed her mind. Just as knowledge is located in time and changes over time, so are knowledge makers located in time, and subject to its influences. It's worth noting further that Nash is writing in the discipline of anthropology—for, besides feminist reasoning, the other radical questioning of scholarly authority in the late twentieth century has come from post-colonial positions. **Post-colonial reasoning** has challenged the authority of Western researchers to produce knowledge of other cultures, and has exposed traditional anthropological knowledge as saturated with colonial values.

Exercise 4

Examine the following abstracts from scholarly articles. Based on these abstracts, describe the method by which knowledge is being made in each article.

ABSTRACT 1

Although late nineteenth century and early twentieth century Canada, the United States, Australia, and New Zealand were all settler societies with a predominantly British ethnic heritage, a comparison reveals intriguing differences in attitudes and practices related to "racial" mixing during this period. The relation to land was the underpinning of the dominant discourses concerning miscegenation in all four countries, and these discourses were grounded in an international pan-European discussion of social and physiological difference. However, constructions of sexuality, class, race, gender, and national values, as well as previous experiences of inter-ethnic contact, all played roles in determining attitudes and policies toward racial mixing in any particular circumstance. The actual forms of mixing that took place, and to a certain extent the discourses about them, were shaped by indigenous as well as European attitudes and agency, and in some instances were shaped as much by male patriarchal authority and male gender solidarity across cultures as by the interests of settler colonialism.

Victoria Freeman 2005 "Attitudes toward 'miscegenation' in Canada, the United States, New Zealand, and Australia, 1860–1914." *Native Studies Review* 16 (1): 41–70, 41.

ABSTRACT 2

Studies the parallelism of the English play "Mary Magdalen" preserved in the Bodleian Library MS Digby 133 and William Shakespeare's "Pericles." Summary outline of "Pericles"; Narrative source of relevant parts of "Mary Magdalen"; Possible gests that make up saints' legends—conversion, martyrdom, miracle and withdrawal from the world.

Peter Womack 1999 "Shakespeare and the sea of stories." *Journal of Medieval & Early Modern Studies* 29 (1): 169–88, 169.

Exercise 5

Examine the two excerpts from scholarly articles below to determine how each writer steps beyond the traditional role of the discursive *I*. (Passage 2 comes from a co-authored article innovatively structured as a dialogue.)

PASSAGE 1

About 2 years ago, I conversed with an American business-man in Mexico about how difficult replacement parts were to come by in that country. Over the next several months, he formed an alliance with Mexican and American partners and investors and formed a company, one with a more specific business goal, namely, to provide rebuilt engine parts from the US to commercial transportation fleets in Mexico.

During meetings over the following year, the American and Mexican partners saw me in action, doing what linguistic anthropologists naturally do—mediating worlds—sometimes in English, sometimes in rusty Spanish, sometimes in both. We mutually decided that I would spend the summer in Mexico City to help start up the company. I dealt with Mexican and American partners, government offices, lawyers, and customers. I worked in the cracks between two different "cultures," cracks described in recent books on Mexican-American relations, books whose titles foreshadow the examples to come: *Distant Neighbors* (Riding, 1985) and *Limits to Friendship* (Pastor and Castaneda, 1988). Kismet turned me into something I had never been before—an "intercultural communicator." The rest of this article is dedicated to figuring out what, in light of that experience, the phrase might mean.

Intercultural communicator

After my baptism by fire, I returned to the university in the autumn and approached the library with a naive question in mind: "What is the field of intercultural communication all about?" The question was naive because the literature is huge, diverse, without agreement on any particular unifying focus (see

Hinnenkamp, 1990, for a related concern with the fundamentals of the field).

Michael Agar 1994 "The intercultural frame." *International Journal of Intercultural Relations* 18 (2): 221–37, 221–22.

PASSAGE 2

I. Introduction: Multiple openings with(in) a dialogue
What, then, are the limitations of our practice? How is our practice complicit with certain established societal structures?

Ming-Yeung Lu

MING-YUEN S. MA: This quote brings up many of the questions that keep coming up in my mind as I work on this project, and I think that they point out the uncertainties in my motives: who am I, a first generation Chinese gay man, who was born but did not grow up in the United States, whose higher education was enabled by my privileged, upper-middle-class background, to write about Asian lesbian and gay writers? What is my placement in the text? What does it mean for us to be writing about works by persons of Asian and Pacific Islander descent in a language that is not our own—though most of us communicate by it?

ALICE Y. HOM: As a second-generation Chinese American, raised in a working-class immigrant family but educated in an Ivy League college, I think there are some complexities to the language issue. Many second-, third-, and fourth-generation Asian Americans do not feel their native language is an Asian language. When talking about Asian Pacific Islander lesbian and gay writing, we have to address the definition of "Asian Pacific Islander." In this case we are speaking of Asian and Pacific Islander immigrants and those born in the United States. The diaspora is limited to the United States although some of the Asian Pacific Islander lesbian writings are coming from Canada. For the most part, we will concentrate on this United States-centred context because most of our research and experiences are from here.

Alice Y. Hom and Ming-Yuen S. Ma 1994 "Premature gestures: A speculative dialogue on Asian Pacific lesbian and gay writing." *Journal of Homosexuality* 26 (2/3): 21–51, 22.

13

Making and Maintaining Knowledge II

In Chapter 11 we met the discursive *I*: the intellectual being who arranged and forecasted the discussion, who pointed to parts of the text, summing up and emphasizing. In Chapter 12 we met the methodological *I*: the researcher in her capacity as a physical agent who conducted research, manipulating equipment or excavating sites. We also met a more radically personal subject position (discussed in Chapter 12C), which makes appearances when researchers feel compelled to emphasize their personal role in the knowledge-making process. As we noted, this need may be due to the discipline (for example, women's studies or ethnographic disciplines like anthropology) or it may arise from a general questioning of the knowledge-making process itself. Below we meet a variant of the discursive *I*—the **knowledge-making *I***—that is pervasive, albeit more shy than the arranger and forecaster of discussion. This "I" is not as personal as the expression of subject position, but it is similar insofar as it marks the presence or role of the researcher in the knowledge-making process. It is perhaps most distinguished by the awareness it exhibits of the limits of its own certainty.

Later in the chapter we will also consider how researchers use tense to trace the development of knowledge over time.

13A **Modality**

Consider the use of the knowledge-making *I* in the example below. In summarizing the views of another writer (Wittig), the writer (Calhoun) appears in the text as a reasoning being, evaluating the statements of others.

> Because lesbians and heterosexual resisters must have, on [Wittig's] account, the same relation to the category "woman," there can be no interesting differences between the two. This, **I think**, is a mistake, and **I will argue** in a moment that lesbians are in a quite special sense not-women.
>
> Calhoun 1994: 564 (emphasis added).

You will note that the second appearance of the "I" in this passage is the discursive, forecasting "I" organizing the argument: "I will argue...." But the first appearance—"I think"—asserts Calhoun's own judgement on the issue under discussion. Since the scholarly genres impose so many restrictions on the presentation of the writing 'self,' we might well scrutinize this special appearance of the writing self to find out what conditions permit it.

What we will find is that the "I think" in the passage above is by no means an isolated case. Rather, it is a variation on a set of expressions that are in fact abundant in the research genres and that tend to occur in just such situations as the passage above exemplifies: situations where the writer is taking a step beyond established knowledge, moving to offer new statements to the research community. To develop some perspective on this set of expressions and their range of occurrence, we will first see how the grammar of "I think" is related to the grammar of some other expressions which are akin to it in function.

Let's say Matthew is inside on a dark night. He hears a sound on the roof. He reports to Thomas:

> It's raining.

Since he is inside, where it is dry, he is *inferring* that it is raining. Matthew could report his finding as a product of his own reasoning—an **estimate from a position of limited knowledge**.

> **I think** it's raining.

Matthew doesn't know if it is raining for sure, so he emphasizes that the statement is based on his own perception. He could include such an estimate in his statement by other means. He could say:

It seems to be raining. **It must** be raining.

Or, if the two men are unfamiliar with the building they're in, and less certain about how it registers the sounds of the outside world, Matthew could express his estimate with less certainty:

THOMAS: What's that noise?

MATTHEW: It **could** be rain. It **might** be rain. **Maybe** it's rain.

"Seems," "must," "could," "might," "maybe" are all expressions embedded in the statement that identify it as the product of inference from a position of limited knowledge. Along with other expressions like "evidently," "apparently," "perhaps," "possibly," "appears," these expressions **modalize** statements. Roughly, they are equivalent to "I think." Although **modality** erases "I" from the surface of the expression, it nevertheless maintains the sense of the statement in which it occurs as being knowledge under construction from a certain location: the speaker's or writer's position in the world.

These traces of reasoning from positions of limited knowledge are typical of scholarly expression. They signify the research community's persistent interest in the production of knowledge. On the one hand, they permit the individual researcher to move into unconfirmed territory—a lone explorer, estimating and reckoning ("I will argue ...")—and, on the other hand, they signal respect for the community's cooperative work of corroborating and recognizing established positions ("This, I think, is a mistake ...").

So strong is this tradition of respect for properly established positions that even when the current researchers are evidently impatient with the dominance of accepted views, and when their own research defies those views, they still identify knowledge deficits through modalized statements. Consider the way in which modalized statements, in the following passages, produce a knowledge deficit. Two researchers (Tiratsoo and Tomlinson) report extensive evidence to overturn the standing idea that trade-union activities have a lot to do with Britain's post-war economic circumstances. They nevertheless approach the standing view with signs of respect, expressed through modality. Here they respond to the work of a distinguished and widely cited scholar:

Olson's work demands to be taken seriously, yet it, too, **seems** to be flawed. Olson has attracted considerable support from economists and economic historians because his methodology conforms to the tenets of individual rational action theory inherent in neo-classical economics. However, this choice of approach **can** be criticised because it encourages a misleadingly simplified view of reality.

* * *

It **may** be right to conclude about Olson, therefore, that what he has produced is not an explanation, but merely an historical set of abstractions. His theory **seems** to provide little more satisfaction than the offerings of far less sophisticated analysts.

At this point, it **appears** wise to turn from the current literature and re-examine the contemporary evidence. Many recent authorities have argued, as we have shown, that restrictionism was strongly evident on Britain's shopfloor after 1945, but not much of what has been written, it **seems** fair to conclude, is very persuasive.

Tiratsoo and Tomlinson 1994: 67, 69 (emphasis added).

Using modalized expressions allows Tiratsoo and Tomlinson to question established positions on the topic and to politely suggest an alternate approach, in this case to return to the "evidence."

You will notice that in the example about rain above, Matthew follows the observation that it "seems" to be raining by saying that it "must" be raining. This confident assertion may seem to contradict the expression of uncertainty conveyed by "might." And yet, while "must" can seem like an expression of certainty, it is in fact a sign of strong but not infallible conviction attending an inference. For example, "It must be nearly 4 o'clock" suggests that the speaker does not have a watch and so can't say for sure what time it is. Along with "must," "obviously" can seem like an expression of certainty, but the next example shows that speakers can use "obviously" (like "must") in the presence of doubt, or **uncertainty**:

... obviously you grew up, although this might not be the case, in a family that encouraged this interest [in music].

Rex Murphy, *Cross-country check-up*, CBC, 23 April 2000, talking to a constitutional expert about music.

From a distance, we might think that the research genres would be the ones that would use expressions of certainty, rather than uncertainty, limitation, and possibility. If we think of research and the sciences—particularly the "hard" sciences—as sources of authority and ultimate fact, we would expect certainty, not **indeterminacy**. But in fact tentative expressions are very common across the research genres. They indicate the writer's reasoning, inference, speculation, and even subjectivity.

Perhaps we would not be surprised at this indeterminacy in the research genres if we recall the research genres' distinctive dependence on reported speech. In a way, the expressions which make a statement indeterminate by showing it to be the speaker's inference from incomplete evidence are something like the statements which are reported as coming from someone other than the writer. So, to return to our rain example, the speaker could also make a claim about the weather by reporting the speech of someone else.

MATTHEW: Mike says it's raining.

THOMAS: Oh.

If Thomas knows that Mike has just come in from outside, then he is likely to credit the statement as valid. It seems to come from a reliable position. On the other hand, if Mike has not been out, and is only speculating, and tends to interpret all noises as rain, Thomas might not be convinced. The context in which the reported statement was produced—the speaker's identity and situation, the timing of the statement—helps the listener to evaluate the statement. Similarly, reporting expressions, documentation, characterization of the source—all these features of scholarly citation help readers evaluate reported statements.

Exercise 1
Identify the modalizing expressions in the following passages. How do they limit the speakers' claims for the knowledge they will produce?

PASSAGE 1
Human representations offer archaeologists the possibility of investigating ancient social categorization and differentiation from within. Of course, we are given only a very partial view. Figurines do not provide maps to complete social systems. Instead, they encode only very selected themes. The anthropomorphic figurines of Early Formative Paso de la Amada [Mexico]

appear to be stylized human images depicting idealized social categories or roles (Lesure 1997). Their specific uses are unknown. Most were deployed, broken, discarded in household contexts. They were probably grouped into sets or scenes in which not only the individual representations but comparisons between them became important (Flannery and Marcus 1976, 382; Marcus 1989, 1996). It therefore seems likely that the message conveyed by the use of figurines involved statements not only about social categories, but about relationships between categories.

Richard Lesure 1999 "Figurines as representations and products at Paso de la Amada, Mexico." *Cambridge Archaeological Journal* 9 (2): 209–20, 209.

PASSAGE 2

An objective way to determine the current nature of the field of personality psychology is to examine what gets published in various journals over a fixed period of time. This is not a foolproof system, since more papers are rejected for publication than are accepted. The ones that do get accepted might thus represent a biased sample. Journal editors serve as 'gatekeepers' and therefore what is accepted might not necessarily be the best but rather may reflect the biases of journal editors and referees or the zeitgeist of psychology.

Nevertheless, what is published in personality journals is probably the closest approximation of the true nature of research in the area, and is certainly a good indicator of what is currently being disseminated.

Norman S. Endler and Rachel L. Speer 1998 "Personality psychology: Research trends for 1993–1995." *Journal of Personality* 66 (5): 621–69, 621.

13B Other Markers of the Status of Knowledge

As we have seen, modality and reporting expressions both indicate that statements come from a position of limited knowledge. In this section we will look at other expressions that indicate the status of statements as knowledge. First, we will examine **limiting expressions**. While modality indicates a lack of certainty on the part of the writer, limiting expressions qualify or place other limits on statements, especially generalizations. Second, we will look at **agentless expressions**, with specific attention to how they indicate consensus about whether a statement is obvious or not. The functions of these different expressions may sometimes seem to overlap, and generally speaking we can regard them as establishing writers' attitudes toward or opinions of the statement they are offering.

By definition, generalizations may seem to defy limits. The opening generalization of the passage below appears at first to ignore the modalizing and reporting tendencies we have been observing in the last section:

> During the course of the twentieth century relationships between minorities and dominant societies have fundamentally altered in wartime....

However, on closer inspection we will see that it in fact conforms to traditions of marking statements for their status as knowledge:

> During the course of the twentieth century relationships between minorities and dominant societies have fundamentally altered in wartime, an assertion which applies to all states. The position of minorities usually deteriorates, particularly if they represent a group which has acted as the traditional scapegoat for the dominant society, or if they are identified with the state facing their land of settlement in war. In such a situation the minorities almost invariably face persecution, varying from controls on movement and expression to internment and even genocide. The response of the dominant group varies according to the political traditions upon which it is grounded. A liberal democracy will usually retain traces of tolerations, while an autocratic state will exercise more arbitrary anti-minority policies (Panayi 1990b). Few exceptions exist to this state of affairs, although in some cases opportunities may arise that allow a minority to make some socio-economic progress. The experience of Afro-Americans and American Indians in the first world war provides an example (Dippie 1982, p. 194; Grossman 1989).
>
> Mark Ellis and Panikos Panayi 1994 "German minorities in World War I: A comparative study of Britain and the U.S.A." *Ethnic and Racial Studies* 17 (2): 238–59, 238–39.

The writers seem to be aware of the risk they take in offering a generalization that is neither reported nor modalized, for they quickly move to characterize it and insist on its generality:

> ... an **assertion** which applies to all states.

Then, as they develop this generality, they gradually and slightly reduce the application of its parts: "all" gives way to "usually," "almost invariably," "usually," "[f]ew exceptions exist," and "some cases." Each of these expressions *limit* the statement in some way. That is, the writers do not commit themselves to saying that any given statement is universally true. That would be too much.

The following statement is from an article reporting results of an experimental study of the ability to remember and learn a written style:

> [T]he subjects **demonstrated a trend toward** mentioning more rules for the marked forms than for the unmarked forms for all three style characteristics.
>
> Jennifer Zervakis and David C. Rubin 1998 "Memory and learning for a novel written style." *Memory and Cognition* 26 (4): 754–67, 764 (emphasis added).

How would this statement sound without the limiting expression?

In effect, expressions like these control the extent of a statement's application. They reduce and monitor how the generalization is applied to cases or instances. They place limits on knowledge by conditioning where and under what circumstances it is valid. While by no means exhaustive, the following list gives a good sense of the range of limiting expressions:

usually	in part
most	at least
some	partly
many	often
generally	sometimes
roughly	typically

Notice the effect that the insertion of appropriate limiting expressions can have in conditioning a broad statement for use in a research setting. Consider this statement:

> Family-wage campaigns supported both patriarchal and corporate interests.

Compare it with this statement:

> Generally, family-wage campaigns supported patriarchal and corporate interests.

Given the scholarly genres' preoccupation with the status of knowledge and the processes by which knowledge is produced, we could expect limiting expressions to cooperate with reporting and modality to sketch the limits of knowledge. In the following example, a writer offers an interpretation of evidence she has presented as to the conditions of labour after the abolition of slavery in Brazil. Note the reporting, modalizing, and limiting expressions in the passage.

> It was this process that **Peter Isenberg called** "modernization without change" and that **has generally been interpreted** as implying a crushing continuity of dependence and poverty for former slaves. While this is **in one sense quite** accurate—indeed, rural northeasterners **may** have been even more malnourished after emancipation than before—an overemphasis on continuity **may** obscure the importance of the access to land that **many** former slaves did achieve....
>
> Even though the physical work performed by labor tenants **might** differ little from that performed by slaves, the orbits of their lives now had a **somewhat** different shape. While slaves had lived in a centralized set of quarters under direct supervision, moradores **usually** built their huts "at scattered points on the estates." An even more general dispersion of the population was **probably** prevented by the development of central mills, but the small-scale dispersion within estates **could** be of crucial importance to the development of a life oriented toward family and neighbors rather than employer. And, to the extent that freedom of movement **could** be maintained, it provided **some** constraint on the exactions that **could** be imposed on rural dwellers.
>
> Rebecca J. Scott 1994 "Defining the boundaries of freedom in the world of cane: Cuba, Brazil, and Louisiana after emancipation." *American Historical Review* February: 70–102, 96 (emphasis added).

Reporting expressions include the citation of Isenberg ("called") and the obscured reference "generally interpreted." Note that Scott continues by calling the reported statements into question. She does so by first using limiting expressions ("in one sense" and "quite") and allowing for the validity of this "one sense" with the modal expression "may." As she proceeds, note how modality is used again ("may," "may," "might," "could," "could") and coupled with different limiting expressions: "many former slaves," "somewhat different shape," "usually built," "some constraint." All these expressions limit the scope of the statement. In that respect, they are pointers to statements' status as knowledge, and to writers' limited position: they are not in a position to say such-and-such is true for all cases.

In addition to limiting statements, we also find scholarly writers expressing attitudes about the **obviousness** of statements. Alongside words like "possibly," "may," "might," or "could," we see them saying things like the following:

> Certainly, *x*
> It is evident that *x*
> Surely *x*
> Apparently *x*
> Undoubtedly *x*

They can even combine apparent confidence with seeming reservation. For example, summarizing the research of "social investigator Ferdinand Zweig," these writers say:

> He concentrated on five main sectors (building and civil engineering, cotton, engineering, iron and steel, and printing) and found that restrictive practices of various kinds were **certainly sometimes** evident.
>
> Tiratsoo and Tomlinson 1994: 70 (emphasis added).

They don't say:

> He ... found restrictive practices of various kinds.

This complex trace of reasoning—the phenomenon is "evident" (to an observer/interpreter), but only "sometimes," but then "certainly"—indicates the status of this statement as knowledge.

To say that something is evident—or apparent, or observable, or recognizable—is to say that it is so *to someone*. Remembering that scholarly writing makes big efforts to attach statements to their sources, we might confront wordings like these and ask, well, *who* finds something evident or apparent, or *who* observes it or recognizes it? At first, these wordings might seem vague, and at odds with other features we have been looking at. But we can account for these typical wordings by noticing how they resemble some other forms we have seen. *Observable, identifiable,* and *evident* are agentless: they omit the agent—the person—who observes, identifies, or finds something evident. So they are like other agentless forms we have seen, for example:

> it is known that *x* ...
> *x* is acknowledged as ...

In the following passage, note the prevalence of agentless expressions:

> The problem of deep oceanic convection induced by localized surface cooling has received considerable attention in the last years. Results from field observations (e.g., in the Greenland Sea or the Gulf of Lions), laboratory experiments, and numerical simulations have led to some theoretical predictions concerning the structure of the convective region like plume scale, chimney scale, and rim current by, for example, Klinger and Marshall (1995), Send and Marshall (1995), and Viseck et al. (1996). The comparison of these scaling arguments with real ocean data on deep connection is somewhat restricted due to the lack of detailed measurements of convective plumes and chimneys, although field experiments have provided very impressive cases of deep ocean convection (e.g., Morawitz et al. 1996; Schott et al. 1996).

> S. Raasch and D. Etling 1998 "Modeling deep ocean convection: Large eddy simulation in comparison with laboratory experiments." *American Meteorological Society* 21: 1786–1802, 1786.

Who attends? Who observes? Who experiments? Who designs simulations? Who predicts? Who produces results? Who compares? The answers to these questions are not given. In the passage, "attention" and "observations" are agentless. They take away the person who attended and the person who observed. Notably, if we ask *who* uses theory to predict, examples are given: Klinger and Marshall (1995), Send and Marshall (1995), and Viseck et al. (1996). Why are Raasch and Etling so imprecise about some things and so precise about others? Apparently they assume that readers are generally familiar with the earlier findings that led to the work of Marshall and others.

Expressions such as "it is known that ..." seem to distribute knowledge: it is not just the present speaker who sees this or knows it. Similarly, in the case of expressions like "evident" or "observable," the commentary on the status of knowledge includes not so much an estimate of its probability (as "possibly" or "may," for example, would provide), or not only a trace of its source (something someone reported), but a measure of the position from which x is known. As—

> it is known that *x* ...
> *x* is acknowledged as ...

—suggest that more than one person knows this, so—

> evident
> apparent
> observable
> identifiable

—suggest that, from any reasonable position, people would see this. "Reasonable position," however, by now should occur to us as a social rather than purely cognitive (and universal) measure. And we can now recognize the role of presupposition in such expressions (see Chapter 5G). In scholarly circles, reasoning goes on in social contexts, among people of similar experience.

These markers of obviousness can take the form of "evident," "apparent," "recognized/recognizable," or "observed/observable," or the more pronounced forms of "surely," "certainly," and "clearly," which insist that the statement should be acceptable to reasonable readers. Most compelling, perhaps, of these forms is "of course." "Of course" signals that the statement is so evident that readers are only being reminded of what they already know:

> It is now well-established, **of course**, that the majority of British employers looked to the apprenticeship system rather than formal education in the classroom as the appropriate training for the bulk of their employees.
>
> Keith Burgess 1994 "British employers and education policy, 1935–45: A decade of 'missed opportunities'?" *Business History* 36 (3): 29–61 (emphasis added).

Here "of course" signals that the writer takes his readers (business historians) as already knowing that it is known that British employers favoured apprenticeship training. "Of course" signals the status of this knowledge as widely distributed in the community which forms the audience for this article.

In a way, "of course" is an expression of politeness: it constructs readers as knowledgeable, as not needing to be told something they already know. But what if you *didn't* know that apprenticeship was the preferred form of training? In this case, "of course" would inform you that the topic is common ground for the intended audience, a well-known consensus in that community.

Yet, while "of course," "certainly," "to be sure," or "clearly" can create the impression of consensus, these expressions of obviousness can also suddenly alienate a reader. On the one hand, we should be aware of the power of certain expressions to appear to distribute knowledge: we use them to signal to readers that we know we are not delivering brand-new ideas, but, rather, ideas that are broadly entertained in the community. On the other hand, these expressions incur some risk that our reader may not find something as clear, evident, or matter-of-course as we suggest.

> MATTHEW: Clearly, Dickens' verbal art is a precursor of cinematic art.

> THOMAS: Wait a minute. That's not clear at all.

While "of course" and related expressions say "This statement is in keeping with what you and I (and others like us) know about the world," words like "surprisingly" say "This statement is *not* in keeping with what you and I (and others like us) know about the world."

> Most analyses of the various proposals to date (including the so-called Flat Tax, a national sales tax, the "USATax," etc.) have concentrated on the distributional impact of the plans, along familiar lines of progressivity and regressivity. **Surprisingly** little critical attention has been paid to the macroeconomic implications of these tax reform plans, particularly to the claims about saving.
>
> Neil H. Buchanan 1999 "Taxes, saving, and macroeconomics." *Journal of Economic Issues* 33 (1): 59–75, 60 (emphasis added).

"Of course," "obviously," and "surprisingly" signify a solidarity amongst those convened by what we called writer's orchestration (see Chapter 6). They reflect a kind of identification on the part of the writer with the scholarly community: shared attitudes and experiences in research disciplines.

We could also see expressions like "of course," "obviously," and "surprisingly" as expanding the identity of the discursive *I*, for they emphasize a position—from which something is well known ("of course") or clearly to be seen ("obviously") or never seen before ("surprisingly"). Although academic writing is often considered impersonal, or neutral, or anonymous, in fact there are many signals of subjectivity in scholarly style: expressions of attitude—and even feeling (of a sort). Here two economists are "astonish[ed]" by something which might not stir such feeling in people who do not share their position in the world:

> From 1929 to 1932, Argentina imported severe deflationary pressures and adverse terms-of-trade shocks from the international economy: the external terms of trade declined by 24 percent and the foreign (US) price level fell by 26 percent.
>
> In this context it is **astonishing** that the Argentine Great Depression was so mild and short-lived by international standards.
>
> Gerardo della Paolera and Alan M. Taylor 1999 "Economic recovery from the Argentine Great Depression: Institutions, expectations, and the change of macroeconomic regime." *Journal of Economic History* 59 (3): 567–98, 569 (emphasis added).

Exercise 2

In the passage below, the writers begin to reinterpret evidence. Identify the modal and limiting expressions they use as they begin to evaluate available knowledge.

Taken together, these various accounts appear to constitute a formidable indictment, yet closer inspection once again exposes flaws. Some industrial correspondents did, of course, have good contacts in business and may have accurately reported what they were told. Nevertheless, it is not certain what employers' complaints really added up to: grumbles from the boardroom were, of course, nothing new. Moreover, some of the press accounts have a formulatory ring and may well have been shaped more by the pressure to grab the reader's attention than the desire to present accurate facts.

Tiratsoo and Tomlinson 1994: 69–70.

Exercise 3

Inspect essays you have recently written or are currently drafting. Do you find the modalizing and limiting expressions that we have been examining in published scholarship? If they are missing, can you explain their absence? Does your writing situation differ from that of professional scholars in ways that lead you away from expressions of position and limitation? If it doesn't, and you find modalizing and limiting expressions missing from your academic writing, try introducing them at appropriate points, and observe the effect.

Exercise 4

Identify in the following passages signs of attitude (something is good, or bad) and feeling (something has taken the writers by surprise).

PASSAGE 1

In many less developed countries the government resorts to minimum wage laws in a bid to raise the living standards of the workers. In India, for example, the Minimum Wages Act of 1948 laid down standards of minimum wage. The objective was "not merely ... the bare sustenance of life but ... for some measure of education, medical requirements and amenities."[1] In other countries also, such laws and regulations were motivated by similar concerns.

Unfortunately, however, there is little concern about the possible detrimental effects of such laws on the level of employment, as these laws may induce the firms to cut down on the number of workers employed.

Note

1 Committee for Fair Wages appointed by government of India, 1948.

Saikat Datta and Prabal Roy Chowdhury 1998 "Management union bargaining under minimum wage regulation in less developed countries." *Indian Economic Review* 33 (2): 169–84, 169–70.

PASSAGE 2

The complex and often fitful transition from central planning to the market in China and the Warsaw Pact countries has been a hot topic during the past decade. Notably, the United States made a similar transition after World War II. Indeed, the reconversion from a wartime command economy to a market-oriented postwar economy, a transition accomplished with astonishing speed and little apparent difficulty, constitutes one of the most remarkable events in US economic history. Nevertheless, economists and economic historians have devoted little attention to that episode, and their explanations of it are, on close inspection, extremely problematic.

Robert Higgs 1999 "From central planning to the market: The American transition, 1945–1947." *The Journal of Economic History* 59: 600–23, 623.

PASSAGE 3

Unfortunately, this methodological assumption treats the media as passive "channels" of communication or neutral and objective observers and recorders of events, a view that for some time now has been rejected by scholars of the media (e.g., Gans 1981; Herman and Chomsky 1988; Shoemaker and Resse 1991), as well as refuted by studies of the media coverage of collective events (Danzger 1975; Franzosi 1987; McCarthy, McPhail, and Smith 1996; Meuller 1997a; Snyder and Kelly 1977).

Oliver and Myers 1999: 39.

13C Tense and the Story of Research

Students are often told to "be consistent" in tense, and they are generally advised to use present tense. It is true that the simple present is the most common form for reporting expressions in the research genres, but it is often joined by other forms of the present tense as well as the past tense. With this array of tenses, scholarly writers tell the story of statements occurring, staging or dramatizing the making of knowledge. In this story, knowledge is not timeless and immutable, but historical, located in time.

Most of the **reporting verbs** we have been looking at seem to prefer the simple present form in the research genres.

Rouse **presents** a novel challenge to spatial images, highlighting the nature of postmodern space. He **points out** that members of a "transnational migration" circuit can be parts of two communities simultaneously. However, he **argues**....

Chavez 1994: 55 (emphasis added).

Although, clearly, the speech actions of arguing or pointing out occurred in past time (before Chavez wrote the above), they are presented in present tense.

In a sample summary in Chapter 3, we followed the trend and used the simple present too:

Calhoun (1994) **explains** how heterosexual society makes heterosexuality seem natural and creates a "negative social reality" for lesbians and gay men. She **identifies** social practices like dating, sex education, and erotica that construct sex/gender dimorphism. She also **catalogues** social conventions (e.g., joint invitations to husband-and-wife) and legal and economic structures (e.g., adoption procedures, spousal health benefits) which produce the "single unit" of man and woman.

Consider how this would sound if we changed the verb from simple present to simple past:

Calhoun (1994) **explained** how heterosexual society makes heterosexuality seem natural and creates a "negative social reality" for lesbians and gay men. She **identified** social practices like dating, sex education, and erotica that construct sex/gender dimorphism. She also **catalogued** social conventions (e.g., joint invitations to husband-and-wife)....

An academic reader could stop, or misstep, noting the past tense. Later, we will consider how such a reader might interpret this way of talking about Calhoun's research. What is important for the moment is that the simple present tense appears to be an important way to bring scholarly conversations to life. Why is this so?

Consider the role of the simple present in this example of everyday conversation:

So this guy **comes** over and **says** is that your car and **I'm like** yeah and he **goes** you gonna leave it there and **I'm like**—*what?*

Studies of simple present (e.g., Chafe 1994) in conversational citation suggest that it coincides with speakers' evaluation of what they are saying as particularly impressive: they dramatize their report of important moments by switching to simple present, creating an effect of immediacy. Scholarly "conversation" may be borrowing some of this immediacy in its preference for the simple present.

However, this is not the whole story of tense and citation. Simple present can be, in some instances, overtaken by present progressive ("-ing" forms of the verb):

> Here Rouse **is questioning** the....

This verb form may be likely to occur with **direct-speech** citation—where the cited speaker is quoted in their own words. The present progressive intensifies this moment of the conversation, improving even on the immediacy provided by the simple present. It is as though the current writer is interacting directly with the cited author, initiating a new stage in the conversation. Present progressive occurs in other situations too, like this one:

> ... the latent structure of childhood negative emotions **is** only **beginning** to be conceptualized in detail (e.g., Joiner, Catanzaro, and Laurent, 1996).
>
> Chorpita, Albano, and Barlow 1998: 74 (emphasis added).

Here the researchers present the focus of their study—the "latent structure of childhood negative emotions"—as a particularly fertile field of research: the current understanding, they suggest, is in flux—it is under ongoing, active construction.

More common than present progressive is present perfect. Consider its effect in this passage:

> The bulk of the empirical work on migration determinants **has studied** how wage and unemployment differentials affect migration flows under the Harris-Todaro (1970) hypothesis of risk neutrality of an individual migrant. [...] The role of other factors than expected wages **has been emphasized** in the new migration literature.
>
> Francesco Daveri and Ricardo Faini 1999 "Where do migrants go?" *Oxford Economic Papers* 51: 595–622, 596 (emphasis added).

Present perfect is a sensitive form in English—second nature to speakers of English as a first language, perhaps, but difficult to explain—and called on to execute speakers' perception of what is close or distant in time. In conversation, it says something is done (notice the *past* action in present perfect—*has studied, has been emphasized*), but only *just* done—recent enough to be still an aspect of the *present* situation (and often occurs with "just"). Writers in the research genres sometimes select the present perfect, as we see above and in the next example:

> Premack and Woodruff (1978) asked "Does the chimpanzee have a theory of mind?" Since it was posed 20 years ago, Premack and Woodruff's question **has dominated** the study of both social behavior in nonhuman primates [...] and cognitive development in children, but progress in the two fields **has been** markedly different. Developmentalists **have established** empirical methods to investigate children's understanding of mentality, and forging links with philosophy of mind and philosophy of science, they **have mustered** the conceptual resources for disciplined dispute about the origins [...], on-line control [...], and epistemic stance [...] of human folk psychology (e.g., Goldman 1993; Gopnik 1993; Gopnik and Wellman 1994). In contrast, those working with primates **have continued** to struggle with the basic question of whether any primate has any capacity to conceive of mental states.
>
> C.M. Heyes 1998 "Theory of mind in nonhuman primates." *Behavioral and Brain Sciences* 21: 101–48, 101 (emphasis added).

The first sentence of the example above also shows that writers in the research genres can also pick the simple past for reporting verbs: "Premack and Woodruff (1978) *asked* 'Does the chimpanzee have a theory of mind?'" In the next example, the writers begin their article on a new model of social interaction by citing a prominent contributor to this field, and use the simple past in conjunction with a positive evaluation ("celebrated") of the work's reception:

> In his celebrated essay on "The Architecture of Complexity," Herbert Simon ([1962] 1969) **developed** the argument that all complex systems shared certain structural features. These features emerged, he **showed**, by virtue of what appeared to be a universal partitioning

principle—the tendency for strongly interacting entities to group together into subsystems.

Thomas S. Smith and Gregory T. Stevens 1999 "The architecture of small networks: Strong interaction and dynamic organization in small social systems." *American Sociological Review* 64: 403–20, 403 (emphasis added).

Similarly, writing about undocumented immigrants in the US, Leo R. Chavez uses the simple past as he cites the ancestral, founding statements of social theorists:

Classical theorists **wrestled** with the notion of community, particularly the forces that held together complex societies. For Marx (1967 [1867]), the community or society **was** the arena within which interest groups defined by their relation to the means of production, competed.... Early anthropological work on tribal societies, the "classic" ethnographies of Malinowski (1961 [1922]), Evans-Pritchard (1972 [1940]), and others **were concerned** with issues of social solidarity and village life, social structure, and organization. It was Redfield (1956) who ... **brought** the notion of the "little community" into full anthropological gaze.

Chavez 1994: 53 (emphasis added).

Eventually, the record emerges from history and touches the present (in the perfect aspect):

The subfield of human anthropology, drawing on both Redfield and the Chicago School, **has produced** a wealth of interesting research on communities around the world (Hannerz 1980).

Chavez 1994: 52 (emphasis added).

But when does the present begin? In 1980? Or in 1950, as in this article from meteorology?

By combining surface observations, cloud-motion winds, and upper-air observations from kites and balloons, Bjerknes (1919) and Bjerknes and Solberg (1922) **set forth** the conceptual framework for understanding three-dimensional air-flows and associated weather within cyclones and about fronts by establishing the "Norwegian frontal-cyclone model." Inspection of even earlier observational analyses over North America (e.g., Bjerknes 1910; Rossby and Weightman 1926; Palmn and Newton 1951; Sanders 1955), however, **reveals** that frontal-cyclone evolutions over the central United States do not always mirror the conceptual model developed in Northern Europe. Recognition of the differences in topography and land-water distribution between northern Europe (where the Norwegian cyclone model originated) and the central United States **has** subsequently **led** to more complex conceptual models of surface frontal-cyclone evolutions and their attendant precipitation systems (e.g., Newton 1950, 1963; Carlson 1980; Hobbs et al. 1996).

Paul J. Neiman, F. Martin Ralph, M.A. Shapiro, B.F. Smull, and D. Johnson 1998 "An observational study of fronts and frontal mergers over the Continental United States." *Monthly Weather Review* 126: 2521–52, 2521 (emphasis added).

Inspecting the example below, we might notice that the simple present emerges with the research question—when the current writer *replies* to the reported statements, and initiates a new stage in the conversation.

The subfield of human anthropology, drawing on both Redfield and the Chicago School, **has produced** a wealth of interesting research on communities around the world (Hannerz 1980)....

Suffice it to say that despite all the work that has been carried out on communities, the question still **remains**: What **underlies** a sense of community? Anderson (1983) **examined** this question and **suggested** that communities are "imagined." Members of modern nations....

Such a view allows for a redefinition of *community*. Since it is imagined, a sense of community is not limited to a specific geographic locale (Gupta and Ferguson 1992). Immigrants are said to live in "binational communities" (Baca and Bryan 1980), "extended communities" (Whiteford 1979), "transnational communities" in "hyperspace" (Rouse 1991), and "transnational families" (Chavez 1992). These concepts **highlight** the connections migrants maintain with life in their home communities....

Chavez 1994: 54 (emphasis added).

What can we learn from the example above? Past tenses seem to occur in reporting expressions as a writer represents founding statements which led to other statements: so, after reaching the present in 1980 (and the chance to ask a question), we are back in the past with "Anderson (1983) examined." With this in mind, let's reconsider our question concerning the use of the past tense in the summary of Calhoun above ("Calhoun (1994) **explained** how heterosexual society makes heterosexuality seem natural ..."). A reader might interpret Calhoun's cataloguing as preliminary or foundational work, rather than the immediate motivation of the present research. Reporting expressions in scholarly writing may favour the present tenses because these tenses signal an essential motivation for scholarly work: the scholar listens to what is being said; then, from his or her position, has a question to ask, and takes a turn in the conversation. The present tenses cue the *writer's* motivation.

Sometimes, markers write in the margins of student papers—

Watch your tenses!
Tense!
Be consistent in tense.

—suggesting that academic readers are sensitive to these signals which indicate the story of knowledge being made. Staging the construction of knowledge, the verb forms writers use also indicate *their* version of this story: their sense of the sequence of knowledge, its contexts of production, the remoteness in time of some statements (remote but still audible, and enduring or echoing despite the passage of time) and the proximity of others (some so nearby in time that they are re-spoken as if in the present moment). On the one hand, the staging of statements in time is a dimension of a writer's particular perspective on the scholarly conversation. On the other hand, it displays the writer's familiarity with the progress of knowledge in the discipline. This perhaps explains scholarly readers' sensitivity to tenses, and to (what may seem to them) misrepresentations of the progress of knowledge, and may also explain the difficulty that newcomers to the disciplines can have in locating statements in time—choosing among present and past tenses, simple and perfect aspects—in ways that make sense to readers very familiar with the scholarly conversation.

Exercise 5

Examine the passage below and identify verb tense in reporting expressions. What do the shifts in tense imply about how knowledge is located in time?

Eugenics theory powerfully influenced late nineteenth- and early twentieth-century US policies concerning the groups then known as "the dependent, defective, and delinquent classes" (Henderson 1901, US Department of the Interior 1883). In essence, eugenics held that the "fit" should be encouraged to reproduce ("positive" eugenics) and the "unfit" prevented from doing so ("negative" eugenics). Historians generally agree that between 1900 and 1920 this doctrine formed the basis for a full-fledged social movement with research centers, propaganda vehicles, and strong middle-class support (Haller 1963, Kevles 1985, Ludmerer 1972, Pickens 1968). Less commonly acknowledged is the fact that eugenics theory affected public policy for decades before becoming the social movement's foundation and that eugenic ideas outlived the movement itself, in ways that a new generation of historians is just starting to explore (Dann 1991, Noll 1990, Reilly 1991). Even today, eugenics arguments occasionally make their way into debates about such matters as population growth and crime control (e.g., Wattenberg 1987, Wilson 1989; for a recent analysis see Duster 1990).

Nicole H. Rafter 1992 "Claims-making and socio-cultural context in the first U.S. eugenics campaign." *Social Problems* 39 (1): 17–34, 17.

Exercise 6

Inspect a research essay you have recently written or are currently drafting. What tense(s) do you use for reporting verbs? What does your use of tense imply about how knowledge is—or has been—constructed? Could you rework your essay by employing a combination of tenses to emphasize changes to the state of knowledge over time? Do you feel you are in a position to tell the story of knowledge in a field?

14

Conclusions and the Moral Compass of the Disciplines

This chapter will look at some of the ways in which the knowledge-making demands of research writing shape conclusions. These demands make the conclusion more complex than you might expect if you think that the main feature of a conclusion is to summarize what you have already said or if you've previously been given the rule not to introduce new ideas in a conclusion.

One way to begin to understand how the knowledge-making demands of the research genres inform conclusions is to consider that conclusions of lab reports require writers to draw inferences based on experimental results. Rather than simply repeating and summarizing the earlier parts of the report, the lab-report conclusion may interpret the data and evaluate the hypothesis. The lab report thus demonstrates more conspicuously what is true for conclusions more generally in research writing. Conclusions in research writing often engage in a distinct mode of address, as if the reader of the conclusion were different from the reader of the introduction.

This chapter will also look at how some of the features we have examined in past chapters—modality and limiting expressions, the state of knowledge, and abstractions—play key roles in conclusions to academic writing.

Finally, we will examine the types of **moral statements** that sometimes appear in the conclusions of research writing. These moral statements will lead to a more in-depth consideration of the values and beliefs that characterize different academic disciplines—the **moral compass of the disciplines**.

14A Conclusions

How do conclusions contribute to the reader's understanding of research writing? Certainly, the conclusion is the writer's last chance to make sure that connections between parts of the discussion are secure in readers' minds; it is the last chance to invoke the complex, high-level abstractions which motivated the discussion, made sense of its specifics, and contributed to the ongoing scholarly conversation. It is therefore best to think of conclusions as not concluding so much as *confirming* what has gone before.

Conclusions which merely restate the introduction can be troubling for readers of the research genres. This isn't to say that repetition does not occur in scholarly writing in general or conclusions in particular. As we saw in Chapter 9, reinstating abstractions can help readers manage their mental desktops by interpreting detail and bringing material back to attention. However, exact repetition in a conclusion can sound strange, because the reader who is addressed at the end of an essay is not exactly the same reader who is addressed at the beginning. At the end, the reader is familiar with the details and course of the argument: he or she has just been through it. To simply repeat the introduction suggests that the reader hasn't heard what the writer said.

So conclusions in research writing tend to address the reader as *a different reader* from the one who read the introduction. In the intervening pages, the reader has encountered detailed analysis and illustration, the claims derived from evidence. The reader at the end of the paper needs reminders of key abstractions and important findings to confirm the results and significance of the essay. The conclusion essentially advances the writer's claim in its final—rather than preliminary—form.

But scholarly writers also go beyond confirming claims in conclusions. They indicate the *limits* of new knowledge. In our discussion of introductions in Chapter 8, we noted that signs of limited knowledge come with modality and limiting expressions. In conclusions, where writers locate new knowledge deficits, we might expect to find modality and other signs of limits. This concluding section from an article on plain language shows the researchers still speculating and inferring:

As in the case of consultation between health-care professionals and consumers, it is **possible** that legal concepts are difficult to understand because, even when explained in plain language, they are complex or because they are in conflict with folk theories of the law. The subjects in this study (and lay people in general), **may** have been relying on inaccurate prior knowledge of the law or on their own intuition about justice, which **frequently** does not reflect the legal reality. These results **suggest** that plain language drafting alone will take us only part way to the goal of making the law more broadly understood. It must be supported by other measures such as public legal education and individual counselling of persons faced with legal obligations.

Michael E.J. Masson and Mary Anne Waldron 1994 "Comprehension of legal contracts by non-experts: Effectiveness of plain language redrafting." *Applied Cognitive Psychology* 8: 67–85, 79 (emphasis added).

As well as using modality, writers can point to a new knowledge deficit by explicitly remarking on what we don't know. In the following example, the writer confirms the main point of the essay and the knowledge deficit it addressed, then directly refers to the study's "limitations" and indicates what remains to be done:

Through his association of writing with speech, Malivha immersed *Inkululeko* in the pre-existing forms of communication, and thus ensured the paper's accessibility to its audience. As *Inkululeko* was read some fifty years ago, we are at a disadvantage in getting a clearer picture of how readers interacted with the newspaper. Questions about how the paper was distributed, read and discussed among the people would undoubtedly enrich our understanding of the role played by *Inkululeko* in mobilising for the ZBA, but what is left of these today will certainly be general impressions and memories.

In spite of these limitations, it is hoped that this essay has highlighted issues otherwise largely overlooked by existing social-historical studies seeking to understand questions of popular responses to political mobilisation in the countryside. The processes of forced removal, dispossession, and community destruction undoubtedly generated political consciousness which varied with region and time. But a focus on these processes alone, this essay argued, ignores a host of other factors which can also help explain questions of popular responses to political mobilisation in the countryside. Using the ZBA as a case study, the essay focused on how ideas about these processes were communicated to the Zoutpansberg people by looking at the language and style of mobilisation, and the methods as well as the media of communication the organisation used. We believe that more detailed and thorough research in this direction will enrich our understanding of how some organisations are able to attract popular following in the countryside.

Thiathu J. Nemutanzhela 1993 "Cultural forms and literacy as resources for political mobilisation: A.M. Malivha and the Zoutpansberg Balemi Association." *African Studies* 52 (1): 89–102, 100–01.

As well as confirming the main point of the essay, and the knowledge deficit it addressed, this conclusion directly refers to its own "limitations" by mentioning them, and indirectly refers to limitations by saying, in the last sentence of the passage, what still has to be done. Did you notice the use of self-reference ("this essay") and the use of knowledge-making verbs in the past tense ("argued," "focused")? As the example also shows, conclusions not only gesture toward the future, making a promise for greater knowledge still, they also tend to return the reader to the highest level of abstraction: here, such terms as "dispossession" and "political consciousness." This move makes sense because these prestige abstractions are the high-status terms that gave the introduction rhetorical force—the Big Issues which warrant claims on readers' attention and identify the writer as someone in touch with established concerns.

Accordingly, conclusions are one place where we see the otherwise relatively rare kind of expression we could call moral statements. While the research genres are generally relatively free of statements of moral obligation like this—

People **should** learn to respect the environment.
We **must** preserve our neighbourhoods.
Sports celebrities **ought to** be role models.

—there are nevertheless some occasions when obligation is expressed. Sometimes these obligations are about research itself. Something needs to be examined more closely; something should be explained in relation to something else. We can see an example of such an expression of obligation here, in the last sentence of an article on the experience of German minorities in Britain and the US in World War I (notice as well the major abstractions—*xenophobia, control, intolerance*—that are invoked by this ending):

> In each case, the experience of the German minority **needs** to be placed within traditions of xenophobia in the two countries, but, more especially, the war atmosphere which led to increasing control of all citizens and a growth of more general intolerance towards all perceived outgroups.
>
> Mark Ellis and Panikos Panayi 1994 "German minorities in World War I: A comparative study of Britain and the U.S.A." *Ethnic and Racial Studies* 17 (2): 238–59, 255–56 (emphasis added).

Sometimes the expression of obligation extends to the *application* of the research, as the passage by Masson and Waldron at the beginning of this chapter shows. Plain language redrafting, the authors conclude, is not enough to make legal documents understandable:

> It **must** be supported by other measures such as public legal education and individual counselling of persons faced with legal obligations.
>
> Michael E.J. Masson and Mary Anne Waldron 1994 "Comprehension of legal contracts by non-experts: Effectiveness of plain language redrafting." *Applied Cognitive Psychology* 8: 67–85, 79 (emphasis added).

And, sometimes, researchers can conclude with statements that resemble the calls to specific action or attitude we find in other genres, such as newspaper editorials or partisan political briefs. This is from a conclusion the writer has labelled "Policy implications":

> Human capital differences may be addressed by establishing programs to help women complete their education. We **should** offer scholarships and financial aid for women at both the high school and college levels. We **must** also establish programs to allow women who were forced to drop out of school to return and complete their education. These educational programs **must** be supplemented by others that provide job training and retraining. Many women worked prior to leaving the waged labor force to bear and/or rear children. Their occupational skills often became outdated during their absence and **must** be brought up to date. [...]
>
> My own analysis has revealed that young children in the home are a major barrier to married women's participation in the waged labor force. It is possible that this reflects a negative evaluation of mothers

with young children working outside the home, but it could also reflect the absence of safe, affordable day care. We cannot or perhaps **should** not do anything about the former possibility, but we can certainly address the latter. We **must** establish federally funded and federally supervised day care centers. It would be especially desirable if these day care centers could combine custodial with educational functions to provide a "head start" where needed.

James A. Geschwender 1992 "Ethgender, women's waged labor, and economic mobility." *Social Problems* 39 (1): 1–16, 12 (emphasis added).

In this article, "conclusion" and "action-to-be-taken" seem almost equivalent. This conclusion goes further toward real-world action/application than many research genres would permit. As we will see in the final section of this chapter, these calls for government action are themselves limited by some powerful constraints: even though, out of context, these moral statements may sound like those coming from editorials or campaigns, they have a different force and a different authority.

The preceding (and following) examples show that "moral" statements are not entirely missing from the scholarly genres—although they may occur in different degrees and with different focus in different disciplines.

Different disciplines have different kinds of connections with the world beyond the research domain—and the variations in "moral" statements (what *should* be done) that we have observed in the samples in this section are signals of these different connections. In the conclusion to an article from the journal *Estuaries*, for example, "marsh creation" is a positive goal—a *good*—and conditions which "retard" advance towards this goal are *ills*.

The recent decline in fur demand has depressed the industry so that nutria- [an aquatic rodent] trapping in Louisiana's coastal marshes is no longer economical, yet control of nutria populations is essential to maximize growth of newly created marshes. Marsh creation is a major policy objective of the state of Louisiana and of the Federal government. Dealing with the population size of an introduced mammalian species is a part of that policy issue.

We have shown that an introduced species—the nutria—alone or in combination with native migrating waterfowl can seriously retard marsh development in the deltaic environment. This demonstration of the importance of herbivory in the Atchafayala Delta has practical applications for the northern Gulf of Mexico coast where coastal wetland loss rates are the highest in North America (65 km^2 year, Britsch and Dunbar 1993).

Elaine D. Evers, Charles Sasser, James Gosselink, Deborah Fuller, and Jenneke Visser 1998 "The impact of vertebrate herbivores on wetland vegetation in Atchafayala Bay, Louisiana." *Estuaries* 21 (1): 1–13, 12.

As the passage indicates, nutria population is an obstacle, so "control of nutria populations is essential to maximize growth of newly created marshlands": nutria *should* be reduced in numbers. (Nutria themselves or their advocates may look at things differently.) Did you notice that the arguments recommending marshland as *good* are presupposed rather than reviewed? This presupposed positive understanding is captured in the claim that "[m]arsh creation is a major policy objective of the state of Louisiana and of the Federal government."

As this example shows, research interests in some disciplines or sub-disciplines involve a direct connection with interests in the public domain. The next section will help you analyze your discipline's internal way of thinking about what is desirable or undesirable.

Exercise 1

The passage below comes from the conclusion of the article on the effects of "low-ability" grouping by Gamoran (1993) that you encountered in Chapters 8 and 11. In this passage, "Mrs. Turner" and "Mrs. Grant" were two of the successful teachers of low-ability classes observed by the writer. Identify the expressions that limit the researcher's findings.

Yet another limitation of this study, also a form of narrowness, is that it relied on higher-than-expected achievement as a sign of effectiveness without considering other sorts of outcomes. Critics of ability grouping, however, maintain that low-track assignment is stigmatizing, producing harmful social outcomes apart from effects on achievement (see, e.g., Schwartz 1981; Oakes 1985). Cases studied by Valli (1986) and by Camarena (1990) seemed to open the possibility of counteracting this problem. However, in this study, Mrs. Turner commented in the year-end interview that assigning students to a remedial class stigmatizes them and depresses their motivation, and she views this as reason to avoid assigning them to a separate class. In fact, both Mrs. Turner and Mrs. Grant told us that, although they see the ability-grouping question as complex and multisided, on balance they both prefer mixing low-track students with other students. Thus, our examples of teachers who succeeded with low tracks—at least with respect to instruction and achievement—would actually prefer to end that arrangement. Perhaps, then, these are simply examples of good teachers, who would be effective regardless of how students were assigned. In any case, given the likelihood that ability grouping will continue to be used, we need to know much more about how to use it well.

Adam Gamoran 1993 "Alternative uses of ability grouping in secondary schools: Can we bring high-quality instruction to low-ability classes?" *American Journal of Education* 102: 1–22, 18–19.

Exercise 2

Examine the calls for action in the passages below. What should be done? What is good or bad? What kinds of outcome are in sight?

PASSAGE 1

There are at least four reasons why studying gaze aversion and disengaging from the environment may be of more than passing interest. First, the behavior is so frequent as to be characterized as "commonplace" (Kundera, 1996). Second, the results bear a family resemblance to the irrelevant speech effect (LeCompte, 1994) and to the analysis of attentional demands on retrieval (Craik, Govoni, Naveh-Benjamin, and Anderson, 1996). Third, this sort of behavior has been noted as relevant by investigators in at least two other domains: social behavior (Argyle and Kendon, 1967), and law enforcement. In the latter context, Fisher and Geiselman (1992) recommend closing the eyes as a component of the cognitive interview designed to facilitate accurate recall of information from eyewitnesses to crimes.

Finally, Glenberg (1997) has proposed that disengaging from the environment may be a significant source of individual differences in cognition. That is, planning, recollective memory, and language all seem to require some ability to disengage from the current environment. If there is reliable variability in the capacity or skill needed to disengage (see Ehrlichman and Weinberger, 1978, for data on this), this variability ought to be systematically related to the execution of a wide variety of cognitive and behavioral skills.

Arthur M. Glenberg, Jennifer L. Schroeder, and David A. Robertson 1998 "Averting the gaze disengages the environment and facilitates remembering." *Memory and Cognition* 26 (4): 651–58, 657.

PASSAGE 2

The rewards of working with TEK are commonly expressed using the future tense. While improvements are certainly possible, available methods of documenting TEK, such as the one used in this study, are effective. What remain to be developed are better means of integrating TEK approaches with those of Western science, better ways of using TEK in resource management, and a better understanding of how TEK can help conservation, including sustainable use of living resources.

This research shows that an effective methodology used in a collaborative research process with elders and hunters can document a wide range of useful and detailed information. The benefits of such research include a better understanding of the ecology of a region or a species, as well as cooperation in research, which aids the cooperative management strategies that are increasingly common in Alaska and elsewhere in the Arctic. Effective processes for applying documented indigenous knowledge to management, conservation, and biological research, however, remain elusive, and require additional investigation.

Henry Huntington et al. 1999 "Traditional knowledge of the ecology of beluga whales (*Delphinapterus leucas*) in the Eastern Chukchi and Northern Bering Seas, Alaska." *Arctic* 52 (1): 49–61, 59.

PASSAGE 3

Finally, we must bear in mind that preservation of ecosystems is a primary goal of preventing global warming, and the destruction of ecosystems to prevent global warming would be a counterproductive and perverse strategy. Therefore, the cooling that could potentially arise from deforestation outside the tropics should not necessarily be viewed as a strategy for mitigating climate change because, apart from their potential climatic role, forests are valuable in many aspects. They provide natural habitat to plants and animals, preserve the biodiversity of natural ecosystems, produce economically valuable timber and firewood, protect watersheds through prevention of soil erosion, and indirectly prevent ocean acidification by reducing atmospheric CO_2. In planning responses to global challenges, therefore, it is important to pursue broad goals and to avoid narrow criteria that may lead to environmentally harmful consequences.

G. Bala, K. Caldeira, M. Wickett, T.J. Phillips, D.B. Lobell, C. Delire, and A. Mirin 2007 "Combined climate and carbon-cycle effects of large-scale deforestation." *Proceedings of the National Academy of Sciences* 104 (16): 6550–55, 6554.

14B The Moral Compass of the Disciplines: Research Ethics

If research is a truth-seeking pursuit, who could object to it? The fact that reasonable people do raise or anticipate objections suggests that research is not so strictly neutral a pursuit, that it has some interests of its own, and that these may conflict with other valid interests.

Universities themselves watch for such conflicts. They establish committees to scrutinize the **ethics** of research carried on by their faculty. These committees guard the interests of those who participate in research projects. Some of these participants are animals whose welfare must be protected as far as possible. Others are people taking part in clinical trials of pharmaceuticals and other therapies. We can imagine the risk to both animals and people in research which, in the process of seeking knowledge, may expose its participants to harm. But other participants, who are not so obviously at risk, still attract the attention of research-ethics committees. These others are people who agree to be interviewed, answer questionnaires, or, in an experimental situation, express their thoughts or manipulate objects. Other kinds of participants might be those who agree to a researcher's presence in a real-life situation: a classroom or a workplace or a family dinnertime, for example. Less personally, others might agree to have their life information—on health, income, place of residence, family situation, for example—combined with information from thousands of other people and made available to researchers. To get permission to conduct research which includes in its methodology interviews, surveys, questionnaires, on-site observation, social-psychological experimentation, or data banks, researchers must present to **ethics committees** detailed accounts of their procedures. Most important, they must explain how they will get from participants their **informed consent**. That is, researchers must tell potential participants the purpose of the research, and how the results will be used, including assurances that individual participants' identities will not be exposed. Researchers must explain to participants what they will be asked to do, and how long it will take. Researchers must identify their own affiliations, including in some cases the sources of funds for conducting their study. Researchers must make sure that participants understand all this information as they decide whether or not to take part.

Informed consent can be a controversial issue. Sometimes potential participants might be willing to take part, but they find the consent process tedious and not to be taken seriously. They don't want to listen to the explanation or read the consent form. Other times, full disclosure of research premises could distort participants' responses. For example, if researchers want to compare the responses of younger and older people to female political leaders, those with reservations about women leaders might adjust their responses if they know what researchers will be watching for. Information on the gendering of politics could be useful to democratic reform, but to get accurate information, researchers may look for ways to inform participants only generally or partially. Where is the line between full information and reasonable consent? How are the interests of knowledge-making to be reconciled with those of **research subjects**? If some people sincerely believe that male leaders are more capable, do they have a right to disguise these beliefs, or to withhold them from research that would reveal them?

It is possible that in some cases an ethics committee's concerns may be exaggerated. But history warns us of a tendency of research inquiries to corroborate what privileged groups want to know about groups they dominate. Early in the twentieth century, women were found, by a linguist of great reputation, to be incapable of producing logical sentences, a disability warranting their guidance by men.

Historically, people of profound disadvantage—the poor, the afflicted, the incarcerated, the vagrant or dispossessed—were found to have deviant characteristics which warranted not only their disadvantage but also the intervention of the privileged in their lives. Even today, so pronounced has been the inclination of middle-class researchers to study underclass groups that some have called for a moratorium on research focused on disadvantaged people. Such calls may be issued more as a matter of principle than practice. Nevertheless, in Canada, national policy statements, while setting out the broad principles for protecting research subjects from potential harm, make special comment on "research involving aboriginal people":

> There are historical reasons why Indigenous or Aboriginal Peoples may legitimately feel apprehensive about the activities of researchers. In many cases, research has been conducted in respectful ways and has contributed to the well-being of Aboriginal communities. In others, Aboriginal Peoples have not been treated with a high degree of respect by researchers. Inaccurate or insensitive research has caused stigmatization. On occasion, the cultural property and human remains of Indigenous Peoples have been expropriated by researchers for permanent exhibition or storage in institutes, or offered for sale. Researchers have sometimes treated groups merely as sources of data, and have occasionally endangered dissident Indigenous Peoples by unwittingly acting as information-gatherers for repressive regimes. Such conduct has harmed the participant communities and spoiled future research opportunities.
>
> Canadian Institutes of Health Research, Natural Sciences and Engineering Research Council of Canada, Social Sciences and Humanities Research Council of Canada *Tri-Council Policy Statement: Ethical Conduct for Research Involving Humans* 1998 (with 2000, 2002, and 2005 amendments) www.pre-ethics.gc.ca/english/policystatement/introduction.cfm.

We may think that today's research activities are cleansed of the class, gender, and racialist interests of earlier generations, but the guidelines which follow the statements cited above suggest that we cannot take for granted the purity of knowledge making. And it may be that some degree of bias, or some form of social involvement, is inherent to research. We explore this possibility in the next and final section of this book.

Exercise 3

As a student of academic writing and a new member of a research community, you are in a position to reflect seriously on ethical questions posed by different research scenarios. The following scenarios ask you to consider the potential clash of interest between those who make knowledge and their research subjects—those from whose lives data are extracted. Imagine the possibilities of harm—embarrassment, injury to life chances, or even physical danger—to research participants.

1. A researcher is investigating a site in a rural village far from home. The people the researcher has got to know want to talk, and they invite her into their confidence. But they have no time for the consent form. They find it irrelevant or incomprehensible: it's a nuisance to listen to the lengthy explanation of the project. They put their trust in their personal relationship with the researcher. Should the researcher be given permission to conduct her research? What more would you want to know about the project to make your decision?

2. At mammography clinics, data relevant to the incidence of breast cancer have been collected from 100,000 women. Participants have been informed of the purpose of data collection, and they have given their consent. Another research project now proposes to review the data for a purpose other than studying incidence of breast cancer. What would you have to know to approve the new study?

3. What harm could come to participants in a study of diet and diabetes? Of workplace bullying? Of religious conviction? Of spousal assault? Of internet shopping habits? Of political coalitions in opposition to land development? What would you need to know about the studies in question to estimate whether the potential for harm could be reduced? Can you think of situations where the harm could not be mitigated, and the research should not be undertaken, despite benefits?

Exercise 4

In the 1960s, psychologist Stanley Milgram conducted a series of controversial studies on obedience and authority. Research subjects were told that they were participating as "teachers" in a study on the relation between electric shock and learning. These "teachers" asked questions of "learners," and they applied an increasing amount of electric shock when the "learners" answered incorrectly. If a "teacher" asked the researcher to stop because the electric shock was too high or the "learner" was in pain, the researcher instructed the "teacher" to continue. The majority of subjects obeyed the authority of the researcher, even when the shock appeared to be almost lethal and the "learner" appeared to be unconscious. In fact, the "learners" were actors who pretended to experience electric shock. The "teachers" were the actual focus of the study: Milgram wanted to see if they would obey an authority even when the action went against their own sense of right and wrong. This study has been criticized by those who believe that the stress of the deceptive experiment could have caused permanent damage to the research subjects. Others argue that such deception is necessary because the "teachers" would not have obeyed if they knew that they were the ones being observed. Discuss the merits of each position. Should Milgram have been allowed to conduct this type of experiment? Was it ethical? (For the original study, see Milgram 1963.)

14C The Moral Compass of the Disciplines: Moral Statements

In the first section of this chapter (14A), we observed that moral statements in the form of expressions of obligations are not common in research writing, but they do appear. When can you, as a student researcher, make explicit recommendations for action? Are such statements at odds with your role as a researcher? Aren't the research genres neutral and impersonal? Even those who study the research genres consider them to be so, saying that experts in an academic field avoid language "commonly employed to place somebody under an *obligation*.... Their mastery, instead, is shown by the adoption of a more *neutral* tone ..." (Gotti & Dossena, 2001: 14, emphasis added).

But are these expressions of moral obligation impersonal or neutral?

- Corporations **should** live up to the commitments they have made to retired workers.
- Consumers **should** cut back on their use of plastic credit.
- People **ought to** take responsibility for their own health.
- You **need to** be more assertive.

The first three of these obligations are less imposing than the last one: addressees would have to identify themselves as credit-voracious or health-irresponsible or corporate-complicit to feel the imposition. (Yet even if they didn't so identify, they would still be hearing others imposed on, in a moral tone.) But all of these statements of obligation participate in the force of the last one. These statements get *personal*. At the same time, each expression of obligation implicitly estimates what is *good* and *bad*: it's *good* to be assertive; *bad* to indulge in fatty foods, to buy things you can't afford, to enhance profits by going back on promises. Since the research genres are taken to be impersonal and neutral, we might think that these moral wordings—*should, must, have to, ought to*—will not appear. But they do, as we have seen:

> The experience of the German minority **needs to** be placed within traditions of xenophobia in the two countries ...
>
> Ellis and Panayi 1994: 255–56 (emphasis added).
>
> [Plain language redrafting] **must** be supported by other measures such as public legal education and individual counselling of persons faced with legal obligations.
>
> Masson and Waldron 1994: 79 (emphasis added).

To be sure, the **modals of moral obligation** are not so frequent in research writing as the modals which limit the status of knowledge. But because the moral expressions carry such a social charge—personal and value-laden—they are high-profile features. They can stop readers in their tracks. And because their appearance may remind students of expressions of obligation well regarded in high-school essays (e.g., "We must protect the environment"), it is worthwhile to look into the incentives to and constraints on moral expression in academic writing. We will learn more about the moral compass of research, and more about the student writer's position.

The principal author of this book was curious about the apparent contradiction between the research genres' reputation for impersonal neutrality and their tolerance of certain moral expressions. Her curiosity was sparked by her familiarity with research into scholarly genres themselves and her observation of expressions of moral obligation in research articles. She had also noticed how students could sometimes hit the wrong note in their writing when they took a moral stand and called for action: e.g., if a student wrote, "We must learn to respect other people's cultures." Selecting three disciplines—forestry, social psychology, and urban geography—she assembled a one-million-word sample of academic writing, searched electronically for expressions of moral obligation, and then analyzed the results to discover the settings which permitted or called for these expressions. Roughly, these expressions were found in two settings.

The first setting involved researchers themselves and their knowledge-making activities: *We **must** find this out, and we **must** do it this way.* Examples were found in all three disciplines. In forestry, researchers tell other researchers that "the structural and functional components of resistance and resilience **must** be distinguished" and "one **should** remember the **necessity** to take account of the species identity for the definition of any appropriate silvicultural system." In urban geography, researchers argue to other researchers that "race **should** be understood as socially constructed" and "inferences **must** be model-based." In social psychology, researchers tell each other that "we **should** ask why people are pessimistic" and "future research **should** examine these possible contingencies and assess the effects of these factors more systematically." Although these are "moral" statements, they can still be explained within the "neutral" and "impersonal" stance of the research genres. The obligations around method speak to the value of reliable (and therefore "neutral" rather than "subjective") means of making knowledge. These obligations focus on the object of inquiry, and in doing so they confirm research goals already agreed on in the discipline: shared and scholarly rather than "personal." While all three disciplines showed these patterns around the method and object of inquiry, they displayed them differently, suggesting that different disciplines use these resources for establishing methods and goals in different ways.

The second setting for expression of moral obligation involved calls for action by people who were not involved in knowledge making: in other words, real-world applications of the results of research. These calls to action are issued through narrow channels. Urban geographers advise city planners or health officials, or traffic-flow managers—in other words, designated professionals. Forestry researchers address managers of timber industries and decision makers who compose the many regulations governing timber harvest. So urban geographers tell professionals in the field that "intervention strategies **should** focus on old and poor neighbourhoods and minority neighbourhoods, without undue emphasis on the latter" and that "land use and transport planners **must** work with the reality of the two-car family." Forestry researchers tell professionals in the field and decision makers that "cooperation **must** be maintained" and that "the harvesting or tree selection method used **should** be appropriate to the timber species' regeneration requirements."

We can now begin to specify how these two disciplines put a limit on calls for action in the world. First, these calls are only issued on the basis of *research-attested* findings—rather than on some other basis, such as sympathy, religious conviction, or respect for authority, or love of country. Statements of obligation in these research genres are a way of saying that the results of research are valid and significant. So, if a student wrote that "We must learn to respect other people's cultures," an academic reader would ask about the research basis for such an obligation: by what research methods has this been found out? Second, the obligation is imposed on a social group—professionals working in a field—rather than broadly, on everybody. You can see how these moral statements differ from those which, in a high-school essay, take a stand for spirituality, vegetarian diet, or an end to schoolyard bullying or cruelty to animals.

You may also see, in conjunction with the type of neutrality maintained by the first condition (that actions are only prescribed from research-attested findings), that the research disciplines are involved in the world. They instruct professional and social groups whose activities can impinge on our everyday lives: our experience of woodlands and our use of watersheds; our experience of traffic and neighbourhoods. Here we will not go into the results of more detailed analysis of the moral style of research writing in these two disciplines. We will just say that such analysis showed forestry's complex involvement not only with the economics and biology of timber harvest but also with government regulation and the interests of people who don't want trees cut down at all. Further analysis showed, in some sectors of urban geography, an involvement with the interests of people who were liable to be dispossessed by middle-class uses of the city. These more complicated patterns of conflicts and collusions confirm the importance of ethics committees' scrutiny of research projects. So does the more general finding that expressions of moral obligation are intended for particular social sectors, which may have their own interests to advance or protect.

In explaining this overall pattern, we haven't mentioned social psychology. Even though social psychology studies things most people would be interested in and might want advice about—memory, judgement, creativity, optimism, stereotyping, for example—it seems that social psychologists do not tell people what to do. Beyond knowledge making, statements of obligation by means of the "moral" wordings we have inspected do not seem to play as big a role in social psychology as they do in some other disciplines. It is notable that different disciplines have such different ways of articulating moral obligation, and that these differences can't necessarily be predicted based on common sense.

Just as the million-word sample of research writing contained statements of moral obligation, so can the study of the sample issue some of its own obligations. As knowledge makers, we *should* investigate the puzzle presented by social psychology, and we *should* inquire further into the social involvement of research activities. These are knowledge-making obligations. For those of you who will be pursuing your own research and joining research cultures as writers, the "should" statements could take the form of the following advice: moral statements carry a social charge in any context. In academic contexts, the social charge flows to attested research findings and out into the world through designated professionals. Students *should* consider whether their findings warrant the emphasis of moral statements and whether the findings warrant being transmitted—even figuratively—to people in the field. (Are you in a position to instruct designated professionals?) Students *should* also be aware of the different ways these high-charged expressions are used in different disciplines. And then, more generally, and in keeping with the spirit of this book, which invites students to join the activities of the disciplines, these findings suggest that students *should* be aware that research is not separate from real life, but rich with the complexities of its interests and values.

Exercise 5

a) The case of social psychology remains a puzzle for us. What is it about the discipline that makes researchers withhold rather than deliver recommendations? Can the following episode suggest where we might look for missing pieces of the puzzle?

> In a radio interview, a social psychologist reports findings from a recent study. He and his colleagues found that, when people contemplate a "relationship change," they overestimate the distress they will feel. In other words, breaking up is not as hard as people expect. The interviewer asks, "So people *should* go ahead anyway, even though they are afraid of what they will feel?" The researcher repeats his findings and also qualifies them: not every single subject found breaking up easier than expected and there was a range of difference between expectation and eventuality. (CBC August 2008)

b) *Corporations should live up to commitments they have made to retired workers*: this was one of the examples, offered above, of a statement of moral obligation. Can you think of a writing situation where such a statement would be warranted—that is, a situation where it was attested by research findings? What disciplines would offer the methodologies capable of producing such findings?

c) We have some (limited) information on the appearance of expressions of moral obligation in research writing. Knowing the restrictions on their appearance, what role do you think they might play in your own academic writing? We also know that different disciplines use these expressions differently. Amongst the disciplines in which you have studied or are now studying, can you anticipate differences in the use of statements of moral obligation?

Glossary

abstract the brief SUMMARY that sometimes precedes an article or accompanies bibliographical information found in an index (CH. 12C).

abstractions, abstract words concepts, ideas, and entities that could be said to have essentially mental existence, for example, "power" or "racial antagonism." We develop abstractions from concrete data and GENERALIZATIONS. Abstractions occupy the highest levels of generality and perform a cognitive function: that is, they play an important role in reasoning. PRESTIGE ABSTRACTIONS also perform important social functions: high-value abstractions attract the attention of members of a particular academic community; display the writer's allegiance to the interests and knowledge-making methods of that community; and establish the writer's right to speak as a member of the community. For example, "voluntary employee turnover" or "relationship marketing" can establish a speaker's position as a member of the management-studies community (CH. 3B, 4, 7B–7D, 9A, 10E).

academic discipline a particular branch of academic study. A discipline can be construed broadly (history, biology) or narrowly (cognitive psychology, medical entomology) (CH. 1D).

academic writing peer-to-peer communication about knowledge and inquiry within research communities. In this book, academic writing is also referred to as scholarly writing, the research genres, and writing in the disciplines (CH. 1B).

313

agentlessness/agentless expressions a way of highlighting the activity rather than the actor, by eliminating the person (or "agent") doing the activity (CH. 8B, 10D, 11C, 12B). *See also* PASSIVE CONSTRUCTIONS and FORECASTS.

ambiguity the capacity for a word or phrase to be interpreted in two or more ways. Ambiguity is associated particularly with NOUN PHRASES containing two or more nouns, for example, "labour supply decision-making" (CH. 10D).

anticipatory-it, it-extraposition the use of "it" at the beginning of a sentence as a means of deferring important material to the end of the sentence (CH. 11D). *See also* END-WEIGHT PRINCIPLE.

apposition/appositive a grammatical structure, signalled by commas, dashes, a colon, parentheses, "or," and "i.e.," that puts an equivalent expression next to a term that the writer estimates as important but difficult for a reader. The appositive may define and narrow the meaning and application of an important word or it may expand and amplify the sense of the term (CH. 7B).

asserting, assertion the speech action of making a statement for the new information of the reader—as if the reader did not know this information (CH. 5G). *See also* PRESUPPOSITION.

citation the customary practice of attributing words, phrases, or statements to another speaker (CH. 2, 8A).

cleft sentence, cleft construction a syntactic construction commonly used for EMPHASIS. Cleft constructions take the form "It was X that did such-and-such" rather than "X did such-and-such" (e.g., "It was geological evidence that supported the Alvarez hypothesis" rather than "geological evidence supported the Alvarez hypothesis") (CH. 11D).

cognitive response vs. social response the response of a reader based on understanding or reasoning vs. the response based on social expectations, though the distinction is blurred in actuality. Most people experience similar cognitive responses, reflecting the general psychological conditions of comprehension and communication. Social responses come from shared habits of reasoning and preferred procedures for constructing knowledge in particular research communities (CH. 5, 9). *See also* MUTUAL KNOWLEDGE.

common sense vs. uncommon sense (expertise) unexamined but widely accepted assumptions arising out of everyday experience and popular discourse vs. statements arising out of the domains of research (CH. 10A). *See also* PLAIN LANGUAGE.

cultural situation circumstances that define the relationship between writer and reader; a distinct occasion in a culture. Looking for work and the job interview are examples of cultural situations (CH. 1).

definite expressions a noun phrase beginning with "the" or "this," marking the entity as familiar to both writer and reader (e.g., "the recipe on the spaghetti box"). When used in academic discourse, the definite expression (e.g., "the choice-theoretic paradigm") encodes a community of researchers (writers and readers) (CH. 5G). *See also* PRESUPPOSITION.

definition a statement clarifying how a term is to be used in a particular context. Definition is a remarkably complex phenomenon, and statements can be clarified by a variety of means. Moreover, the approaches to definition vary from ACADEMIC DISCIPLINE to discipline, with some disciplines preferring definitions based on TAXONOMY and others allowing the meaning of use of a term to be adapted for the immediate purposes of the argument at hand (CH. 7). *See also* APPOSITION, FORMAL DEFINITION, and SUSTAINED DEFINITION.

direct speech reported speech that represents the exact words used by someone else in another context. The simplest form of reported speech is quotation (x said "y"), a verbatim record of another's speech (CH. 8B, 13C).

discipline *see* ACADEMIC DISCIPLINE.

discourse action an action that can be represented by a reporting verb (x describes, x observes, x proposes) or reporting noun (x's description, x's observation, x's proposal). Discourse actions are associated both with CITATION and the DISCURSIVE *I,* and the choice of verb can be influenced by the discipline in which a writer is working (CH. 11B).

discourse community a group of people identifiable (or recognizable) not only by their shared values, beliefs, and specialized knowledge about the world but also by the way they talk or write: their use of language embodies their shared values and special knowledge. For example, mountain bikers and developmental psychologists both constitute distinct discourse communities because each group exhibits characteristic patterns of communication that its members find meaningful and efficient ("vegetable tunnel" and "yard sale" being useful and economical expressions of experience for the first group, but incomprehensible and irrelevant to the experiences and interests of the second) (CH. 1, 10).

discursive *I* the use of "I" to refer to the writer in his or her capacity as a researcher/writer. The discursive *I* may also appear in the plural form, as "we". (CH. 8D, 11B).

documentation a two-part tracking system that aids the reader's movement from REPORTED SPEECH in the body of the text to the full documentation of sources in footnotes, endnotes, and the "References" or "Works Cited" pages (CH. 8C).

double reporting, reporting reporting the activity of reporting information cited by a source, i.e., when a writer accounts for a source's summarizing activity (CH. 3E).

emphasis expressions drawing attention to key points, as in, for example, "of particular importance here" or "the point I want to stress here …" (CH. 11D).

end-weight principle the tendency to shift important material to the end of the sentence (e.g., "It has been routinely argued that the advances in obstetrical knowledge in the eighteenth century undermined the traditional role of the midwife") (CH. 11D).

estimate from a position of limited knowledge modality and modalizing expressions such as "I think" and "seems" indicate that a statement issues from the writer as knowledge maker (CH. 13A). *See also* KNOWLEDGE-MAKING *I*.

ethics, research ethics norms or rules for deciding whether an action, in this case research, is acceptable or not. Research ethics are especially important when the people or animals being studied may be harmed by the research or are otherwise vulnerable (CH. 14B). *See also* ETHICS COMMITTEES and INFORMED CONSENT.

ethics committees groups that provide oversight and guidance for researchers working with vulnerable research subjects (CH. 14B). *See also* ETHICS.

expert vs. non-expert generally speaking, the distinction between those who are members of a research community and those who are not. However, the boundaries between the two categories can be contested (CH. 3F).

failed-then-revised hypothesis the revisions to one's understanding of a NOUN PHRASE as one works through it. For example, as a reader works through the noun phrase "the letter-carrier union representative meeting" it becomes necessary to revise one's understanding of the noun phrase with each successive word (CH. 10C).

feminist reasoning related to ways of thinking following women's rights movements in the nineteenth and twentieth centuries, feminism sometimes critiques the historically masculinist basis of knowledge making, and has often insisted on emphasizing the role of the subject in the knowledge-making process (CH. 12C).

forecasts statements about how the argument will be organized, what readers can expect (CH. 11C).

form elements readers recognize as patterns in the wordings or overall shape of writing. Form is the particular way in which "content"—the writing's ideas or meaning—is expressed, rather than an independent entity. Someone might say that a statute takes the form of a preamble, a series of clauses, and a proclamation; or that a high-school essay has a "five-paragraph form" (an introduction, one paragraph on each of three points, and a conclusion)—and that each of these elements has a role to play in establishing the text's meaning. "Form" can also be used to refer to phrases that frequently occur in certain kinds of writing. When we hear once again "we are gathered here today" or "Once upon a time," the features we recognize could be called formal (or even formulaic) (CH. 1B–C).

formal definition the classical form of a DEFINITION consisting of a single sentence in which the term being defined is the grammatical subject, which is followed by a form of the verb "to be" and a subject complement that identifies the general class the term belongs to and then provides characteristics distinguishing the term from all other members of that class. A version of the classical example of the formal definition is "A human is a rational animal" (human = the term to be defined, animal = the general class humans belong to, rational = the distinctive feature that distinguishes humans from other animals) (CH. 7C).

generalization a statement that typifies large numbers of instances (intermediate level of generality), as in "Through the 1980s, the baby-boomers were the most relentless consumers the marketplace has ever seen." A typified or generalized action or event can itself become an ABSTRACTION (higher level of generality), such as "materialism," and further specified through details (lowest levels of generality), such as "cars, condos, electronic appliances." Both generalizations and abstractions are products of reasoning (CH. 8A, 9A, 12A, 13B). *See also* LEVELS OF GENERALITY.

genre traditionally defined in terms of form and used for categorization, genre has been reconceptualized as involving SITUATION and FORM (situation + form = genre) and, thus, involves not only the type of communication but also the situation that the communication serves (CH. 1, 5). *See also* FORM and CULTURAL SITUATION.

genre-specific expectations readers' often unconscious expectations of specific genres' stylistic conventions, which, among academic readers, reflect disciplinary values and preferred methods for constructing knowledge (CH. 5). A reader of an English paper, for example, expects to see quotations from a literary text that demonstrate or illustrate a writer's statements about meaning. Traditional marking comments, such as the request for more "evidence," often obscure the specificity of these tacit expectations (CH. 5B). *See also* UNITARY VIEWS OF LANGUAGE and GENRE VIOLATION.

genre theory dating to Aristotle, genre theory attempts to explain and categorize communication into types based on formal similarities. Recent genre theory rethinks the emphasis on FORM and sees TYPE as developing from the situational needs and habits of communication (CH. 1B, 5B, 7D, 9A, 10A–B).

genre violation the misapplication of the norms, expectations, or needs regarding communication in one situation to those of another situation. This can occur in writing (e.g., a scholar uses technical terminology when addressing an audience of laypeople) or in reading (e.g., a lay reader criticizes the lack of "clarity" in a research publication) (CH. 10A).

gist the main point of a passage of writing. Recording gists is a way of taking notes that avoids the original sentence-level phrasing and direct copying, using brief words or phrases (recorded in the margin or elsewhere) that can be adapted to report and summarize the reading (CH. 3A–3C).

hypothesis a statement that is deemed plausible but that is, so far, untested and will be shown to be tested in the course of the research study (CH. 8D).

imprint the mark left on language by salient features of a CULTURAL SITUATION. Recent GENRE THEORY predicts that formal features of language develop from and serve recurring situations. When language is used in a way that becomes typical of situation, it is imprinted by that situation (CH. 1). *See also* TYPE, TYPIFICATION.

indeterminacy *see* UNCERTAINTY.

indirect speech REPORTED SPEECH that represents the words of another speaker by using new words: paraphrase or SUMMARY. Indirect speech, unlike DIRECT SPEECH, involves changes in the wording to fit a new and different context. In academic writing especially, it often leads to NOMINALIZATION (CH. 8B).

informed consent permission received from research subjects to participate in a study. Researchers need to inform potential participants about the purpose and risks of the research; participants need to decide to take part in the research (CH. 14B). See ETHICS and ETHICS COMMITTEES.

knowledge deficit the gap in established knowledge—what hasn't been said, what needs to be said, some error in what is held to be true. The knowledge deficit is what justifies the present research project. The location of knowledge deficits often comes with MODALITY and LIMITING EXPRESSIONS (CH. 2C, 6F, 8D–8E, 11A, 13A, 14A).

knowledge-making *I* *see* DISCURSIVE *I*, MODALITY, METHODO-LOGICAL *I*, MODAL EXPRESSIONS (CH. 13).

levels of generality the structure of information in a given passage, moving from the highest, most abstract concepts through general concepts down to specific details. Levels of generality can be represented in diagram form, with abstractions appearing at the top, generalized or contextualized at midpoints, and specific details at the lowest levels. The levels diagram reveals relationships among ideas and specific details; it also sketches our experience of reading as we negotiate the big issues, the writer's general claims, and the specific references used to illustrate and demonstrate those claims (CH. 3B–3C, 4, 8A). *See also* ABSTRACTIONS and GENERALIZATION.

limiting expressions terms that place limits on a GENERALIZATION ("in most cases," "a majority of interviewees") (CH. 13B).

listeners' centre of attention an estimate of the responses of a reader that is based on a writer's own social and cultural expectations and experiences with forms of expression (CH. 5A).

management device a metaphor for how a reader manages information while reading; the way a reader detects, organizes, and assigns priority or RELEVANCE. A writer can anticipate and attempt to assist how a reader manages information (CH. 9B). *See also* MENTAL DESKTOP.

mental desktop a metaphor for how a reader processes information while reading: a space on which statements arrive, one after the other, as the reader advances through a text (CH. 9B). *See also* MANAGEMENT DEVICE.

messages about the argument features including the DISCURSIVE *I*, SELF-REFERENCE, FORECAST, and EMPHASIS that help a reader understand the organization of academic writing (CH. 11).

methodological *I* the use of "I," usually in the METHOD SECTION to refer to the writer in his or her capacity as a practitioner of research methods. The methodological *I* is often associated with verbs expressing physical actions (e.g., "we drilled" or "we excavated") and may also appear in the plural form (CH. 12B).

methods procedures by which knowledge has been produced (CH. 12). *See also* QUANTITATIVE and QUALITATIVE.

method section an explicit account of how the researchers produced the knowledge they are now reporting. In the sciences and social sciences, such accounts are often in a section called "methods" (CH. 12B).

modality, modal expressions words or phrases such as "I think" or "seems" that indicate that a statement is an inference from a position of limited knowledge (CH. 13A, 14A).

modalize the marking of statements as being knowledge under construction—usually with the recognition that the knowledge is limited in some way—from a certain location: the speaker's or writer's position in the world (CH. 8D, 13A).

modals of moral obligation wording like "should" or "must" that expresses the moral need for an action or change based on research findings (CH. 14C). *See also* MODALITY, MODAL EXPRESSIONS, and MODALIZE.

moral compass of the disciplines the values and beliefs that characterize different academic disciplines (CH. 14C).

moral statement a statement, sometimes occurring in conclusions, that expresses research imperatives or obligations—what actions "must" be taken, what "should" be done. Moral statements may presuppose their disciplines' beliefs about what is good and bad, and they often connect the interests and activities of research to concerns in the public domain. The presence or lack of moral statements and the types of imperatives and obligations they propose are discipline specific (CH. 14). *See also* SUBJECT POSITION.

mutual knowledge an estimate of what can be safely assumed as shared background knowledge (CH. 5A).

narrative a sequence of events organized chronologically—a story. Narratives are especially difficult to summarize because they tend not to contain LEVELS OF GENERALITY that explain the details and conditions in the story (CH. 4C).

nominalization the process of word transformation when verbs (actions) and qualities are converted into nouns: "observe," for example, becomes "observation" (CH. 8B, 10). *See also* NOMINAL STYLE, NOUN PHRASE, SYNTACTIC DENSITY.

nominal style noun-heavy style; phrasing characterized by nominalization or noun phrases (CH. 10C–10E). *See also* NOMINALIZATION, NOUN PHRASE, and SYNTACTIC DENSITY.

noun phrase a phrase consisting of a noun or pronoun along with its modifiers (e.g., "*nonspecific goal strategy in problem solving*," "*sample-size considerations*"). Often in academic writing, noun phrases may consist of strings of nouns that modify subsequent nouns or noun-groupings (CH. 10C–10E). *See also* NOMINALIZATION, NOMINAL STYLE, and SYNTACTIC DENSITY.

objectivity the attempt to avoid personal bias or the limits of personal perspective and experience in the production of knowledge (CH. 12A). *Contrast* SUBJECTIVITY.

obviousness an expression of attitude regarding a statement (e.g., "of course") in a given DISCIPLINE or field of research that indicates there is some consensus or common ground with regard to it (CH. 13B).

orchestration a dialogue of two or more speakers (often writers from different research publications) arranged by a writer by way of direct and/or indirect reported speech (CH. 6).

passive construction, passive voice the grammatical construction whereby the object that a transitive verb acts upon is moved from after the verb to before, becoming the subject of the sentence. For example, "I ate all your Easter chocolate" (the active voice) becomes "All your Easter chocolate was eaten by me" *or* "All your Easter chocolate was eaten." The second form of the passive construction is also an example of an AGENTLESS EXPRESSION (CH. 11C).

plain language the use of language designed to be understood by a general readership. When standards of plain language are invoked to criticize the complexities of other kinds of discourse—for example, academic or legal writing—a UNITARY VIEW OF LANGUAGE is in evidence (CH. 10A, 14A).

position a relational stance or perspective negotiated through REPORTED SPEECH and the place from which a writer speaks. REPORTING EXPRESSIONS identify writers' proximity to and distance from statements made by others. The development of interpretive abstractions from concrete data positions writers both cognitively and socially as members of a community of writers (CH. 2, 3, 5, 6, 8B, 13). *See also* COGNITIVE RESPONSE vs. SOCIAL RESPONSE.

post-colonial reasoning a critical tendency that emerges in twentieth-century discourse to challenge the authority of Western researchers to produce knowledge of other cultures, and that exposes traditional anthropological knowledge as being saturated with colonial values (CH. 12C).

prestige abstraction ABSTRACTIONS that have particular social value for a given academic community. Prestige abstractions attract the attention of others in the community, and they signal the writer's contribution to existing research (CH. 7D, 14A).

presupposing, presupposition the phenomenon of some propositions being assumed rather than asserted (*see* ASSERTION). Presupposing expressions are those that construct the reader as knowing—as sharing a set of inferences about the world. They include social, political, and cultural assumptions, as well as assumptions about the physical world and the relationship between things and between people. Whereas here certain information is *asserted*—"Babur had an influence on South Asian life writing"—here the same information is *presupposed*: "The influence of Babur on South Asian life writing ..." (CH. 5G, 13B).

qualitative a METHOD of study that focuses on a case study or direct observation of a small sample or group over a prolonged period of time (CH. 12).

quantitative a METHOD of study that seeks to set aside biases caused by an individual's beliefs or immediate experience of the world by observing and numerically measuring controlled studies or experiments using as broad a sample as possible (CH. 12).

relevance the condition that makes a statement understandable. The relevance of a statement is a function of the context in which it is meaningful. The harder it is to find this context, the less relevant a statement will seem to be (CH. 8A). *See also* RELEVANCE THEORY.

relevance theory the branch of linguistics concerned with studying the contexts that condition readers' understanding and interpretation of language (CH. 9A).

reported speech a projected representation of another's words, directly or indirectly; we use reported speech whenever we convey what someone else has said. Reporting the statements made by other speakers, the writer positions himself or herself in relation to those statements. Reported speech is an important component of POSITION (CH. 2, 8B, 8D).

reporting expressions words and phrases that report sources of information: the writer's name, the title of the work, the date of publication, and the reporting verb (CH. 2, 3D–3E, 8B–8C).

reporting reporting *see* DOUBLE REPORTING (CH. 3E).

reporting verb the verb, in a REPORTING EXPRESSION, that names or characterizes the action of another work, and describes the development of the discussion. Summarizers can develop a POSITION in relation to another work in their choice of reporting verbs (CH. 2, 8B).

research genres types of writing (e.g., published peer-reviewed articles, article reviews, and poster presentations) that appear in scholarly journals and other scholarly venues (e.g., academic conferences); distinguishing features of the research genres reflect discipline-specific research activities (CH. 1D, 5B, 6D, 13A, 14C).

research proposal a detailed account of a research project that is still in its early stages. Research proposals survey the STATE OF KNOWLEDGE, identify a KNOWLEDGE DEFICIT and propose a means of answering a RESEARCH QUESTION (CH. 6F).

research question a question, emerging out of the KNOWLEDGE DEFICIT, that the research seeks to answer (CH. 6F, 8D). See also RESEARCH PROPOSALS, INTRODUCTIONS.

research subject(s) human participants of a study; those who are the focus of research (CH. 3F, 14B). *See also* INFORMED CONSENT.

secured generalization the generalization that has been cited to indicate that it is the product of a tradition of inquiry (CH. 8A).

self-reference a MESSAGE ABOUT THE ARGUMENT in which a work (e.g., article or essay) or a part of a work (e.g., a conclusion) is referred to directly. For example: "In this essay ..." or "By way of concluding ..." (CH. 11, 14A).

situation *see* CULTURAL SITUATION and GENRE (CH. 1, 9A).

sociality of knowledge the ways in which knowledge is the product of social activities (CH. 7D).

social response *see* COGNITIVE RESPONSE vs. SOCIAL RESPONSE (CH. 9A).

socio-cognitive *see* COGNITIVE RESPONSE vs. SOCIAL RESPONSE (CH. 10C).

state of knowledge a writer's estimate of the degree of stability in a designated area of knowledge: established knowledge, limits of knowledge, the conditions under which it was produced, and the positions from which statements issue (CH. 2C, 6A, 6F, 8D).

subjectivity the personal (social and cognitive) point of view or experience of the world (CH. 12C, 13B). *Contrast* OBJECTIVITY.

subject position relevant personal (social and political) elements of a researcher's experience of the world that may influence or be relevant to the knowledge he or she produces (CH. 12C).

summarizer's position the POSITION or perspective developed by a summarizer in relation to reported statements, evident in the way the summarized material is characterized (in the REPORTING VERB) and in the ABSTRACTIONS used to interpret details in the original (CH. 2, 3, 4, 6). *See also* POSITION and REPORTED SPEECH.

summary REPORTED SPEECH that compresses and may rearrange what another speaker has said or written (CH. 2, 3, 4).

sustained definition a strategy whereby a writer locates a phenomenon among other related phenomena in the world. The sustained attention paid to the phenomenon serves to extend or advance the inquiry (CH. 7C). *See also* APPOSITION/APPOSITIVE and FORMAL DEFINITION.

syntactic density the effect resulting from the capacity of NOUN PHRASES to expand by incorporating other sentence elements (adjectives, verbs, adverbs, other nouns) and creating noun "strings" (CH. 10C). *See also* NOUN PHRASE, NOMINAL STYLE, and NOMINALIZATION.

taxonomy schemes for classifying and ordering phenomena, schemes that depend on naming (using nouns) for things (CH. 10E).

think-aloud protocol a tool for professional writers and a technique for researching the reader's experience of using a text. The readers read and report out loud what's going on in their mind while reading; the writer gets a chance to watch someone making meaning from what he or she has written. Think-aloud protocols help writers understand the reading process by learning to anticipate and predict readers' responses to their text; their subsequent adjustments follow the reader's experience of the text rather than UNITARY VIEWS OF LANGUAGE usage (CH. 5, 9A).

tradition of inquiry a scholarly practice including topics considered relevant and worthy of ongoing inquiry, the preferred methods of inquiry, and the research community's style of CITATION (CH. 8A).

tree diagram a graphic representation of the structure of reasoning, with branches connecting lowest levels of detail to higher levels of abstraction (CH. 3B). *See also* LEVELS OF GENERALITY.

typified group a term that generalizes and categorizes large numbers of individual speakers or writers as members of an identifiable community (e.g., interviewees, psychoanalytic critics); when used in reporting and framing, the names of particular members are eliminated (CH. 8B). *See also* AGENTLESS EXPRESSIONS.

uncertainty/indeterminacy expressions that indicate doubt about statements, place limits on GENERALIZATIONS, identify gaps or inadequacies in existing research, and otherwise emphasize that knowledge is under construction. These expressions and tendencies can create a sense of uncertainty or a lack of determinate knowledge about a subject. MODALITY, LIMITING EXPRESSIONS, and REPORTING EXPRESSIONS are all associated with uncertainty (CH. 13A). *See also* KNOWLEDGE DEFICIT.

unitary views of language the idea that a single set of standards can be applied to all forms of writing or speech. Unitary views of language often manifest themselves in set rules (e.g., never begin a sentence with "and," always place a thesis statement at the end of the first paragraph, never end a paragraph with a quotation) (CH. 5B).

unpack to analyze a passage or a statement by examining its components in detail (CH. 10E).

References

Agar, Michael. 1994. "The intercultural frame." *International Journal of Intercultural Relations* 18 (2): 221–37.

Alcock, J.E., D.W. Carment, and S.W. Sadava. 1994. *A textbook of social psychology*, 3rd ed. Scarborough, ON: Prentice Hall.

Allen, Ann Taylor. 1999. "Feminism, social science, and the meanings of modernity: The debate on the origin of the family in Europe and the United States, 1860–1914." *The American Historical Review* 104 (4): 1085–1113.

Amit-Talai, Vered. 1995. "The waltz of sociability: Intimacy, dislocation and friendship in a Quebec high school." In *Youth cultures: A cross-cultural perspective*, ed. Vered Amit-Talai and Helena Wulff (pp. 144–65). London: Routledge.

Anselment, Raymond A. 1989. "Small pox in seventeenth-century English literature: Reality and the metamorphosis of wit." *Medical History* 33 (1): 72–95.

Arata, Stephen. 1990. "The Occidental tourist: 'Dracula' and the anxiety of reverse colonization." *Victorian Studies* 33 (4): 621–45.

Arnold, Bettina. 1999. "'Drinking the feast': Alcohol and the legitimation of power in Celtic Europe." *Cambridge Archaeological Review* 9 (1): 71–93.

Bala, G., K. Caldeira, M. Wickett, T.J. Phillips, D.B. Lobell, C. Delire, and A. Mirin. 2007. "Combined climate and carbon-cycle effects of large-scale deforestation." *Proceedings of the National Academy of Sciences* 104 (16): 6550–55.

Bar-Yosef, Ofer, and Steven L. Kuhn. 1999. "The big deal about blades: Laminar technologies and human evolution." *American Anthropologist* 101 (2): 322–38.

Batey, Mark, and Adrian Furnham. 2006. "Creativity, intelligence, and personality: A critical review of the scattered literature." *Genetic, Social, and General Psychology Monographs* 132 (4): 355–429.

Beaumont, Matthew. 2006. "Red Sphinx: Mechanics of the uncanny in 'The Time Machine.'" *Science Fiction Studies* 33 (2): 230–50.

Bhabha, Homi K. 1994. "How newness enters the world." In *The Location of Culture* (pp. 303–37). London: Routledge.

Berry, Esther. 2008. "The Zombie commodity: Hair and the politics of its globalization." *Postcolonial Studies* 11 (1): 63–84.

Bodley, John H. 1997. *Cultural anthropology: Tribes, states, and the global system*, 2nd ed. Mountain View, CA: Mayfield.

Bruggink, Thomas H., and Kamran Siddiqui. 1995. "An econometric model of alumni giving: A case study for a liberal arts college." *American Economist* 39 (2): 53–60.

Buchanan, Neil H. 1999. "Taxes, saving, and macroeconomics." *Journal of Economic Issues* 33 (1): 59–75.

Burgess, Keith. 1994. "British employers and education policy, 1935–45: A decade of 'missed opportunities'?" *Business History* 36 (3): 29–61.

Calhoun, Cheshire. 1994. "Separating lesbian theory from feminist theory." *Ethics* 104: 558–82.

Cameron, Deborah. 1990. "Demythologizing sociolinguistics: Why language does not reflect society." In *Ideologies of Language*, ed. John E. Joseph and Talbot J. Taylor (pp. 79–86). London: Routledge.

Cameron, Deborah. 1995. *Verbal hygiene*. London: Routledge.

Canadian Institutes of Health Research, Natural Sciences and Engineering Research Council of Canada, Social Sciences and Humanities Research Council of Canada. *Tri-council policy statement: Ethical conduct for research involving humans* 1998 (with 2000, 2002, and 2005 amendments). www.pre-ethics.gc.ca/english/policystatement/introduction.cfm

Caprotti, Federico, and Joanna Romanowicz. 2013. "Thermal eco-cities: Green building and urban thermal metabolism." *International Journal of Urban and Regional Research* 37 (6): 1949–67.

Carr, Michael H., and James W. Head. 2010. "Geologic history of Mars." *Earth and Planetary Science Letters* 294 (3): 185–203.

Chafe, Wallace. 1994. *Discourse, consciousness, and time*. Chicago: U of Chicago P.

Chakravorty, Mrinalini. 2013. "The dead that haunt *Anil's Ghost*: Subaltern difference and postcolonial melancholia." *PMLA* 128 (3): 542–58.

Chavez, Leo R. 1994. "The power of the imagined community: The settlement of undocumented Mexicans and Central Americans in the United States." *American Anthropologist* 96 (1): 52–73.

Chorpita, Bruce F., Anne Marie Albano, and David H. Barlow. 1998. "The structure of negative emotions in a clinical sample of children and adolescents." *Journal of Abnormal Psychology* 107 (1): 74–85.

Clark, Herbert. 1992. *Arenas of language use*. Chicago: U of Chicago P.

Clifford, James. 1997. *Routes: Travel and translation in the late twentieth century*. Cambridge, MA: Harvard UP.

Cluley, Robert. 2013. "What makes a management buzzword buzz." *Organization Studies* 34 (1): 33–43.

Coates, Jennifer. 1996. *Women talk: Conversation between women friends*. Cambridge: Blackwell.

Coffey, David J. 1977. *The encyclopedia of aquarium fishes in color*. New York: Arco.

Cohen, Sheldon, Denise Janicki-Deverts, and Gregory E. Miller. 2007. "Psychological stress and disease." *JAMA* 298: 1685–87.

Corrigan, Patrick W. 2007. "How clinical diagnosis might exacerbate the stigma of mental illness." *Social Work* 52 (1): 31–39.

Counts, Dorothy Ayers, and David R. Counts. 1992. "'They're my family now': The creation of community among RVers." *Anthropologica* 34: 153–82.

Cowan, Ann, Janet Giltrow, Sharon Josephson, and Michele Valiquette. 1998. "Feedback: Its uses, reliability, and design." Paper presented at annual meeting of Canadian Association of Teachers of Technical Writing, Ottawa.

Datta, Saikat, and Prabal Roy Chowdhury. 1998. "Management union bargaining under minimum wage regulation in less developed countries." *Indian Economic Review* 33 (2): 169–84.

Daveri, Francesco, and Ricardo Faini. 1999. "Where do migrants go?" *Oxford Economic Papers* 51: 595–622.

della Paolera, Gerardo, and Alan M. Taylor. 1999. "Economic recovery from the Argentine Great Depression: Institutions, expectations, and the change of macroeconomic regime." *Journal of Economic History* 59 (3): 567–98.

deMaynadier, Phillip G., and Malcolm L. Hunter, Jr. 1995. "The relationship between forest management and amphibian ecology: A review of the North American literature." *Environmental Review* 3: 230–61.

Douglas, Mary. 1996. "The choice between gross and spiritual: Some medical preferences." In *Thought styles*. London: Sage.

Dreses-Werringloer, Ute, Jean-Charles Lambert, Valérie Vingtdeux, Haitian Zhao, Horia Vais, Adam Siebert, Ankit Jain, Jeremy Koppel, Anne Rovelet-Lecrux, Didier Hannequin, Florence Pasquier, Daniela Galimberti, Elio Scarpini, David Mann, Corinne Lendon, Dominique Campion, Philippe Amouyel, Peter Davies, J. Kevin Foskett, Fabien Campagne, and Philippe Marambaud. 2008. "A polymorphism in CALHM1 influences Ca^{2+} homeostatis, Ab levels, and Alzheimer's disease risk." *Cell* 133 (7): 1149–61.

Early, Margaret, and Sondra Marshall. 2008. "Adolescent ESL students' interpretation and appreciation of literary texts: A case study of multimodality." *Canadian Modern Language Review* 64 (3): 377–97.

Eckes, Thomas. 1994. "Features of men, features of women: Assessing stereotypic beliefs about gender subtypes." *British Journal of Social Psychology* 33: 107–23.

Ellis, Mark, and Panikos Panayi. 1994. "German minorities in World War I: A comparative study of Britain and the U.S.A." *Ethnic and Racial Studies* 17 (2): 238–59.

Endler, Norman S., and Rachel L. Speer. 1998. "Personality psychology: Research trends for 1993–1995." *Journal of Personality* 66 (5): 621–69.

Englund, Mary. 1981. "An Indian remembers." In *Now you are my brother*, ed. Margaret Whitehead. Victoria, BC: Provincial Archives.

Evers, D. Elaine, Charles Sasser, James Gosselink, Deborah Fuller, and Jenneke Visser. 1998. "The impact of vertebrate herbivores on wetland vegetation in Atchafayala Bay, Louisiana." *Estuaries* 21 (1): 1–13.

Foot, David K., and Daniel Stoffman. 1996. *Boom, bust & echo: How to profit from the coming demographic shift.* Toronto: Macfarlane Walter & Ross.

Fowler, James H., and Nicholas A. Christakis. 2009. "Dynamic spread of happiness in a large social network: Longitudinal analysis of the Framingham Heart Study social network." *British Medical Journal* 338: 23–27.

Freeman, Victoria. 2005. "Attitudes toward 'miscegenation' in Canada, the United States, New Zealand, and Australia, 1860–1914." *Native Studies Review* 16 (1): 41–70.

Gamoran, Adam. 1993. "Alternative uses of ability grouping in secondary schools: Can we bring high-quality instruction to low-ability classes?" *American Journal of Education* 102: 1–22.

Geschwender, James A. 1992. "Ethgender, women's waged labor, and economic mobility." *Social Problems* 39 (1): 1–16.

Giddens, Anthony. 1990. *The consequences of modernity.* Stanford, CA: Stanford UP.

Giltrow, Janet. 2000. "'Argument' as a term in talk about student writing." In *Learning to Argue in Higher Education*, ed. S. Mitchell and R. Andrews. Portsmouth, NH: Boynton Cook/Heinemann.

Glenberg, Arthur M., Jennifer L. Schroeder, and David A. Robertson. 1998. "Averting the gaze disengages the environment and facilitates remembering." *Memory and Cognition* 26 (4): 651–58.

Gotti, Maurizio, and Marina Dossena, eds. 2001. *Modality in specialized texts: Selected papers of the 1st CERLIS Conference.* Bonn.

Gravina, Brad, Paul Mellars, and Christopher Bronk Ramsey. 2005. "Radiocarbon dating of interstratified Neanderthal and early modern human occupations at the Chatelperronian type-site." *Nature* 438 (3): 51–56.

Greening, Daniel W., and Barbara Gray. 1994. "Testing a model of organizational response to social and political issues." *Academy of Management Journal* 37 (3): 467–98.

Grossman, Herschel I. 1999. "Kleptocracy and revolutions." *Oxford Economic Papers* 51: 267–83.

Guerin, Bernard, and Yoshihiko Miyazaki. 2006. "Analyzing rumors, gossip, and urban legends through their conversational properties." *Psychological Record* 56 (1): 23–33.

Gurnis, Michael, Mark Turner, Sabin Zahirovic, Lydia DiCaprio, Sonja Spasojevic, R. Dietmar Müller, James Boyden, Maria Seton, Vlad Constantin Manea, and Dan J. Bower. 2012. "Plate tectonic reconstructions with continuously closing plates." *Computers and Geosciences* 38 (1): 35–42.

Halliday, M.A.K., and J.R. Martin. 1993. *Writing science: Literary and discursive power.* Pittsburgh: U of Pittsburgh P.

Hamilton, Gary G., and Nicole Woolsey Biggart. 1988. "Market, culture, and authority: A comparative analysis of management and organization in the Far-East." *American Journal of Sociology* 94: 552–94.

Hancock, Dana B., Eden R. Martin, Gregory M. Mayhew, Jeffrey M. Stajich, Rita Jewett, Mark A. Stacy, Burton L. Scott, Jeffery M. Vance, and William K. Scott. 2008. "Pesticide exposure and risk of Parkinson's disease: A family-based case-control study." *BMC Neurology* 8: 6.

Harrison, Claire. 2003. "Visual social semiotics: Understanding how still images make meaning." *Technical Communication* 50 (1): 46–60.

Hawkins, Ronnie Zoe. 2002. "Seeing ourselves as primates." *Ethics & the Environment* 7 (2): 60–103.

Helsen, Michiel M., Michiel R. van den Broeke, Roderik S.W. van de Wal, Willem Jan van de Berg, Erik van Meijgaard, Curt H. Davis, Yonghong Li, and Ian Goodwin. 2008. "Elevation changes in Antarctica mainly determined by accumulation variability." *Science* 320 (5883): 1626–29.

Herben, Tomáš, Zuzana Nováková, Jitka Klimešová, and Lubomír Hrouda. 2012. "Species traits and plant performance: Functional trade-offs in a large set of species in a botanical garden." *Journal of Ecology* 100 (6): 1522–33.

Heyes, C.M. 1998. "Theory of mind in nonhuman primates." *Behavioral and Brain Sciences* 21: 101–48.

Higgs, Robert. 1999. "From central planning to the market: The American transition, 1945–1947." *Journal of Economic History* 59: 600–23.

Hom, Alice Y., and Ming-Yuen S. Ma. 1994. "Premature gestures: A speculative dialogue on Asian Pacific lesbian and gay writing." *Journal of Homosexuality* 26 (2/3): 21–51.

Hoppitt, Will, Jamie Samson, Kevin N. Laland, Alex Thornton. 2012. "Identification of learning mechanisms in a wild meerkat population." *PLoS ONE*, 7 (8): 1–11.

Huntington, Henry, and the Communities of Buckland, Elim, Koyuk, Point Lay, and Shaktoolik. 1999. "Traditional knowledge of the ecology of beluga whales (*Delphinapterus leucas*) in the Eastern Chukchi and Northern Bering Seas, Alaska." *Arctic* 52 (1): 49–61.

Hurwitz, Gregg. 2002. "A tempest, a birth and death: Freud, Jung, and Shakespeare's *Pericles*." *Sexuality & Culture* 6 (3): 3–73.

Husbands, Christopher T. 1994. "Crises of national identity as the 'new moral panics': Political agenda-setting about definitions of nationhood." *New Community* 20 (2): 191–206.

Hyland, Ken. 1999. "Academic attribution: Citation and the construction of disciplinary knowledge." *Applied Linguistics* 20 (3): 341–67.

Irvine, Leslie, Kristina N. Kahl, and Jesse Smith. 2012. "Confrontations and donations: Encounters between homeless pet owners and the public." *Sociological Quarterly* 53 (1): 25–43.

Jackson, Sue. 2002. "To be or not to be? The place of women's studies in the lives of its students." *Journal of Gender Studies* 9 (2): 189–97.

Kabeer, Naila. 1994. "The structure of 'revealed' preference: Race, community and female labour supply in the London clothing industry." *Development and Change* 25: 307–31.

Kelm, Mary-Ellen. 1999. "British Columbia First Nations and the influenza pandemic of 1918–19." *BC Studies* 122 (Summer): 23–47.

Kerwin, Scott. 1999. "The Janet Smith Bill of 1924 and the language of race and nation in British Columbia." *BC Studies* 121: 83–114.

Khalid, Adeeb. 1994. "Printing, publishing, and reform in Tsarist Central Asia." *International Journal of Middle East Studies* 26: 187–200.

Kidd, Dustin. 2007. "Harry Potter and the functions of popular culture." *The Journal of Popular Culture* 40 (1): 69–89.

Kieffer, Christine C. 2013. "Rumors and gossip as forms of bullying: Sticks and stones?" *Psychoanalytic Inquiry* 33 (2): 90–104.

Killingray, David. 1994. "The 'rod of empire': The debate over corporal punishment in the British African colonial forces, 1888–1946." *Journal of African History* 35: 210–16.

Koch, Shelley L., and Joey Sprague. 2014. "Economic sociology vs. real life: The case of grocery shopping." *American Journal of Economics and Sociology* 73 (1): 237–63.

Kolodny, Annette. 1994. "Inventing a feminist discourse: Rhetoric and resistance in Margaret Fuller's *Woman in the Nineteenth Century*." *New Literary History* 25 (2): 355–82.

LaFollette, Hugh. 2000. "Gun control." *Ethics* 110: 263–81.

Lashley, Conrad, and Alison Morrison. 2013. *In search of hospitality.* Hoboken: Taylor and Francis.

Lee, Thomas W., and Terence R. Mitchell. 1994. "An alternative approach: The unfolding model of voluntary employee turnover." *Academy of Management Journal* 19 (1): 51–89.

Lesure, Richard. 1999. "Figurines as representations and products at Paso de la Amada, Mexico." *Cambridge Archaeological Journal* 9 (2): 209–20.

Lin, Chia-Chin. 2000. "Applying the American Pain Society's QA standards to evaluate the quality of pain management among surgical, oncology, and hospice inpatients in Taiwan." *Pain* 87: 43–49.

Lopes, Paul. 2006. "Culture and stigma: Popular culture and the case of comic books." *Sociological Forum* 21 (3): 387–414.

Lu, Min-Zhan. 1992. "Conflict and struggle: The enemies or preconditions of basic writing?" *College English* 54 (8): 891–913.

Lupton, Deborah, and John Tulloch. 1999. "Theorizing fear of crime: Beyond the rational/irrational oppositions." *British Journal of Sociology* 50 (3): 507–23.

MacDonald, Susan Peck. 1994. *Professional academic writing in the humanities and social sciences*. Carbondale: Southern Illinois UP.

Masson, Michael E.J., and Mary Anne Waldron. 1994. "Comprehension of legal contracts by non-experts: Effectiveness of plain language redrafting." *Applied Cognitive Psychology* 8: 67–85.

Matas, Robert. 2007. "Witness admits seeing 'lots of blood' in trailer." *The Globe and Mail*. 6 September: A7.

Mayes, Patricia. 1990. "Quotation in spoken English." *Studies in Language* 14 (2): 325–63.

McCorristine, Shane. 2013. "Searching for Franklin: A contemporary Canadian ghost story." *British Journal of Canadian Studies* 26 (1): 39–57.

Meizel, Katherine. 2009. "Making the dream a reality (show): The celebration of failure in American Idol." *Popular Music and Society* 32 (4): 475–88.

Middleton, Joyce Irene. 1993. "Orality, literacy, and memory in Toni Morrison's *Song of Solomon*." *College English* 55 (1): 64–65.

Milgram, Stanley. 1963. "Behavioral study of obedience." *Journal of Abnormal and Social Psychology*. 67 (4): 371–78.

Milroy, James, and Lesley Milroy. 1991 [1985]. *Authority in language: Investigating language prescription and standardisation*, 2nd ed. London: Routledge.

Mistry, Rohinton. 1995. "Prologue: 1975." In *A Fine Balance*. Toronto: McClelland & Stewart.

Morwood, M.J., T. Sutikna, E.W. Saptomo, K.E. Westaway, Jatmiko, R. Awe Due, M.W. Moore, Dwi Yani Yuniawati, P. Hadi, J.-x. Zhao, C.S.M. Turney, K. Fifield, H. Allen, and R.P. Soejono. 2008. "Climate, people and faunal succession on Java, Indonesia: Evidence from Song Gupuh." *Journal of Archaeological Science* 35: 1776–89.

Muir, Angela. "Kosovo." In *The Oxford Companion to Wine*, ed. Jancis Robinson. Oxford: Oxford UP.

Murphy, Rex. 2000, April 23. *Cross-country check-up*, CBC Radio.

Myers, Greg. 1999. "Functions of reported speech in group discussions." *Applied Linguistics* 20 (5): 376–401.

Nash, June. 1994. "Global integration and subsistence insecurity." *American Anthropologist* 96 (1): 7–30.

Negrave, Greta. 2013. "Selfie generation: Simulacrum of individuality." Research essay completed for Interdisciplinary Studies 100: Popular Culture and University Writing, Vancouver Island University.

Neiman, Paul J., F. Martin Ralph, M.A. Shapiro, B.F. Smull, and D. Johnson. 1998. "An observational study of fronts and frontal mergers over the Continental United States." *Monthly Weather Review* 126: 2521–52.

Nemutanzhela, Thiathu J. 1993. "Cultural forms and literacy as resources for political mobilisation: A.M. Malivha and the Zoutpansberg Balemi Association." *African Studies* 52 (1): 89–102.

O'Connor, Denis. 1987. "Glue sniffers with special needs." *British Journal of Special Education* 14 (3): 94–97.

Olick, Jeffrey K. 1999. "Genre memories and memory genres: A dialogical analysis of May 8, 1945 commemorations in the Federal Republic of Germany." *American Sociological Review* 64: 381–402.

Oliver, Pamela E., and Daniel J. Myers. 1999. "How events enter the public sphere." *American Journal of Sociology* 105 (1): 38–67.

Ottawa Citizen, reprinted in *The Vancouver Province*, 5 July 1994, A14.

Perrault, Charles. 1969. "Little Thumb." In *The Blue Fairy Book*, ed. Andrew Lang. New York: Airmont.

Peterson, Sara-Anne. 2006. "China's eco-city sets example." *Edmonton Journal*. 22 May: A17.

Prestwich, Patricia E. 1994. "Family strategies and medical power: 'Voluntary' committal in a Parisian asylum, 1876–1914." *Journal of Social History* 27 (4): 799–818.

Pringle, Heather. 1988. "Boneyard enigma." *Equinox* May–June: 87–104.

Quintero, Gilbert A., and Antonio L. Estrada. 1998. "Cultural models of masculinity and drug use: 'Machismo,' heroin, and street survival on the U.S.–Mexican border." *Contemporary Drug Problems* 25: 147–65.

Raasch, S., and D. Etling. 1998. "Modeling deep ocean convection: Large eddy simulation in comparison with laboratory experiments." *American Meteorological Society* 21: 1786–1802.

Rafter, Nicole H. 1992. "Claims-making and socio-cultural context in the first U.S. eugenics campaign." *Social Problems* 39 (1): 17.

Rauch-Elnekave, Helen. 1994. "Teenage motherhood: Its relationship to undetected learning problems." *Adolescence* 29 (113): 91–103.

Reiger, Kerreen M. 1989. "'Clean and comfortable and respectable': Working-class aspirations and the Australian 1920 Royal Commission on the Basic Wage." *History Workshop* 27: 86–105.

Reynolds, Jennifer F., and Elaine W. Chun. 2013. "Figuring youth citizenship: Communicative practices mediating the cultural politics of citizenship and age." *Language and Communication* 33 (4): 473–80.

Roberts, R. Michael, and Susan J. Fisher. 2011. "Trophoblast stem cells." *Biology of Reproduction* 84 (3): 412–21.

Rosenhan, David. 1973. "On being sane in insane places." *Science* 179 (4070): 250–58.

Sandlin, Jennifer A., and Jennifer L. Milam. 2008. "'Mixing pop (culture) and politics': Cultural resistance, culture jamming, and anti-consumption activism as critical public pedagogy." *Curriculum Inquiry* 38 (3): 323–50.

Sawicki, Gregory S., and Mont Hubbard. 2003. "How to hit home runs: Optimum baseball bat swing parameters for maximum range trajectories." *American Journal of Physics* 71 (11): 1152–62.

Schnabel, Jim. 1994. "Puck in the laboratory: The construction and deconstruction of hoaxlike deception in science." *Science, Technology, & Human Values* 19 (4): 459–92.

Schriver, Karen. 1994 [1992]. "What document designers can learn from usability testing." *Technostyle* 19 (3/4).

Scott, Rebecca J. 1994. "Defining the boundaries of freedom in the world of cane: Cuba, Brazil, and Louisiana after emancipation." *American Historical Review* (February): 70–102.

Seymour, Susanne. 1994. "Gender, church and people in rural areas." *Area* 26 (1): 45–56.

Shieffelin, Bambi B., and Rachelle Charlier Doucet. 1994. "The 'real' Haitian creole: Ideology, metalinguistics, and orthographic choice." *American Ethnologist* 21(1): 176–200.

Shimizu, K., K. Suhara, M. Ikumo, M. Eremets, and K. Amaya. 1998. "Superconductivity in oxygen." *Nature* 393: 767–69.

Smith, Thomas S., and Gregory T. Stevens. 1999. "The architecture of small networks: Strong interaction and dynamic organization in small social systems." *American Sociological Review* 64: 403–20.

South, Scott J., and Kyle D. Crowder. 1999. "Neighborhood effects on family formation: Concentrated poverty and beyond." *American Sociological Review* 64: 113–32.

Speck, Dara Culhane. 1987. *An error in judgement: The politics of medical care in an Indian/white community.* Vancouver, BC: Talonbooks.

Sperber, Dan, and Deirdre Wilson. 1986. *Relevance: Communication and cognition.* Cambridge, MA: Harvard UP.

Stockton, Sharon. 1995. "Writing in history: Narrating the subject of time." *Written Communication* 12 (1): 47–73.

Stratman, James F. 1994. "Investigating persuasive processes in legal discourse in real time: Cognitive biases and rhetorical strategy in appeal court briefs." *Discourse Processes* 17: 1–57.

Susskind, Leonard. 2013. "String theory." *Foundations of Physics* 43 (1): 174–81.

Swales, John. 1990. *Genre analysis: English in academic and research settings.* Cambridge: Cambridge UP.

Tannen, Deborah. 1990. *You just don't understand: Women and men in conversation.* New York: Ballantine Books.

Thompson, Lee, and Julie Cupples. 2008. "Seen and not heard? Text messaging and digital sociality." *Social & Cultural Geography* 9 (1): 95–108.

Tiratsoo, Nick, and Jim Tomlinson. 1994. "Restrictive practices on the shopfloor in Britain, 1946–60: Myth and reality." *Business History* 36 (2): 65–84.

Todaro, Michael P. 1997. *Economic Development.* New York: Longman.

Tri-City News. [*Letter to the editor*]. 26 April 2000.

Valentine, Gill, and Sarah Holloway. 2001. "On-line dangers?: Geographies of parents' fears for children's safety in cyberspace." *Professional Geographer* 53 (1): 71–83.

Ventura, Abbie. 2011. "Predicting a better situation? Three Young Adult speculative fiction texts and the possibilities for social change." *Children's Literature Association Quarterly* 36: 89–103.

Verkuyten, Maykel, Wiebe de Jong, and Kees Masson. 1994. "Similarities in anti-racist and racist discourse: Dutch local residents talking about ethnic minorities." *New Community* 20 (2): 253–67.

Waern, Yvonne. 1988. "Thoughts on texts in context: Applying the think-aloud method to text processing." *Text* 8 (4): 317–50.

Wassink, Alicia Beckford. 1999. "Historic low prestige and seeds of change: Attitudes toward Jamaican Creole." *Language in Society* 28: 57–92.

Wearne, Phillip. 1996. *Return of the Indian: Conquest and revival in the Americas.* London: Cassell.

Weinberger, Daniel A. 1998. "Defenses, personality structure and development: Integrating psychodynamic theory into a typological approach to personality." *Journal of Personality* 66 (6): 1061–77.

Wells, Deborah. 2004. "A review of environmental enrichment for kennelled dogs, *Canis familiaris.*" *Applied Animal Behaviour Science* 85: 307–17.

Wenzel, George W. 1999. "Traditional ecological knowledge and Inuit: Reflections on TEK research and ethics." *Arctic* 52 (2): 113–24.

Whittington, H.B. 1971. "The enigmatic animal *Opabinia regalis,* middle Cambrian, Burgess Shale, British Columbia." *Philosophical Transactions of the Royal Society, London.*

Willott, Sara, and Chris Griffin. 1999. "Building your own lifeboat: Working-class male offenders talk about economic class." *British Journal of Social Psychology* 38: 445–60.

Womack, Peter. 1999. "Shakespeare and the sea of stories." *Journal of Medieval & Early Modern Studies* 29 (1): 169–88.

Wong, Siu Kwong. 1999. "Acculturation, peer relations, and delinquent behavior of Chinese-Canadian youth." *Adolescence* 34 (133): 107–19.

Wulder, Michael A., Stephanie M. Ortlepp, Joanne C. White, Nicholas C. Coops, Sam B. Coggins. 2009. "Monitoring the impacts of mountain pine beetle mitigation." *Forest Ecology and Management* 258 (7): 1181–87.

Zervakis, Jennifer, and David C. Rubin. 1998. "Memory and learning for a novel written style." *Memory and Cognition* 26 (4): 754–67.

Zwick, Michael B., Paul W.H.I. Parren, Erica O. Saphire, Sarah Church, Meng Wang, Jamie K. Scott, Philip E. Dawson, Ian A. Wilson, and Dennis R. Burton. 2003. "Molecular features of the broadly neutralizing immunoglobulin G1 b12 required for recognition of human immunodeficiency virus type 1 gp120." *Journal of Virology* 77 (10): 5863–76.

Subject Index